Columbus Delano Whitehead,
his Ancestors, his Descendants

Columbus Delano Whitehead,
his Ancestors, his Descendants

Including associated families, Wilson, Maxwell, Anderson,
Gaston, Needles, Bray, Odell and Schultz

Robert D. McCloud
Cheryl McCloud Helm

Genealogy Publishing Group
Amherst, Massachusetts

Published 2021 by Genealogy Publishing Group, a division of White River Press
PO Box 3561, Amherst, MA 01004
genealogypublishinggroup.com

ISBN: 978-1-887043-97-7

Cover Design by Lufkin Graphic Designs
Norwich, Vermont • www.LufkinGraphics.com

Library of Congress Cataloging-in-Publication Data

Names: McCloud, Robert D. (Robert Davis), 1938- author. | Helm, Cheryl
   McCloud, 1973- author.
Title: Columbus Delano Whitehead, his ancestors, his descendants :
   including associated families Wilson, Maxwell, Anderson, Gaston,
   Needles, Bray, Odell and Schultz / compiled by Robert D. McCloud, Cheryl
   McCloud Helm.
Description: Amherst, Massachusetts : Genealogy Publishing Group, 2021. |
   Includes index. | Summary: "A genealogy book on the life of Columbus
   Delano Whitehead and his ancestors and descendants, including associated
   families Wilson, Maxwell, Anderson, Gaston, Needles, Bray, Odel and
   Schultz."-- Provided by publisher.
Identifiers: LCCN 2021015709 | ISBN 9781887043977 (hardcover)
Subjects: LCSH: Whitehead family. | Whitehead, Columbus Delano,
   1848-1919--Family. | United States--Genealogy.
Classification: LCC CS71.W591 2021 | DDC 929.20973--dc23
LC record available at https://lccn.loc.gov/2021015709

Contents

Forward

The Whitehead surname is linked to names in England and Scotland. It means fair haired or white hair. These families probably come from the same origin. The factor separating the English names from the Scottish name was religion. Scottish Whiteheads worshiped in the Presbyterian faith. The early Whiteheads of this family were staunch Presbyterians. The fact they married into other Scottish Presbyterian families, sort of settles the question.

Exactly where they picked up that faith probably has a lot to do with the history of the Protestants settlements in Ireland in what is now known as the Ulster Scots or Northern Ireland. A very complicated history there, of over three hundred years.

Dedication

This collection of genealogical information is dedication to the loving memories of William Bray Whitehead and Winona Ruth Odell Whitehead.

William Bray and Winona Odell Whitehead

The Revolutionary War plaque dedicated to Onesimus Whitehead

The following article "Patriot Ancestor: Onesimus Whitehead" was taken from the *George Mason Chapter, Virginia Society, Sons of American Revolution* dated March 11, 2013:

"Onesimus Whitehead, the patriot ancestor of Rear Admiral Joel Whitehead, was a member of a family with a strong military tradition since well before the Revolution. The immigrant ancestor of this branch of the Whitehead Family, Isaac Whitehead I, served in the New Haven Colony Militia in Connecticut as early as 1643. The Whitehead family moved westward in 1666 to become founders of the Elizabethtown Colony in New Jersey. The family later moved to Morristown where Onesimus served in the New Jersey Militia when George Washington brought his Continental Army of 10,000 soldiers to encamp during the winters of 1777 and 1779. The latter encampment occurred during the "hard winter" that still remains the coldest on record for New Jersey. Onesimus Whitehead died in Morristown, as fortune would have, on July 4th, 1814.

Most of the Whitehead family in Morristown including Isaac Whitehead IV moved to the Finger Lakes of New York about 1700. The family remained there until about

1826 when they again moved westward to Ohio after opening of the Erie Canal. The family military tradition continued with the Admiral's father who entered the Army during World War II and served over 20 years, retiring as a Lieutenant Colonel. Hs brother Scott is a Marine who recently retired as a Colonel in the Marin Corps Reserve. The Admiral's Coast Guard service spanned a career of over 38 years, with him retiring at the rank of Rear Admiral after serving as the Commander of the Eight Coast Guard District in New Orleans."

There are three known membership applications made to the U.S. Sons of the American Revolution by descendants of Onesimus Whitehead.

Harrie Pennington Whitehead applied on March 22, 1895 and was approved on June 14, 1895. In the application, Harrie Pennington Whitehead was born on February 25, 1861 in Buffalo, Erie County, New Jersey. He was the son of Ira C. Whitehead and Mary Elizabeth Davis, the grandson of Asa Whitehead and Phoebe Pennington, the great grandson of Silas Whitehead and Ruth Condit and the great-great grandson of Onesimus C. Whitehead and Rebecca Condit. According to the application Onesimus Whitehead was a "private in the New Jersey Militia from Morris County N.J. enlisting underneath name of Onis Whitehead." The reference was provided by "Gen. W.S. Stryker's Book "officers and men of New Jersey in the Revolutionary Army" for "Onis" Whitehead 818."

Charles R. Whitehead applied on May 25, 1903 and was approved on June 12, 1903. In the application, Charles R. Whitehead was born on September 1, 1860 in Morris Township, Morris County, New Jersey. He was the son of Aaron D. Whitehead and Harriet E. Lee, the grandson of Sylvester R. Whitehead and Abby Freeman, the great grandson of Ezekiel Whitehead and Mary Condit and the great-great grandson of Onesimus Whitehead and Rebecca Condit. According to the application Onesimus Whitehead was a "private in the State troops from New Jersey. Enlisting under the name of Onis and known by that name." The reference was provided by "Gen. W.S. Stryker's Books officers and men of New Jersey in the Revolutionary Army page 818."

Herbert L. Whitehead applied on May 6, 1905 and was approved on November 1, 1905. In the application, Herbert L. Whitehead was born on August 17, 1865 in Indianapolis, Marion County, Indiana. He was the son of Moses Stuart Whitehead and Anna J. Suffith Whitehead, the grandson of Alfred P. Whitehead and Sophia Cooley Whitehead, the great grandson of Isaac Whitehead and Elizabeth Payne of

Long Island and the great-great grandson of Onis Whitehead and Rebecca Condit. According to the application Onesimus Whitehead was a "private County Militia." The reference was provided by "Officers and men from New Jersey in the Revolutionary War by Gen. W.S. Stryker."

CHAPTER ONE

The Whitehead Family of
Morris County, New Jersey and
Licking County, Ohio

ISAAC WHITEHEAD was born circa 1688 in Morris County, New Jersey. The research of V. B. Smith of Spring Lake, MI states Isaac Whitehead was the son of Isaac Whitehead and Abigail Crane. He is believed to be the third of his family to hold that name in succession. Isaac Whitehead married Sarah Van Courtland in Morris County, NJ. Sarah was born in Union County, NJ.

Isaac Whitehead died on February 11, 1777, in Morristown, NJ. Sarah Van Courtland Whitehead died at the age of "104" on August 4, 1804.

Isaac and Sarah Whitehead were the parents of seven known children.

1. Sarah Whitehead, born about 1720
2. William Whitehead, born about 1723
3. Mary Whitehead, born about 1726
4. Rebecca Whitehead, born about 1733
5. Elizabeth Whitehead, born about 1737
6. Onesimus Whitehead
7. Ruth Whitehead, born about 1742

ONESIMUS WHITEHEAD was born in Morris County, New Jersey on August 1, 1741, the son of Isaac and Sarah Whitehead. Onesimus Whitehead married Rebecca Condit on October 31, 1764. Rebecca was the daughter of Phillip Condit and Mary Day. The Condit named has also been found misspelled as Condict by several researchers. Onesimus Whitehead was a farmer.

A plaque was placed November 4, 1996, in the Presbyterian Churchyard, Morristown, NJ by the Hannah Cobb Chapter of the DAR honoring Onesimus and Rebecca Whitehead. The George Mason Chapter, Virginia Society, of the Sons of the American Revolution later featured the plaque honoring Onesimus Whitehead and his wife Rebecca on their web page. This was on March 11, 2013, commemorating the ancestors of Admiral Joel Whitehead for his Coast Guard service spanning 38 years serving as the Commander of the Eighth Coast Guard in New Orleans.

The plaque states Onesimus Whitehead served as a Prv (private) of New Jersey militia. Information on this SAR web site states the immigrant ancestor of this branch of the Whitehead Family, Isaac Whitehead I, served in the New Haven Colony Militia in Connecticut as early as 1643. The Whitehead family moved westward in 1666 to become founders of the Elizabethtown Colony in New Jersey. The family later moved to Morristown where Onesimus served in the New Jersey Militia when George Washington brought his Continental Army of 10,000 soldiers to encamp there during the winters of 1777 and 1779.

Several Whitehead family members from Morristown moved to the Finger Lakes area of New York. Certain family members remained there until about 1820 when they moved again westward to Ohio after the opening of the Erie Canal. Ohio was formed on March 1, 1803, from a partition under the provisions of the Northwest Ordinance. Many of the settlers from New York and Morris County, New Jersey settled in Licking County, Ohio after it was formed there on January 30, 1808.

The will of Onesimus Whitehead's father-in-law Phillip Condit was dated April 3, 1800 and approved on January 21, 1802. The executors were Jabez Condit, a son of Phillip Condit, and Onesimus Whitehead. The personal estate was divided between the daughters, not named, while the real estate went to Jabez Condit.

Rebecca Condit Whitehead died September 3, 1805, she was buried in the First Presbyterian Churchyard in Morristown, New Jersey. Onesimus Whitehead died in Morristown, NJ on July 4, 1814. It is believed he was buried beside his wife.

Onesimus and Rebecca Condit Whitehead were the parents of nine known children.

1. Ezekial Whitehead
2. Silas Whitehead
3. Huldah Whitehead
4. Asa Whitehead
5. Isaac Whitehead
6. Elizabeth Whitehead
7. Hannah Whitehead
8. Abner Whitehead
9. Ruth Whitehead

EZEKIAL WHITEHEAD was born on May 7, 1765, in Morris County, New Jersey, the son of Onesimus Whitehead. Ezekial married Mary Condit, the daughter of Jabez Condit.

SILAS WHITEHEAD was born January 31, 1767, in Morris County, New Jersey, the son of Onesimus Whitehead and Rebecca Condit Whitehead. Silas married Ruth Condit, the daughter of Jonathan Condit.

HULDAH WHITEHEAD was born on July 30, 1769, in Morris County, New Jersey, the daughter of Onesimus Whitehead. Huldah married Samuel Williams of Essex County, New Jersey. This family moved to Jersey, Ohio. Huldah died in Jersey, Ohio on June 10, 1846 and Samuel died there in June 1858.

ASA WHITEHEAD was born May 4, 1771, in Morris County, New Jersey, the son of Onesimus Whitehead and Rebecca Condit Whitehead. Asa married Abigail Lacy

Bates, the widow of John Bates; most likely in Morris County, New Jersey. Abigail was born about 1780 in New Jersey. This family moved to Caledonia, Genesee County, New York; the family was found there for the 1810 census. The family then moved to Franklin County, Ohio and still later to Licking County, Ohio, where they were found there for the 1820 census.

Asa's brother Abner Whitehead settled in Jersey Township of Licking County, Ohio in September 1816. In 1817, Onesimus Whitehead, possibly another brother, also settled in the area. Asa and his family settled in the township in 1820. In fact, it appears the Jersey Township was composed of people primarily from the Williams family, the Condit family and the Whitehead family, all formerly of Morris County, New Jersey.

Asa Whitehead died in Licking County, Ohio on March 24, 1822. The 1850 Licking County census shows Abigail was then living with her son Silas Whitehead. She was 69 years old and noted as born in New Jersey. Abigail Lacy Whitehead died in Licking County, Ohio in 1856.

Asa and Abigail Lacy Whitehead were the parents of six, possibly seven, children.

1. Silas Whitehead
2. Abram Lacy Whitehead
3. Rebecca C. Whitehead
4. Isaac Whitehead
5. Phebe Whitehead
6. Eliza Whitehead
7. Hannah Whitehead

SILAS WHITEHEAD was born in Morris County, New Jersey, in 1802, the son of Asa and Abigail Lacy Whitehead.

ABRAM LACY WHITEHEAD was born May 1, 1805, in Genesee County, New York the son of Asa and Abigail Lacy Whitehead. The family moved from New York to Franklin County, Ohio in 1813 and to Licking County in 1820.

Abraham(sic) L. Whitehead married Mary Green in Licking County, Ohio on April 27, 1828, in a ceremony performed by the Justice of the Peace Benjamin Beem. Mary Green was born October 14, 1809, at Greens Chapel in Licking County, Ohio, the daughter of Richard Stoneman Green and Sarah Davis Green. It has been passed down in the Whitehead family that Mary was the first white child born in Lima Township, Ohio. Abram and Mary's son Columbus Delano Whitehead wrote in a 1905 Wabash College Alumni questionnaire that his "Father's stock on his father's side is English & Scotch, his mother's side Irish. Mother's father Richard Green was a full blood Hollander, her mother Emily Davis was Welsh."

Abram Lacy and Mary Green Whitehead

The Davis side of the Green family traces its heritage back to Samuel Davis who was born in Virginia on October 15, 1768. Samuel married Mary Stone in Hardy County, Virginia about the year 1790. Samuel and Mary Stone came to Licking County, Ohio in 1806. They were the parents of five known children, Sarah, James, Rhoda, Elizabeth and Rebecca. Sarah Davis was born April 22, 1792, in Virginia. She married Richard Stoneman Green in Licking County on December 12, 1809. Sarah Davis Green died on October 23, 1858 and was buried in Pataskala Cemetery in Pataskala, Ohio.

Mary Green's father Richard Stoneman Green was born on February 18, 1786, in Maryland. Richard's father was Benjamin Green who was born April 26, 1754. Richard's mother was Katherine Boehm, her surname was later changed to Beem. Benjamin and Katherine would have been most likely married in Maryland. Katherine Beem Green died in 1822. Benjamin Green died on September 28, 1835. His tombstone reads, "His body consigned to the cold tomb/ concealed from mortal sight/ the happy spirit has gained its home/ at God's right hand/ in the sweet world of light."

Richard Stoneman Green was at the time of his death on April 16, 1872, the oldest living pioneer of Licking County, Ohio. He came to Licking County when he was sixteen years old. He helped man the boat leaving Marietta for Zanesville with all the family's belongings. He later became a trustee of Lima Township. He and his wife Sarah are recorded on the same tombstone in Pataskala Cemetery along with their daughter Anna Woolard. Sarah Davis Green died on October 23, 1858.

Following her marriage to Abram Whitehead, Mary Green Whitehead transferred her church membership to the Presbyterian Church at Pataskala. The Abram Lacy Whitehead family was located in Licking County for the 1850 census. There were six children in the home at that time, S. D., Richard B., Ezra L., Asa F., Wickliff C., and Delano S. Abram's sister Hannah Horn and her son Asa W. Horn were also living in the home.

Abram Lacy Whitehead died without a will on October 18, 1884, at the age of seventy-nine. He was buried in Pataskala Cemetery. An Application for Letters of Administration was submitted to the court on the 9th day of December 1884. In this application was a listing of the heirs;

S.D Whitehead, son, Pataskala, Ohio
John M. Whitehead, son, New Mexico
Emily J. Osborn, daughter, Jersey, Ohio
Ezra L. Whitehead, son, Austin, Texas
Asa L. Whitehead, son, Cincinnati, Ohio
Wickliff C. Whitehead, son, Pataskala, Ohio
C. Delano Whitehead, son, Maryville, Missouri
Daniel G. Whitehead, son, Jersey, Ohio

Mary Green Whitehead died on Saturday, June 22, 1895, at the home of her son W. C. Whitehead. She was eighty-five years old. Her obituary found in the June 28, 1895 issue of *Newark Semi-Weekly American* noted her death "removes another link connecting the present generation from a far distant past." The article also noted she was the parent of ten children with five living at the time of her death. Services were held at the Presbyterian Church at Pataskala with the Rev. S. M. Shook officiating.

Abram Lacy and Mary Green Whitehead were the parents of ten known children. Six of the children listed below, items 5 through 10, are verified by the 1850, 1860 and 1870 Licking County, Ohio census. A son identified as Lafayette Whitehead on the 1860 census is missing because it was uncertain where he fitted into the family enumeration. He was listed as a nineteen-year-old shoemaker on the 1850 census. This most certainly had to be Asa Fayette listed below.

1. Emily Jane Whitehead
2. Samuel Davis Whitehead
3. John Mark Whitehead
4. Phoebe Whitehead
5. Richard Baxter Whitehead
6. Ezra Lacy Whitehead
7. Asa Fayette Whitehead
8. Wycliff Condit Whitehead
9. Delano Sterns Whitehead
10. Daniel Gierhart Whitehead

EMILY JANE WHITEHEAD was born in Franklin County, Ohio on November 12, 1829 the daughter of Abram and Mary Green Whitehead. Emily married Enos Osborn.

He was born 1826 and died in 1897; Emily died on July 27, 1892 in Jersey, Licking County, Ohio and is buried in Jersey Presbyterian Cemetery.

Enos and Emily Whitehead Osborn were the parents of eight children.

1. Bertram Pierson Osborn, 1849-1928
2. Larkin David Osborn, 1852-1904
3. Mary Ellen Osborn Condit, 1854-1940
4. George L. Osborn, 1859-1904
5. Alma P. Osborn Puffer, 1863-1955
6. John W. Osborn, 1864-1944
7. Enos L. Osborn, 1864-1958
8. Lucy M. Osborn Bourne, 1868-1964

SAMUEL DAVIS WHITEHEAD was born in Delaware County, Ohio on February 9, 1831, the son of Abram L. and Mary Green Whitehead. Samuel married Hannah Marie Condit on ____. She was the daughter of ____.

Samuel D. Whitehead died on January 14, 1893, he was buried Pataskala Cemetery, Licking County, Ohio. Hannah Condit Whitehead died in 1910. They were the parents of eight known children.

1. Alice Mary Whitehead, 1855-1942
2. Lewis Condict Whitehead, 1857-1859
3. James Whitehead, 1858-1861
4. Jennie Maria Whitehead Brown, 1861-1895
5. Timothy Condict Whitehead,1862-1879
6. Harry Whitehead, 1868-1868
7. Rose E. Whitehead Thomas, 1869-1950
8. Abram Ray Whitehead, 1871-1876

JOHN MARK WHITEHEAD was born in Licking County, Ohio on February 4, 1833, the son of Abram L. and Mary Green Whitehead.

John Mark Whitehead served with the Union forces in Kansas 7th Cavalry Co. I. He began his service as a Hospital steward, but later served in the field. During his time serving, he also attended as an animal doctor, which was a needed service for the Cavalry Unit.

Left photo, John Mark Whitehead Right photo, left to right Ada Margaret, Martha Estelle Mathers, Mary Ora, John Mark and Emma Belle Whitehead

John Mark's married Martha Mathers on _____. Martha Mathers was born on January 25, 1841 in Indiana. During their time in Kansas, John supported his family as a famer. Martha died on September 11, 1878. After his wife's death, John moved from Kansas to New Mexico to assist in establishing and managing a Harvey House on the railroad line. John married his sister-in law Margaret Mathers on _____.

In June of 1889 John Mark signed papers to homestead 160 acres outside Guthrie, Oklahoma Territory. John, his wife Margaret and his youngest daughter, Ada moved to Guthrie. OK. John died on February 27, 1909 in Guthrie, Logan County, Oklahoma and is buried at Summit View Cemetery. He lived to see nine grandchildren.

John and Martha Mathers Whitehead were the parents of three known children.

1. Emma Belle Whitehead, born in Ohio
2. Mary Ora Whitehead, born in Kansas
3. Ada Margaret Whitehead, born in Kansas

RICHARD BAXTER WHITEHEAD was born in Licking County, Ohio on January 16, 1837, the son of Abram L. and Mary Green Whitehead. Richard died on June 9, 1854 (aged 17). Burial was in Jersey Presbyterian Cemetery, Jersey Licking County, Ohio.

EZRA LACY WHITEHEAD was born in Licking County, Ohio on December 11, 11, 1840, the son of Abram L. and Mary Green Whitehead. Ezra married Hattie Clark. Ezra and Hattie Clark Whitehead were the parents of five children.

7

E. L. Whitehead, age 78, died at his home, 946 Arlington street, Houston Heights at 6:15 p.m. Thursday. He is survived by one son, L.K. Whitehead of Texarkana, and four daughters, Mrs. C. E. Hargraves, of Sour Lake, Mrs. G. C. Stalnaker of Austin, Mrs. Claire Sinclair Calahan and Mrs. Pearl Terrell, both of Houston. Burial was in Glenwood Cemetery, TX., Houston, Harris County, TX.

Ezra Lacy and Hattie Clark Whitehead were the parents of six known children.

1. Pearl T. Whitehead Broadrick, 1867-1947
2. Roy Lacy Whitehead, 1871-1916
3. Lewis Karl Whitehead, 1873-1924
4. Claire Jane Whitehead, 1977-1945
5. Elizabeth Isabelle Whitehead Hargraves, 1880-1920
6. Beulah Beatrix Whitehead Stalnaker, 1883-1975

ASA FAYETTE WHITEHEAD was born in Licking County, Ohio on May 2, 1843, the son of Abram L. and Mary Green Whitehead. During the Civil War, Asa enlisted on May 2, 1864 and discharged on September 1, 1864.

After the war Asa earned his living as a boot and shoemaker. In April of 1869, Asa married Hannah M. Williams.

During the early 1880s, Asa attended Lane Seminary and for the remainder of his life was a Presbyterian Minister.

Due to his was service Asa's health was compromised. He died in 1892 at the age of 48. The Minutes of the Annual Meeting of the Synod of Michigan listed his death and his years of service. "The Reverend Asa F. Whitehead died February 6, 1892, aged 48 years, after a lingering illness of two years. He was graduated from Lane Seminary in Cincinnati, Ohio in 1886. He labored three years thereafter in Tennessee. He was received by the Michigan Synod from Presbytery of Kingston on October 9, 1889, and then labored with the Church of the Covenant in West Bay City, Michigan."

Asa Fayette and Hannah Williams Whitehead were the parent of one known child.

1. Minnie Whitehead born in October 1870

WICKLIFF CONDIT WHITEHEAD was born in Licking County, Ohio in 1845, the son of Abram L. and Mary Green Whitehead. Wickliff C. Whitehead was a student at Wabash College, graduating in 1871. The 1870 Indiana census of the school shows he went by the name of Condit Whitehead. Following graduation, he studied law and became a lawyer.

Wickliff Condit Whitehead
Written on back "Height 6 ft.3, weight 190 lbs, Age 25 years, Graduate next June."
Tintype taken in Indianapolis, Indiana.

Wickliff married Anna Yount of Yountsville, Indiana on July 25, 1872. Their marriage license was issue from Montgomery County, Indiana. Anna was born April 14, 1845, the daughter of Daniel and Sarah Price Yount. The village of Yountsville, Indiana was named after this family.

It seems two brothers Daniel and Allen Yount came to western Indiana at about 1840 looking for a mill site. By 1849 their factory was turning out a finished product. The mill was powered by a turbine water wheel which powered the factory until 1905. The factory eventually became a successful carding mill and a woolen mill.

According to information found in the *Yountsville History* by Ruth G. Clodfelder McCormick, Wycliff(sic) C. Whitehead, in 1875, became part of a family run organization named "Dan Yount and Sons." It is not known how long Wickliff stayed with this business, but he eventually practiced law.

Wickliff eventually gave up being an attorney and returned home to Ohio where he farmed. Wickliff Whitehead died on October 10, 1900 in Licking County, Ohio and is buried in Pataskala Cemetery. Anna Yount Whitehead died in 1933.

Wickliff C. and Anna Yount Whitehead were the parents of five known children with four living to adulthood.

1. Albert Whitehead
2. Oliver Whitehead

3. Paul Whitehead
4. Andrew Yount Whitehead

DELANO STERNS WHITEHEAD see Chapter Two, page 15.

DANIEL GIERHART WHITEHEAD was born in Licking County, Ohio on December 16, 1851, the son of Abram Lacy and Mary Green Whitehead. Daniel married Alice Didema Beem.

Daniel and Alice where found living in Wichita, Sedgwick County, Kansas, for the 1910 census. None of their children were at that time found living in the home.

Didema Beem and Daniel Gierhart Whitehead

Daniel and Didema Beem Whitehead are believed to be the parents of six children.

1. Gertrude who married George Frazier, family lived in Carthage, MO

REBECCA C. WHITEHEAD was born in Morris County, New Jersey in 1807, the daughter of Asa and Abigail Lacy Whitehead.

ISAAC WHITEHEAD was born in Morris County, New Jersey in 1810, the son of Asa and Abigail Lacy Whitehead.

PHEBE WHITEHEAD was born in Licking County, Ohio in 1812, the daughter of Asa and Abigail Lacy Whitehead. Phebe married Jesse Horn.

ELIZA WHITEHEAD was born in Licking County, Ohio in 1814, the daughter of Asa and Abigail Lacy Whitehead. Eliza married William B. Thompson.

HANNAH WHITEHEAD was born in Licking County, Ohio in 1817, the daughter of Asa and Abigail Lacy Whitehead. Hannah married Abram Horn. Hannah Horn and her three-year-old son Asa W. Horn were found living in the home of her brother Abram L. Whitehead for the 1850 Licking County, Ohio census.

ISAAC WHITEHEAD was born August 28, 1773, in Morris County, New Jersey, the son of Onesimus Whitehead and Rebecca Condit Whitehead. Isaac married Elizabeth Payne(Paine). The family moved to Romulus, New York.

Elizabeth Payne Whitehead died at Jersey, Ohio on June 27, 1851. Isaac Whitehead died at Jersey, Ohio on June 30, 1857.

ELIZABETH WHITEHEAD was born in 1775, in Morris County, New Jersey, the daughter of Onesimus and Rebecca Condit Whitehead. Elizabeth married the Rev. George Callahan of Licking County, Ohio on June 28, 1818, by the Justice of the Peace James Holmes. He was a Methodist clergyman and resided at Jersey, Ohio.

HANNAH WHITEHEAD was born August 28, 1777, in Morris County, New Jersey, the daughter of Onesimus Whitehead and Rebecca Condit Whitehead. Hannah married Jacob Allen(?). Hannah later married Tunis Spear.

ABNER WHITEHEAD was born October 22, 1779, in Morris County, New Jersey, the son of Onesimus Whitehead and Rebecca Condit Whitehead. Abner married Abigail Condit in 1805. She was the daughter of Jabez Condit. The family moved to Jersey, Ohio in September 1816.

Abner and Abigail Condit Whitehead were the parents of nine known children.

1. Jabez Condit Whitehead
2. David S. Whitehead, born Aug. 12, 1807, died Feb. 11, 1808
3. Isaac Whitehead
4. Lucinda Whitehead
5. Asa Horace Whitehead
6. Ira Onesimus Whitehead, born Mar. 8, 1816, died July 8, 1840
7. Ezekiel Whitehead
8. Theodore F. Whitehead
9. Phebe Whitehead, born 1818, died 1819, Jersey, Ohio

ISAAC WHITEHEAD was born September 16, 1809, in Morristown, New Jersey, the son of Abner and Abigail Condit Whitehead. Isaac married Elizabeth Martin in 1830. Elizabeth was born in Sussex County, New Jersey on October 20, 1811. At one year of age her family moved to Charleston, VA and later to Licking County.

Isaac died in Illinois on June 29, 1858. Elizabeth Whitehead of El Dorado, Kansas celebrated her ninety-first birthday in 1902 at the home of her daughter Mrs. G. W. Bowie, with whom she lives.

Isaac and Elizabeth Martin Whitehead were the parents of nine known children.

1. E. E. Whitehead of Dixie, OK
2. I. O. Whitehead of Pawnee, OK
3. Mrs. G. W. Bowie of El Dorado, Kansas
4. D. T. Whitehead of El Dorado, Kansas
5. Lewis M. Whitehead, of Newark, Ohio-liveryman
6. Leander M. Whitehead of Springfield, Ohio
7. Eva Whitehead Martin of Cowden, Illinois

LUCINDA WHITEHEAD was born January 1, 1811, in Morristown, New Jersey, the daughter of Abner and Abigail Condit Whitehead. Lucinda married Enos O. Williams. Lucinda died August 31, 1848, in Jersey, Ohio.

ASA HORACE WHITEHEAD was born December 3, 1813, in Morristown, New Jersey, the son of Abner and Abigail Condit Whitehead. Asa married Mary Carter. Asa died in 1888.

EZEKIEL WHITEHEAD was born on November 11, 1818, in Licking County, Ohio, the son of Abner and Abigail Condit Whitehead. He married Margaret Salts. Ezekiel Whitehead died June 25, 1868.

THEODORE F. WHITEHEAD was born on September 23, 1821, in Licking County, Ohio, the son of Abner and Abigail Condit Whitehead. He married Jane Bushfield. He later married Sarah Anderson.

RUTH WHITEHEAD was born in Morris County, New Jersey on August 22, 1782, the daughter of Onesimus Whitehead and Rebecca Condit Whitehead. Ruth married David Talmadge.

CHAPTER TWO

The Columbus Delano Whitehead Family

COLUMBUS DELANO WHITEHEAD was born on a farm near Pataskala, Jersey Township, Licking County, Ohio, on March 21, 1848, the son of Abram and Mary Green Whitehead. Columbus was born Delano Sterns Whitehead. The 1850 Licking County, Ohio census records his name as Delano S.(Sterns)Whitehead. Delano later changed his name from Delano Sterns to Columbus Delano apparently because of his affection for the city of Columbus, Ohio. In his youth, however, he was known as Dell. His name has also been found written as Del.

During the Civil War Delano ran away from home when he was fourteen to join his older brother in the Union Army, but his father went after him and brought him home. There is also a family story that Dell and several of his friends were at a Union encampment located near the Ohio River when a fever broke out and everyone was quarantined. Fearing for their lives, Dell and several of his friends escaped the camp by swimming across the Ohio River, with one of his friends drowning during the swim.

Columbus Delano and Mary Maxwell Wilson Whitehead

Delano Whitehead was a student at Wabash College in Crawfordsville, Indiana starting in the fall of 1867. The college was founded in 1833 with a strong Presbyterian influence. In 1862, when Dr. Joseph F. Tuttle became President of Wabash College, he was at that time also serving as Pastor of Center Church, a Presbyterian church located in Crawfordsville. President Tuttle served as president of Wabash College until 1892.

Delano was following in the footsteps of his brother Wickliffe Condit Whitehead, who started in preparatory school there in 1865. The Whiteheads of Licking County, Ohio were dedicated members of the Presbyterian church which was probably one of the reasons the brothers attended a Presbyterian school, Wabash College.

Delano was in the college's preparatory school for two years and then four years in the college. The 1870 census for the First Ward of Crawfordsville, Montgomery County, Indiana dated June 21, 1870, shows nearly two pages of individuals listed as attending school which was obviously the college. His name was written as Delano Whitehead and he was listed on this enumeration as a native of Ohio and was 29 years old, which was incorrect. He was younger than that. He listed $50.00 of personal property as did most of the students. Condit Whitehead was also listed on the same census as a student at the school. This turned out to be Delano's brother Wickliff Condit Whitehead, who was recorded as 30 years old and from Ohio. He was a member of the 1871 graduating class.

It does appear that it was during his student days at Wabash College that Delano changed his name. The college records from the 1867-68 school year, shows that it was Delano S. Whitehead who was listed in the preparatory English course. The records for school years 1868-69, however, records his name as C. D. Whitehead. The records of the Center Presbyterian Church of Crawfordsville, Indiana confirm the name change, they show "Columbus D. Whitehead" became a member there on December 12, 1868.

Family stories state Columbus Delano became quite proficient in Latin and Greek and may have, at one time, taught those subjects. What is known of his schoolwork, however, is that he won Second Prize for his Sophomore Declamation. He was a member of the Calliopean which was a literary society which had its own library, weekly programs and gave special exhibitions of oratory and essays. Composing essays, speech making, and oratory were heavily emphasized in the college as skills necessary to a young man's success.

Dell was also a member of the Phi Delta Theta fraternity. A student from the class of 1871, W. H. Ristine, writing years later about the early days of the Phis stated, "... we were all poor, it was epidemic in the fraternity. We held our meetings in attics and caves of the earth, like Knights of the Golden Circle, but on some unusual or state occasions we met in my father's law office, surreptitiously, and there we would regale ourselves, and wallow in a welter of mince pies, peanuts, and lastly but greatest, cider of an ancient brew; this did indeed cheer but not inebriate, to speak of." Dell undoubtedly enjoy his years at Wabash College. His brother Wickliff was also a member of the Phis.

Columbus Delano had three articles published in the school paper, *The Wabash Magazine*. The first article appeared in 1871, it was a biography of the poet J. G. Whittier. The second article appeared in 1872 and the subject was on "Sympathy" and the third article appeared in 1873 and was about his countries policy in "Cuba." Perhaps the article on "Sympathy" give us an insight into some of his values at that time.

> ... The world is getting better if we may judge from the grand display of human kindness. The Cultivation of this feeling is desired by all.

"We pine for kindred natures
to mingle with our own."
Since we know that this is accomplished by correcting and polishing our
affections individually, we should work zealously, privately, and continually
to that end, casting out thoughts unseemly, checking evil imaginations, thereby
working good in the soul and for the world,
"For there is need that on man's heart should fall
A spirit that can sympathize with all"

Dell graduated in 1873 with an A. B. and a M. A. That year a new prize was offered to the graduating seniors called the Baldwin Prize. It was named after the Honorable Daniel P. Baldwin and was cited as a "Prize of forty dollars... offered to that member of the Senior Class who shall compose and pronounce the best English Oration." Columbus Delano Whitehead won the first Baldwin Prize offered at the school. The Prize is still offered at the school today at the beginning of every new school year and is highly prized. One of Dell's graduating classmates who was also competed for the Baldwin Prize was Thomas Riley Marshall who went on to serve as Governor of Indiana and still later as the Vice President of the United States for eight years under President Woodrow Wilson. During one of Marshall's visits to Kansas City, he took the time to share a special visit with his old classmate privately.

In a Wabash Alumni Association questionnaire dated 1905, Delano wrote about his experience at Wabash College, "Worked my way thro' Preparatory & College courses 6 years, was janitor on Center Ch. for 4 years. Worked for Professor David Wood, sheared sheep and sold books and had a good time. Those 6 years at Wabash are the brightest in my life." One final bit of information about Columbus Delano's days at Wabash College. On June 17, 1902, there was a Memorial Tablet dedicated to those who served in the great Civil War. Attached to the north east brick wall of the school's Center Hall, the memorial, a large black cast iron plaque adorned at the top with an eagle in flight, has the name of Columbus Delano Whitehead enrolled there. This certainly gives credence to the story that he ran off and joined the army during the Civil War.

In July 1873, Columbus Delano went to Indianapolis to study law. He read for the law with the firm of Barbour, Jacobs and Williams in Indianapolis. In 1874, the Indianapolis city directory shows he was practicing law at 197 N. Alabama. In 1875 he became a member of the firm of Buchanan, Williams and Whitehead at the 197 N. Alabama address. The firm changed to Buchanan and Whitehead in 1878 and in 1879 the offices were at Rooms 1 and 3, Thorp Block, 873 Market Street, Indianapolis. Curiously, the city directory in 1880 shows there was the firm of Whitehead and Manlove in the book. This information is curious, because by this time Columbus Delano Whitehead and family were living in Maryville, Missouri.

On September 22, 1875, Columbus Delano Whitehead married Mary Maxwell Wilson in Indianapolis, Indiana. Their marriage license was issued from Marion County, Indiana. The marriage ceremony was performed by Stanford A. Edson, Pastor of Memorial Church. Mary M. Wilson was born at South Salem, Ross County, Ohio on October 5,

1850, the daughter of Rev. James Alfred Wilson and Emily McCullough Maxwell. At the time of her marriage, Mary was working as a teacher in Indianapolis.

Left photo, Mary Maxwell Wilson Whitehead Right photo, Emma Coyner, Mary Belle, Howard Maxwell and Joseph Wilson Whitehead

Mary's father James Alfred Wilson was born on a two hundred acres farm in Paint, Township, Ross County, Ohio, on December 18, 1815, the son of William Wilson and Mary Gaston Maxwell. James A. Wilson married Emily McCullough Maxwell at Crawfordsville, Montgomery County, IN on July 24, 1845. Emily M. Maxwell was born near Hanover, Indiana on July 25, 1819, the daughter of Samuel Campbell Maxwell and Jenny Tilford Maxwell. Emily was a granddaughter of Bezaleel Maxwell and Margaret Anderson Maxwell.

Mary Maxwell Wilson and her older brother Samuel Newton Wilson were orphaned at an early age. Samuel was five years old at the time while Mary was only three. Their father became sick while preaching in the pulpit at a church in Covington, Indiana on June 18, 1851, and died shortly thereafter. Emily Maxwell Wilson died on November 11, 1853, at the home of her sister Mrs. Preston Wiley at Kent, near Hanover, Indiana. Mary M. Wilson and her brother Samuel were raised by their father's sister Mary Wilson Coyner, wife of Prof. John M. Coyner. Mary and John M. Coyner were both teachers and lived at Waveland, IN, a small community located a few miles south of Crawfordsville, the county seat of Montgomery County.

In a small publication noted as a "Circular Letter" published in 1879 detailing the events of the graduates of the Class of 1873 at Wabash College, Columbus Delano Whitehead wrote these lines. "In the early part of 1875 I had the trouble so common to all of our kind. I was in love with a fair damsel whom I wooed and won, and on the 22nd day of

16

Sept. '75, married. Her name was Mary M. Wilson, a daughter of Rev. J. A. Wilson. The fruits of this relationship have been, united love, admiration and two girls, Emma C. born Aug. 12, '76, and Mary B. born Nov. 14, '78."

According to stories passed down through the Whitehead family, Mary Maxwell Wilson was educated at Western College for Women in Oxford, Ohio. This college also had a strong Presbyterian history. While a student there, the dormitory in which she was staying burned. She and her roommate made a rope of bed sheets but it broke as they attempted to climb down forcing them to jump from the third or fourth floor. Men below tried to break their fall and did somewhat, but Mary suffered an injury which kept her semi-invalid from then on. She was said to have a floating kidney and would spend two or three days of every weeks in bed. She had dark eyes and hair. She was very bright, witty and well read, often quoting Dickens, and was an excellent seamstress.

There were two well-known fires at the Western College for Women during the 1800's. One occurred on January 19th, 1861, and the other occurred on April 7, 1871. Existing records indicate it was the 1871 fire in which Mary M. Wilson, who was then twenty years of age, was involved. Information from the publication *Western Female Seminary Catalogues-1854-1870,* shows Mary M. Willson(sic) was one of twenty-three students enrolled in the class of 1871. Her home address was given as Cambridge City, Ind. Cambridge City is in Wayne County, Indiana. The publication, *Memorial; Twenty-fifth Anniversary of the Western Female Seminary,* published in 1880, stated, "Mary (Willson) Whitehead taught in Indianapolis, after recovering from injuries received at the fire, till her marriage to a lawyer of that city. She has two little daughters, Emma and Mary." Mary's specific injuries from the fire were not mentioned. This was also the first source of information that related Mary was working as a teacher at the time she married Columbus Delano Whitehead.

Columbus D. Whitehead ran for the elected post of Criminal Court Judge on October 8, 1878 and came in third in a three-man race. He was also a candidate for Mayor of Indianapolis at the election of May 7, 1789. He had no party affiliation and came in a distant third in a four-man race. The fact that he had no party affiliation hurt his chances severely of winning either election because the newspapers at that time were blatantly political and without the support of a newspaper it was virtually impossible to win any election. Two children were born to Columbus Delano and Mary Whitehead while they were living in Indianapolis, Emma was born on August 12, 1876, and Mary Belle was born on November 14, 1878.

The family moved to Maryville, Polk Township, Nodaway County, MO in 1879, where Columbus Delano worked as a grain shipper in a firm entitled Chambers and Whitehead. Two additional children, Howard and Joseph, were born during the family's stay in Maryville. There is a birth record in the Nodaway County records that records the birth of a male child, the 4th child of this marriage, born May 20, 1884, to Mary Wilson Whitehead and Columbus D. Whitehead. Curiously, the information was posted on August 1, 1884, and the child was still unnamed. This child had to be Joseph Wilson Whitehead because that is his birth date and he was the 4th child. One final bit of information from this record gives Columbus D. Whitehead's occupation as "Insurance Agt." which contradicts the grain shipper occupation.

The family lived in Maryville until 1884 when they moved to Kansas City, MO, where Columbus was engaged in the insurance business. Sometime after the move to Kansas City he ran for Congress on the Populist ticket from the 5th Missouri District. At this election he encountered the same problem he had in Indianapolis, lack of political support for independents or third-party candidates from the local newspapers which assured his defeat. In 1898, he worked as a commercial salesman and in 1905 he went to work for the Kansas City branch of the Philips Carey Manufacturing Company of Lockland, Ohio.

Joseph Wilson, Emma Coyner, Howard Maxwell and Mary Belle Whitehead

Mary Wilson Whitehead's uncle, the Rev. Joseph Gaston Wilson, died at her home on Wabash Avenue in Kansas City, MO on January 24, 1886. The newspaper, *Kansas City Star,* dated Monday, January 25, 1886, stated Rev. Wilson "was 74 years old and was born at Hillsboro, O." Hillsboro is the county seat for Highland County, Ohio. The Rev. Joseph Gaston Wilson during his career served as pastor to several congregations, staying twelve years at the Second Presbyterian Church in Lafayette, Indiana. After he was unable to preach because of throat trouble, he served many years as editor of the Ft. Madison, Iowa newspaper the *Plaindealer*. In 1877, President Rutherford B. Hayes appointed Rev. Wilson the U. S. Consul at Jerusalem where he served for five years. When Rev. Wilson returned to the United States, he made his home with his niece, Mary Wilson Whitehead, as all members of his own family were deceased. See page 82.

Mary Wilson Whitehead traveled to Wausau, Wisconsin in June 1906, where she attended the wedding of her niece Mary Margaret Wilson. Mary married Dr. Harry A. Vedder on June 27, 1906, at the Presbyterian Church in Wausau where her father Dr.

Samuel N. Wilson was the pastor. An article about the wedding appeared in the *Marshfield Times,* Marshfield, WI, dated June 29, 1906, and recorded the guest from out of the city and the name of "Mrs. Whitehead of Kansas City" was listed. She apparently traveled to Wausau alone as Mr. Whitehead's name was not mentioned.

Columbus Delano and Mary moved to Wichita, Kansas in 1909. The 1910 census for Sedgwick County, Kansas showed the Whitehead household with just Columbus and Mary listed. Columbus' younger brother Daniel G. Whitehead and his wife Alice were also found listed on the census in Wichita and they were also the only people listed in their household.

Mary Whitehead died shortly after the 1910 census was taken. The obituary for Mary M. Whitehead that appeared in the Thursday, May 5, 1910, publication of *The Wichita Eagle* said her husband was the manager of the Midland Asbestos Manufacturing Company. The obituary, which misspelled Mary Whitehead's name as Whiteside, stated she died at her home on 612 Schiller Avenue from asthma and bronchitis. Mary died on May 3, 1910, she was fifty-nine years old and was survived by three children. Her body was taken over the Santa Fe Railway to Kansas City. The funeral was held on Friday, May 6, 1910, at her former home on 223 Wabash Avenue, Kansas City. Interment was in Elmwood Cemetery, Kansas City. Mary's early death deprived her grandchildren of ever knowing her which was most unfortunate.

Columbus Delano Whitehead married Christine Roth in Kansas City, MO on June 22, 1911. Grandma Tena, as she became known, had previously worked for the Whitehead family in Kansas City. Christine had become an integral part of the household doing the cooking and housework because of Mary Wilson Whitehead's poor health, which was due in part to the accident she suffered in the fall while at college. When Columbus Delano and Mary later moved to Wichita, Kansas, Christine started keeping a boarding house in Kansas City.

At some point after Mary's death, Columbus Delano started his own company called the Whitehead Supply Company located at 145 North Water Street. The company sold material for fire proofing, insulating, water proofing and roofing. The business was successful, and Columbus did better financially with this company than he had with any of his other occupations. An associate with Columbus in the roofing business was a Jim McCloud.

Back row, Hawley W. Drake, Benjamin W. Dwight, Emma Whitehead Dwight, Floribel
Needles Whitehead, Samuel H. Whitehead, and Joseph W. Whitehead
Middle row, Sarah Arbuthnot, Ruth Dwight Uphaus, Mary Dwight Livesay, Catherine
Drake Hoover, Mary Whitehead Drake, Christine Roth Whitehead, Joseph D. Whitehead
Front row, Philip M. Whitehead, Benjamin D. Whitehead, Marian Whitehead
Eichenberger, David W. Whitehead and William B. Whitehead

Columbus was a schoolmate of Vice President Thomas R. Marshall during their time at Wabash College in Crawfordsville, Indiana; both graduating in 1873. Vice President Thomas R. Marshall was on a Lecture Tour where he had an engagement scheduled at the First Presbyterian Church in Wichita the evening of November 13, 1914. In an article that appeared in the *Wichita Beacon* dated November 13, 1914, the Vice President "will be greeted by an old classmate whom he has not seen for years." Columbus D. Whitehead was asked by the reception committee to introduce them to the Vice President since "he is probably the only man in Wichita who knows Mr. Marshall personally."

C. D. Whitehead of 2604 East 15th Street died on May 27, 1919, in Wichita, Kansas as a result of a roofing accident. A family story relates he was showing some of his workers how to work safely on the roof when he accidentally backed off the roof and fell eighteen feet. The article about the accident that appeared in the *Wichita Beacon* on May 28, 1919, however, stated he had been "supervising the placing of roofing on the Freeman Building near Washington and Gilbert Streets, when he slipped from the roof. He was taken to the St. Francis Hospital and died about an hour later." The internal injuries he suffered in the fall combined with his age of 71 years and the fact he was "a large man physically, made his recovery impossible." The article also stated he had been living in Wichita for ten years. His brother Daniel G. Whitehead of 344 North Grove, Wichita, Kansas was mentioned as his only surviving sibling.

Columbus Delano Whitehead

The death certificate for Columbus Delano Whitehead, signed by Christine Whitehead, gave his name as Delano C. Whitehead and stated he died at 4 P.M. The death certificate also stated he was "Mgr. Whitehead Supply Co." Therefore, it is possible he may have been in business with his brother Daniel or other individuals.

Services were held for Columbus Delano Whitehead at the Pentecostal Nazarene Church in Wichita of which he had been an active member. His body was removed to Kansas City, MO, where he was buried in Elmwood Cemetery. Columbus was buried in the same section that contained the remains of his wife Mary Wilson Whitehead and their son Howard Maxwell Whitehead. Following her husband's death Grandma Tena went to live with her stepson Joseph W. Whitehead and his family in Kansas City. Grandma Tena died at her home of a heart blockage on January 17, 1937. She was seventy-five years old. She was buried in Memorial Park Cemetery in Kansas City, MO, in a plot purchased by Joseph W. Whitehead.

Columbus D. Whitehead's granddaughter Ruth Dwight Uphaus, as a young child, remembered him "as a big man with lots of white hair, gentle and patient with us children." Ruth also recalled that on the day of her grandfather's death, he and Grandma Tena had read at their morning devotional a passage from the 34th Psalm in which verse 20 stated, "He keepth all his bones; not one of them is broken." This appears to have been a prophecy concerning his death since none of his bones were broken in the fall.

Columbus Delano, William Bray, Joseph Delano and Joseph Wilson Whitehead

Perhaps the most fitting tribute to the life of Columbus Delano Whitehead were the words he wrote himself in a 1905 Wabash College Alumni questionnaire. He stated, "This is not a brilliant record, but it's made. I can't say that I am particularly proud of it, nor am I ashamed of it. If a failure it is due to environment more than lack of effort. There's a destiny in the affairs of men which shapes their ends rough, hew them how you may."

Columbus Delano and Mary Maxwell Wilson Whitehead were the parents of five children, with four reaching adulthood.

1. Emma Coyner Whitehead
2. Mary Belle Whitehead
3. Howard Maxwell Whitehead
4. Joseph Wilson Whitehead
5. Maxwell Delano Whitehead, born April 24, 1890, died September 3, 1890

EMMA COYNER WHITEHEAD was born August 12, 1876, at Indianapolis, Indiana, the daughter of Columbus Delano and Mary Wilson Whitehead. After graduating from Central High in 1897, Emma attended a summer teacher's training seminar and began teaching in Kansas City at the Irving School which taught sixth and seventh grades.

Emma was an active member in the Methodist Epworth League at the Independence Avenue Methodist Episcopal Church. She had a strong mezzo soprano voice and sang for a time in a paid church quartet. She belonged to a social club called the Idle Hours Outing Club to which young businessmen also belonged. Club members went boating on the Blue River, picnicked, took in plays at the Coates House, and played whist.

It was at one of these outing where Emma met Benjamin Wilbur Dwight. Benjamin was born October 5, 1870, in Logansport, Indiana. Emma and Benjamin were married at the

Independence Avenue Methodist Episcopal Church on June 27, 1907. Emma's address on the marriage license was given as 323 Wabash, Jackson County, Missouri.

Back row, Mary Dwight Livesey, Samuel Howard Whitehead, Joseph Delano Whitehead,
Oscar Leslie Uphaus, Ruth Dwight Uphaus, Joseph Wilson Whitehead,
Front row, John Strother Livesay, Emma Whitehead Dwight, Floribel Needles
Whitehead, Ruth Willoughby Whitehead, Dwight Leslie Uphaus and Esther Lou Uphaus

The family was found for the 1920 Missouri census living in Kansas City, Ward 16, Jackson County, Missouri. Ben's father was noted from Massachusetts, while his mother was born in Iowa. There were two children in the home, Ruth M. Dwight, age 11, and Mary E. Dwight, age 10. A young man recorded as Hawley Drake, age 17, was noted as a nephew to Ben was also listed.

Benjamin W. Dwight was a traveling salesman who worked on a commission. He traveled quite a bit, staying away from home nine months out of a year. He would correspond with his children by letters letting them know his itinerary and where he would be. He was an active member of the First Nazarene Church of Kansas City.

Benjamin W. Dwight died on January 23, 1939, at Lakeside Hospital of prostate surgery complications. Emma and her daughter Mary Ella lived together until Mary's marriage to Strother Ewing Livesay in June 1940. After this time Emma divided her time between her daughters' families. She had developed diabetes after the birth of a third child which was born when she was forty years of age. The child was born dead. The diabetes eventually affected her eyesight. The development of insulin was the only thing that helped stabilized her medical condition.

Emma Whitehead Dwight died of a sudden heart attack at the age of seventy-one at the home of her daughter Ruth Dwight Uphaus near Lexington, MO. Emma was buried, where?

Emma Whitehead and Benjamin W. Dwight were the parents of two children.

1. Ruth Maxwell Dwight
2. Mary Ella Dwight

RUTH MAXWELL DWIGHT was born May 31, 1908, the daughter of Benjamin Wilbur and Emma Whitehead Dwight.

Ruth married Oscar Leslie Uphaus on August 2, 1938. Oscar was born on June 13, 1899, the son of Martin and Elizabeth Uphaus.

Oscar died on December 27, 1970, in Grandview, MO.

Oscar and Ruth Dwight Uphaus were the parents of three children.

1. Dwight Leslie Uphaus
2. Esther Louise Uphaus
3. Charles Maxwell Uphaus

DWIGHT LESLIE UPHAUS was born on June 21, 1939, the son of Oscar Leslie and Ruth Dwight Uphaus.

Dwight married Annalee Janell McFarland on August 18, 1961. Annalee was born in March 1939, the daughter of ___ and ___.

Dwight and Annalee McFarland Uphaus were the parents of three children.

1. Lelsie Ann Uphaus
2. Andra Lynn Uphaus, born February 17, 1969
3. Joel David Uphaus, born July 31, 1971

LESLIE ANN UPHAUS was born on May 6, 1963, the daughter of Dwight and Annalee McFarland Uphaus. Leslie married Randy Wunder on December 17, 1983.

ESTHER LOUISE UPHAUS was born on March 30, 1942, the daughter of Oscar and Ruth Dwight Uphaus. Esther married Stephen Wayne Lockhart in 1967. Stephen was born in September 1942, the son of ___ and ___. They are the parents of one child.

1. Kevin Lockhart, born June 30, 1968

CHARLES MAXWELL UPHAUS was born on October 14, 1947, the son of Oscar and Ruth Dwight Uphaus. Charles married Kathryn Amanda Winter on May 20, 1972. Kathryn was born in October 1946. They are the parents of two children.

1. Adele Kathryn Uphaus
2. Maxwell Benjamin Uphaus, born October 4, 1983

MARY ELLA DWIGHT was born on June 10, 1909, the daughter of Benjamin Wilbur and Emma Whitehead Dwight. The 1940 Missouri census gives Mary's address as East 75th Avenue, Jackson County, Missouri. She was working as a music teacher. Her highest grade completed was college, 4th year.

Mary married Strother Ewing Livesay on June 22, 1940. Strother was born in Lafayette County, Missouri on November 1, 1897, the son of John and Elizabeth Livesay. The 1940 Missouri census finds Strother living with his parents in Blue Township, Jackson County. MO. His occupation was given as deputy.

Strother died on November 12, 1959. He was buried in Salem Cemetery, Independence, MO. Mary Ella Livesay died March 22, 1994, she too was buried in Salem Cemetery, Independence, MO.

Strother and Mary Dwight Livesay were the parents of two children.

1. John Strother Livesay
2. Joseph Dwight Livesay

JOHN STROTHER LIVESAY was born on January 17, 1942, the son of Strothert Ewing and Mary Dwight Livesay. John married Rita Ann Grider on September 5, 1964. They have no children.

JOSEPH DWIGHT LIVESAY was born on May 10, 1945, the son of Strother Ewing and Mary Dwight Livesay. Joseph married Sonja Brown on August 4, 1968.

MARY BELLE WHITEHEAD was born in Indianapolis, Indiana on November 14, 1877, the daughter of Columbus Delano and Mary Wilson Whitehead.

Mary married Willard Royce Drake on June 18, 1901. Willard was from Kansas City and was an artist on the staff of the *Kansas City Star.* Mary was a primary school teacher in Kansas City for forty-plus years. Willard died on February 6, 1910, in Denver, Col. Mary died June 20, 1957, of arteriole sclerosis.

Mary Belle Whitehead Drake

Mary and Willard were the parents of two children.

1. Hawley Wilson Drake, born May 28, 1902, died August 29, 1931
2. Catherine Delano Drake

CATHERINE DELANO DRAKE was born on July 7, 1908, the daughter of Willard Royce and Mary Whitehead Drake. Catherine married Clive Eugene Hoover at the home of her mother at 1162 E. 75th Terrace, Kansas City, MO on December 31, 1933.

Catherine was an artist and seamstress. Clive worked for Eastman Kodak Company. For many years they have spent their summers in Colorado in a cabin they built above Estes Park.

Mary Lynn Hoover, Catherine Drake Hoover, Ruth Willoughby Whitehead and Joseph Delano Whitehead

Clive and Catherine were the parents on one child.

    1. Mary Lynn Hoover

MARY LYNN HOOVER was born in Chicago, Illinois on November 9, 1940, the daughter of Clive Eugene and Catherine Drake Hoover. Mary married Harvey Case in 1960. They are the parents of four children.

    1. Brian Eugene Case, born February 1, 1961
    2. Sherryl Lee Case, born May 23, 1967
    3. Dennis Leonard Case, born February 10, 1970
    4. Cynthia Lynn Case, born January 14, 1973

HOWARD MAXWELL WHITEHEAD was born June 30, 1882, in Maryville, MO the son of Columbus Delano and Mary Wilson Whitehead. Uncle Howard was remembered by his niece Ruth Dwight Uphaus as "a wonderful young man who played football in high school and put up a tremendous battles against tuberculosis. He was a fine Christian man. Grandmother (Mary Wilson Whitehead) took him on a long trip to California hoping it would improve his health, but it was of no avail." Howard died of tuberculosis on January 10, 1902. He was buried in Elmwood Cemetery in Kansas City, MO.

27

Howard Maxwell Whitehead

JOSEPH WILSON WHITEHEAD was born in Maryville, Nodaway County, Missouri on May 20, 1884, the son of Columbus Delano and Mary Wilson Whitehead. There is a Nodaway County birth record that states a male child was born there on May 20, 1884, to Mary Wilson Whitehead and Columbus Delano Whitehead. The child, the 4th for this family, was still unnamed as of August 1, 1884, when the information was filed with the county. Joseph, known by family members as Joe, attended high school in Kansas City, MO.

Joseph W. Whitehead married Floribel Elma Needles on January 1, 1907. They were married by the Rev. Matt L. Hughes of 2411 Independence. Floribel Needles was born in Sedalia, Missouri on November 8, 1885, the daughter of Simgesmer Needles and Elma Florence Bray Needles. Simgesmer Needles was born in Dayton, Montgomery County, Ohio and Elma was born in Millersburg, Holmes County, Ohio.

The 1913 city directory for Wichita, KS list this young couple living on 211 E 8th ST. He was working for the Whitehead Supply Company. A few listings up from Joseph was that of his father Columbus D. (Christine) of Whitehead Supply Company and his uncle Daniel G. (Alice) Whitehead. The Joseph W. Whitehead family was listed in these records for the last time for 1914, apparently returning to Kansas City. Found there for the 1920 census.

Joseph Wilson Whitehead

Joseph worked for and eventually retired from the Sinclair Oil Company. The 1930 Missouri, Jackson County, Kansas City, District 210 census shows this family. Joseph Whitehead's occupation at that time was listed as "General Agent Refining Co." There were eight children listed in the home including Christine (Grandma Tena) Whitehead. Joseph's stepmother.

The 1940 Missouri census locates the Whitehead family living on 3327 Bellefontaine, Kansas City, Missouri. The family had resided at the address since 1935. Joseph's occupation was given as Director of the Travel Bureau for an Oil Refining Company which was probably the Sinclair Oil Company. There were five children still in the home

Joseph and Floribel Whitehead were among the early leading founders of the First Church of the Nazarene in Kansas City. Their devotion to the worldwide growth of the Church of the Nazarene was a lifelong commitment. Floribel's youngest sister Margaret Needles was a missionary to China for many years.

Top left, Joseph Wilson Whitehead, Top right, Floribel Elma Needles Whitehead
Bottom photo, Whitehead home in Kansas City, Missouri

During World War II, Joseph collected letters from various family members and sent them in a collection to other family members so everyone could keep up with what was going on at that time. Their sons David, Sam and Philip were involved in combat and it was a worrisome time for all concerned with the safety of their loved ones. Joseph's granddaughter Priscilla Whitehead McCloud has a three-volume set of these treasured letters.

*Left photo, , Joseph Delano, Marian Elma and William Bray Whitehead Right photo,
back row, Marian Elma, William Bray and Joseph Delano Whitehead front row,
Benjamin Dwight and David Wilson Whitehead*

On December 6, 1950, Floribel Needles Whitehead was accepted as a member of the
Daughters of the American Revolution in the Elizabeth Benton Chapter in Kansas City,
MO. Her membership relative was Asa Bray who served as "Captain, in Connecticut
Troops, Revolutionary Army." Captain Bray first served as a Connecticut State Militia
Lieutenant in December 1774. In November 1776, he was appointed Captain and served
under Col. Thaddeus Cook until March 1777. From March 1777 until June 1777, he
served under Col. Hooker's Militia Regiment. In September 1777, he was with Gen.
Gates Army which defeated Gen. Burgoyne. On July 5, 1779, he marched to New Haven
to repel Tyron and on June 22, 1780, was appointed first on the Committee of the Town
of Southington to raise troops.

Back row, Benjamin Dwight, William Bray and Marian Elma Whitehead
Front row, David Wilson, Philip Maxwell, Samuel Howard and Joseph Delano
Whitehead

Following retirement from the Sinclair Oil Company, Joseph worked in the same capacity for the AAA. Joseph Whitehead finally retired after his wife passed away in 1959.

Floribel Needles Whitehead of 226 West Fifty-third Street, Kansas City MO died of cancer on October 15, 1959. Services were held at the First Church of the Nazarene with the Freeman Mortuary in charge. Burial was in Mount Washington Cemetery, Kansas City MO.

Joseph W. Whitehead eventually sold the house on West 53rd Street and moved to an apartment on Grand Ave. or Street. The remainder of his life he stayed active visiting his children and various grandchildren. He was on hand in Fayetteville, NC, to drive his granddaughter Priscilla Whitehead McCloud home from the hospital after she had given birth to his first great-granddaughter Caroline Ruth McCloud on February 10, 1962.

Back row, Joseph Wilson, Joseph Delano, William Bray and Marian Elma Whitehead
Middle row, David Wilson, Benjamin Dwight and Floribel Needles Whitehead
Front row, Samuel Howard, Margaret Needles and Philip Maxwell Whitehead

A brief testimony to the faith of Joseph W. Whitehead may be found in a letter he wrote to his niece Ruth Dwight Uphaus on January 19, 1961, cited here;

> The Lord is wonderfully blessing me these days. Regardless
> of my great sorrow I can truly say that the past year has been
> the most blessed year of my life for I have found that truly the
> Lord is the God of all comfort.
>
> With my heart condition it is quite possible that I might go at
> any time but I can leave this testimony that I am ready and willing
> to go for I know that instant death will be instant glory for me.
> I have made my peace with God and through His marvelous
> grace I have settled the sin question and know that someday I will
> see Him face to face. Praise His name!!

Joseph W. Whitehead of 5906 Grand, Kansas City, died of heart failure on May 2, 1969. Services were held at the First Church of the Nazarene and conducted by D. W. Newcomer's Sons. Interment was at Mount Washington Cemetery, Kansas City, MO.

Joseph Wilson and Floribel Needles Whitehead

The section of Mount Washington Cemetery where Floribel and Joseph Whitehead are buried also contains the remains of their daughter Marian Whitehead Eichenberger. Floribel's sisters Lida and Lucy Needles are also buried in the same section as is their brother Dr. William Bray Needles.

Joseph W. and Floribel Needles Whitehead were the parents of eight children.

1. Joseph Delano Whitehead
2. William Bray Whitehead
3. Marian Elma Whitehead
4. David Wilson Whitehead
5. Benjamin Dwight Whitehead
6. Philip Maxwell Whitehead
7. Samuel Howard Whitehead
8. Margaret Needles Whitehead

JOSEPH DELANO WHITEHEAD was born November 8, 1908, the son of Joseph Wilson and Floribel Needles Whitehead. Joe was a bookkeeper for Sinclair Oil Company. He served in the U. S. Army during W. W. II, rising to the rank of Captain in the anti-aircraft forces. Joseph married Leona Ruth Willoughby. Joe died of a heart attack at his home in Arkansas on July 3, 1969. Ruth died on December 18, 1996. Joe and Ruth are buried in Mt. Washington Cemetery in Kansas City. There were no children of this marriage.

34

Top left, Floribel Needles and Joseph Delano Whitehead Top right, Joseph Delano and Ruth Willoughby Whitehead Bottom photo, Joseph Delano and Ruth Willoughby Whitehead

WILLIAM BRAY WHITEHEAD was born in Kansas City, MO on February 10, 1911, the son of Joseph Wilson and Floribel Needles Whitehead. William was named for his uncle Dr. William Bray Needles and his grandfather William Bray. William graduated from Central High School in Kansas City. The 1930 Missouri, Jackson County, Kansas City census shows the 19-year-old young man working as a "Cost Clerk' at a furniture store. This had to be Abernathy's Furniture Store, a store that was at the center of many of his stories later in life.

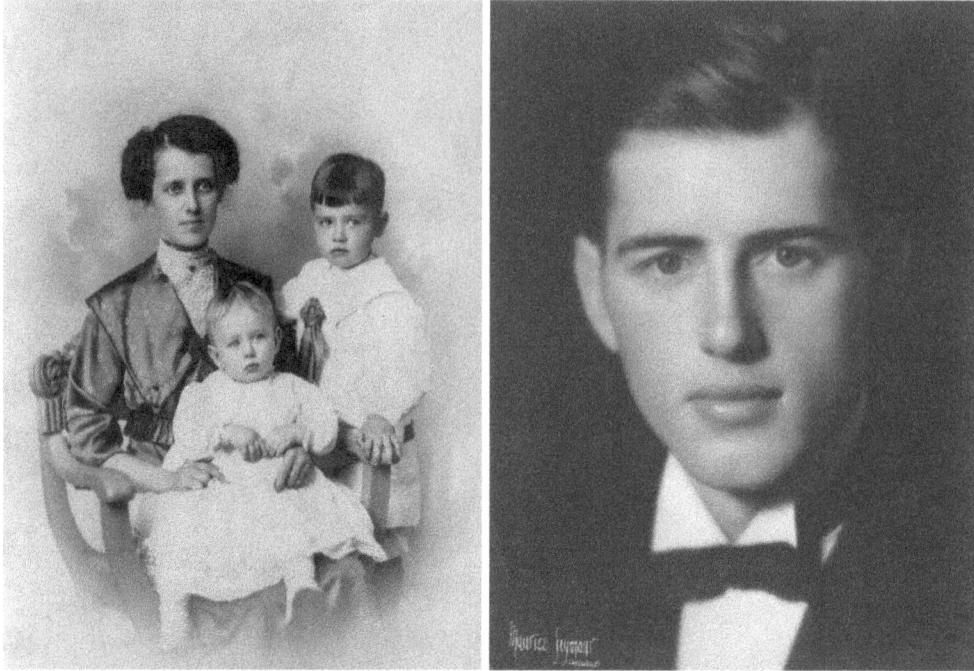

Left photo, Floribel Needles, William Bray and Joseph Delano Whitehead Right photo,
William Bray Whitehead

William left Kansas City, moving to Chicago, IL, where he attended Northern Illinois
College of Optometry graduating from there on June 9, 1933. The optometry school was
owned by his uncle and name sake Dr. William Bray Needles. Following graduation
William took up a teaching position with the school and lived at Drexel Blvd.

William B. Whitehead married Winona Ruth Odell on January 1, 1934, in Chicago, IL.
William and Winona had met while they were both attending the First Nazarene Church
near her home. Winona was born on May 8, 1910, the daughter of Ira N. and Johanna
Schultz Odell.

Maxine Butterfield, Melvin Anderson, Florence Kelly, Raymond Benson, William Bray Whitehead, Winona Odell Whitehead, Joseph Delano Whitehead, Marian Elma Whitehead, Richard Needles, Margaret Scheithe with Cynthia and David Whitsel

An article found in the *Chicago Tribune* states "As the first day of the New Year drew to a close, Winona Ruth Odell, slipped into her long-trained white satin wedding gown, her net veil caught into a satin cap embroidered with pearls, and accompanied her attendants to the First Nazarene church to meet her bridegroom Dr. William Bray Whitehead." Winona's maid of honor was Marian Whitehead of Kansas City, sister to the groom. Her gown was of orchid satin. She wore a silver band over her hair and carried yellow tea roses and sweet peas. The bridesmaids Margaret Scheithe and Florence Kelly were in peach, while Maxine Butterfield wore green. All three held bouquets of Talisman roses.

William's best man was his brother Joseph D. Whitehead of Kansas City. Richard Needles, Melvin Anderson and Raymond Benson were ushers. A reception for 175 guests was held at the G.A.R. Hall at 6223 Princeton Ave. Winona's extended family members in attendance were Louise Hudenburg, Roy Hudenburg, Catherine Hudenburg, Bertha Van Dyk, Albert H. Schultz, Joyce Van Dyk, Jay Van Dyk and Mr. and Mrs. Stanley Van Dyk.

Top photo, Winona Odell Whitehead Bottom left, Winona Odell and William Bray Whitehead Bottom right, Joseph Wilson, Floribel Needles Whitehead with Priscilla Ruth and William Odell Whitehead

Guest from the Wilson side of the Whitehead family was Mrs. Harry Vedder, a first cousin to William's father, and her daughter Mrs. Stanley Morner. Lillian Mae Vedder was the wife of Stanley Morner, better known as the actor Dennis Morgan.

At the time of her marriage, Winona was living with her widowed mother at 6755 Sangamon Street, Chicago, IL. Winona's mother and father had operated a successful electrical business in Chicago for a number of years. However, by the time of the 1930 Illinois, Cook County, census, Winona's father was working as a Realtor-Broker.

Winona and her family were devastated when the unexpected death of her father Ira N. Odell occurred on January 1931. See page 163.

William and Winona lived in an apartment for a while following their marriage. William was then working as an instructor at the Optometry School. To supplement his income, he also saw patients in his home in the evening. A short time after this William and Winona moved in with her mother and lived there for nearly eight years until the family moved to North Carolina in 1943. William also established an upstairs office at his mother-in-law's home where he practiced his profession in the evenings.

Priscilla Ruth, Winona Odell, William Odell and Lawrence Joseph Whitehead

William B. Whitehead was issued a license to practice Optometry in North Carolina on March 17, 1943. After receiving his license, William went alone to Fayetteville, NC where he established his new practice. During this time, he lived in a boarding house on Hay Street near Haymount Hill. After finding an adequate office location, he opened his Optometric practice at the corner of Old and Green Streets. He eventually purchased a home on 2610 Pecan Drive and then brought his family down from Chicago. Winona and their two children came by rail from Chicago to Fayetteville in May 1943. The office was later moved to 549 Hay Street, one block up and across the street from the Prince Charles Hotel and the Sears Department Store.

Shortly after Winona and the children arrived in Fayetteville, her mother became sick with pneumonia. Winona took the train back to Chicago and once her mother was able to travel, Winona brought Mrs. Odell to live with her family in Fayetteville. Mrs. Odell died at her daughter's home on February 22, 1946. Her body was returned to Chicago where she was buried beside her husband at Mount Greenwood Cemetery.

Top photo, William Bray, Priscilla Ruth, Lawrence Joseph, Winona Odell and William Odell Whitehead   Bottom photo, William Bray and Winona Odell Whitehead

William and Winona Whitehead were instrumental in purchasing a lot in Fayetteville and then a building from Fort Bragg when the first church of the Nazarene was established in Fayetteville on Fort Bragg Road. The family also later purchased a home in Punta

Gorda, FL, where they were going to retire one day. But sadly, William and Winona never had the chance to retire together.

Winona Ruth Odell Whitehead died in Scottsdale, Arizona on October 16, 1973, while she and William were visiting his sister Margaret Whitehead Smith. Winona was returned to North Carolina where she was buried at La Fayette Memorial Park, Fayetteville, NC.

William B. Whitehead married Gertrude Chapman Lampher in 1974 in Kansas City, MO. William and Gertrude had known one another since their childhood days in Kansas City. Following their marriage, William and Gertrude established a home in Fayetteville for a while but later moved to Rogers, Arkansas. They then moved to and purchased a home in Bethany, Oklahoma where one of Gertrude's daughters lived. Gertrude died in London, England while on vacation with her daughter in 1984. William had her body returned to the United States and following a funeral in Oklahoma, her body was removed to Kansas City where she was buried beside her first husband.

William Bray and Winona Odell Whitehead

The home in Oklahoma was eventually sold and William moved back to Fayetteville with the help of his grandson Edward W. McCloud. After living alone for about a year and with his health declining, William moved into a small apartment at his daughter's home where he peacefully lived out his final years. William Bray Whitehead died at the home of his daughter Priscilla Whitehead McCloud at 1642 Greenock Avenue, Fayetteville, NC on June 27, 1995. William was buried beside his wife and his son Larry Whitehead in La Fayette Memorial Park, Fayetteville, NC.

William Bray and Winona Odell Whitehead were the parents of three children.

1. William Odell Whitehead
2. Priscilla Ruth Whitehead
3. Lawrence Joseph Whitehead

WILLIAM ODELL WHITEHEAD was born in Chicago, IL on December 7, 1935, the son of William Bray Whitehead and Winona Odell Whitehead. William, known as Bill, moved with his family to Fayetteville, NC in May 1943. Bill graduate from Fayetteville High School in 1953.   He then attended Eastern Nazarene College in Wollaston, MA. Following graduation, he then attended Tuffs Medical School, graduating in 1961. He did his internship at Indiana University and his residency at New England Medical Center, Boston University.

Winona Odell, William Odell and William Bray Whitehead

Bill married Carol Peterson in Boston, MA in 1960. Carol was born on January 13, 1941, in Essex County, Massachusetts, the daughter of Peter Robert Peterson and Alma R. Peterson, Carol's mother is of French-Canadian heritage. Carol was working as a surgical nurse when she and Bill first met.

William Odell Whitehead and Carol Peterson Whitehead

Carol's parents were found for the 1940 Massachusetts census living in Lynn, Essex County. Peter, also known as Pete, was listed as working as a Draftsman working on Electrical Equipment, while Alma was working as a lamp inspector in a lamp works company. Both were listed as 27 years of age, there were no children in the home at this time.

In a recent conversation with Alma's grandson Gregg R. Whitehead, he stated his grandmother's maiden name was Richard and hailed from Prince Edward Island, Canada.

Left photo, William Odell and Carol Peterson Whitehead Right photo, Dawn Elizabeth, William Odell, Gregg Richard, Carol Peterson and Glenn William Whitehead

Carol's father is of Armenian heritage. His parents, Stanley M. Peterson and Carolina Peterson, were both from Lithuanian apparently part of an Armenian contingent in that country. There were five children listed on the 1930 MA Essex County census, the oldest was 20 years old while the youngest was 7 years old. All the children listed were born in Massachusetts. At the time of the census the family was living in Saugus, Essex County on 67 Walden Pond Ave., both parents were working in the Morocco leather industry.

Top photo, middle Commander William Odell Whitehead, M..D. Search and Rescue
Leader, Key West, Florida and crew
Bottom photo, Glenn William, Gregg Richard, Dawn Whitehead Wilson and Carol
Peterson Whitehead

Following his residency for Ophthalmology at Indianapolis, IN, Bill entered the U.S. Navy as a Flight Surgeon. To qualify for this position Bill had to attend flight school where at completion he proudly gained his wings. During his time in the military, there was a three-year tour of duty in England.

Carol's mother passed away on February 24, 1978. She was buried in the Pine Grove Cemetery in Lynn, MA. Peter eventually moved to Lee County, NC where he married again on April 4, 1980, to Clair Langevin. Bill and Carol were there to witness the marriage. Peter died January 5, 1992, in Lee County, NC. He was cremated.

Bill was in private practice in Sanford, NC for several years, but resigned that position to re-enter the Navy. He became a senior medical director on the carrier USS Coral Sea. He retired from the Navy on _____. Following his retirement, he and Carol made their home at Virginia Beach, VA.

Carol Peterson and William Odell Whitehead

William Odell Whitehead died of prostate cancer on November 2, 2007. He was interred in Arlington National Cemetery. His tombstone states he served 26 years seeing service in Vietnam and Persian Gulf War. He was a commander in the U.S. Navy.

Carol Peterson Whitehead died on August 22, 2019 and is buried with William Whitehead at Arlington National Cemetery.

Bill and Carol were the parents of three children.

1. Glenn William Whitehead

2. Dawn Elizabeth Whitehead
3. Gregg Richard Whitehead

DAWN ELIZABETH WHITEHEAD was born August 8, 1963. She married Marty Wilson on June 21, 1987. He was born in Granite Falls, NC. He retired from the North Carolina Rural Water Association. The family lives in Bermuda Run, NC.

Marty Wilson, Dawn Whitehead Wilson, Matthew Wilson, Tyler Lee and Elise Wilson Lee

Dawn and Marty Wilson are the parents of two children.

1. Elise Wilson
2. Matthew Wilson

GREGG RICHARD WHITEWHEAD was born on July 15, 1868. He married Dana Lewis on February 15, 1987. Gregg is the City Manager for Richland, NC. He and Dana are the parents of one child.

Jason, Gregg Richard Whitehead and Dana Lewis Whitehead

1. Jason Whitehead

PRISCILLA RUTH WHITEHEAD was born in Chicago, IL on August 7, 1937, the daughter of William Bray Whitehead and Winona Odell Whitehead. Priscilla moved with her family to Fayetteville, NC in May 1943. She attended the Fayetteville City Schools graduating from Fayetteville High School in 1955. She then attended Eastern Nazarene College in Wollaston, MA from 1955 to 1959.

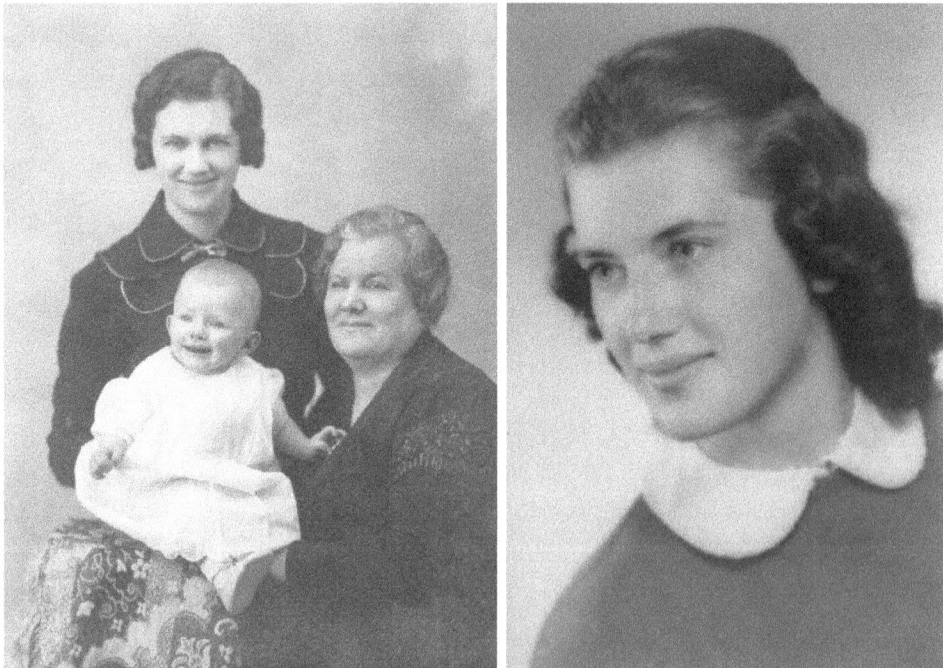

Left photo, Winona Odell Whitehead, Johanna Schultz Odell and Priscilla Ruth Whitehead Right phot, Priscilla Ruth Whitehead

Priscilla married Robert D. McCloud on January 1, 1961, at the Nazarene Church in Fayetteville. Robert was born May 31, 1938, at Warrenton, VA, the son of James E. and Regina Carder McCloud.

Left photo, Priscilla Ruth Whitehead Right photo, Robert Davis and Priscilla Whitehead McCloud Bottom photo, Edward Wilson McCloud, Janet McCloud Firmani, Priscilla Whitehead McCloud, Cheryl McCloud Helm, Annette McCloud Jimmerson and Caroline McCloud Self

Robert D. McCloud graduated from Southern College of Optometry in 1973. He established his first practice with his father-in-law, Dr. W. B. Whitehead, in Fayetteville,

NC, working together until Dr. Whitehead's retirement. Since that time Robert has had a solo practice until his own retirement in December 2015.

Priscilla eventually went to work for the school system in Cumberland County, retiring in 2010.

Priscilla and Robert were divorced in 1992.

Priscilla Ruth Whitehead and Robert D. McCloud were the parents of five children.

1. Caroline Ruth McCloud
2. Edward Wilson McCloud
3. Janet Beth McCloud
4. Annette Leigh McCloud
5. Cheryl Ann McCloud

CAROLINE RUTH McCLOUD was born February 10, 1962, at Cape Fear Valley Hospital, Fayetteville, NC, the daughter of Robert and Priscilla Whitehead McCloud. She was born on the same month and day as her grandfather William B. Whitehead. Caroline's middle name was the same as her grandmother Winona Ruth Odell Whitehead and her mother Priscilla Ruth Whitehead McCloud.

Caroline attended public school in Fayetteville, North Carolina and Southhaven, Mississippi, graduating from Seventy-First High School, Fayetteville, NC in 1983. She then attended East Carolina University, graduating with a degree in Political Science.

Caroline married Gary Schott on December 31, 1983, at the Church of the Nazarene in Fayetteville. Gary, Gerald David Stephen Schott, was born in Germany on April 14, 1961, the son of Lawrence Henry and Rose Marie Kling Schott. Gary was also a graduate of Seventy-First High School and East Carolina University.

Left photo, Caroline McCloud and Ahren Christian Self Right photo, Chelsea Madeline Schott, Caroline McCloud Self and Chad Laurence Schott

At the time of their marriage, Gary was serving with the U S. Air Force near Pasadena, CA. He was a navigator flying C-130 aircrafts. The family eventually moved to North Little Rock Air Force Base, Jacksonville, AK, where he served out the remainder of his tour of duty.

Following his release from the Air Force in 1990, Gary joined Pfizer Pharmaceutical Company. The family lived in Charlotte for a while and then Kings Mountain and finally in Charleston, SC.

Caroline and Gary were divorced in 1997. Caroline married Ahren Christian Self on July 9, 1999. They were married in an evening ceremony on the veranda of Lowndes Plantation on the Ashley River in Charleston. Ahren was born on February 26, 1973, in West Virginia, the son of Ron Self and Louise Miles. Ahren, a 1995 graduate of the Citadel, was a former football player and later football coach for the Citadel. In 2004, Ahren left the Citadel coaching staff to take a position with the Elon College football program at Elon, NC.

In 2005, Ahren left Elon and took a coaching position with the University of Tennessee at Chattanooga. Ahren then accepted a coaching position at a high school in Athens, GA. Carolina worked for the historical Lyndon House Arts Center in Athens. The family living in the Athens area for five years.

In 2016, Ahren then took a coaching position in Summerville, SC school system. Caroline is currently an Artist and Insurance Broker in Summerville, SC.

Caroline McCloud Self is the parent of two children.

1. Chadwick Laurence Schott
2. Chelsea Madeline Schott

CHADWICK LAURENCE SCHOTT was born on October 22, 1985, in Jacksonville, AK, the son of Caroline McCloud and Gary Schott. Chadwick, better known as Chad, graduated from James Island Charter High School, Charleston, SC, on May 26, 2004, at a ceremony held at the Citadel.

Chad is employed by Accenture and resides in Austin, Texas.

Chad Laurence Schott, Chelsea Madeline Schott and Caroline McCloud Self

CHELSEA MADELINE SCHOTT was born on February 2, 1989, in Jacksonville, AK, the daughter of Caroline McCloud and Gary Schott. Chelsea graduated from Emory University, Atlanta, GA majoring in Business. She graduated from Stanford University in June 2018 with her MBA in Business.

Chelsea is employed by Bain Capital and resides in Seattle, Washington.

Dan LeClerc and Chelsea Madeline Schott

EDWARD WILSON McCLOUD was born on June 26, 1963, at Cape Fear Valley Hospital, Fayetteville, NC, the son of Robert and Priscilla Whitehead McCloud. Edward's middle name was given because there are Wilsons from both the Whitehead and the McCloud sides of his family.

Edward attended public school in Fayetteville, NC and Southhaven, MS. He graduated from Seventy First High School in Fayetteville on June 10, 1981.

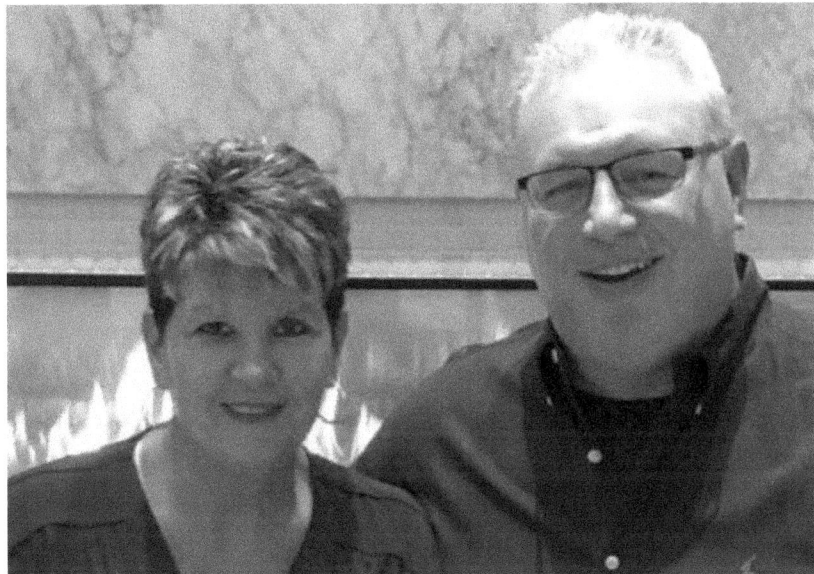

Jacqueline Melvin and Edward Wilson McCloud

Edward married Jacqueline Marie Melvin on November 7, 1992, in a ceremony at the Hay Street Methodist Church in Fayetteville. Jacqueline was born April 13, 1966, the daughter of Joe Harrington and Marie Darden Melvin. She was a graduate of E. E. Smith and the University of North Carolina at Greensboro.

Jacqueline works for Macy's Department Store as a Manager. Edward works for Mark IV as a shipping specialist. They make their home in Fayetteville.

JANET BETH McCLOUD was born on March 13, 1966, at Cape Fear Valley, Fayetteville, NC, the daughter of Robert and Priscilla Whitehead McCloud. Janet attended public school in Southaven, MS and Fayetteville, NC. She graduated from Seventy-First High School in Fayetteville in 1984.

Janet's son with Gary Decker, Alexander Bray McCloud, was born on February 7, 1991, at Cape Fear Valley Hospital.

Left photo, Janet McCloud and Mark Christoph Firmani Right photo, Janet McCloud Firmani and Alexander Bray McCloud

Janet married Mark Christoph Firmani on May 23, 1998, at Hay Street Methodist Church in Fayetteville. Mark is the son of Robert Lee and Marjorie Haynes Firmani. Mark was born on March 21, 1967 at Womack Army Hospital, Fort Bragg, NC and graduated from Douglas Byrd High School in 1985.

Janet accepted a position as a medical scheduler for Caroling Imaging, a diagnostic center. She is currently a Scheduling Organization Specialist with Novant Hospital Systems. Mark worked at Smith International for 16 years before accepting a position at

Carolina International in Darlington SC as a parts salesman. He is now employed at the Conway, SC office of the company.

Mark and Janet lived in Hope Mills, NC for 6 years until Marks parents both passed away in 2005 and now reside in Fayetteville, NC.

Janet is the parent of one child.

1. Alexander Bray McCloud

ALEXANDER BRAY McCLOUD was born at Cape Fear Hospital, Fayetteville, NC, on born February 7, 1991, the son of Janet B. McCloud and Gary Decker. He graduated from ECU in Greenville, NC in December 2013, with a degree in Communications.

Alexander is a News Producer at KSAT 12 in San Antonio, Texas.

Alexander Bray McCloud

ANNETTE LEIGH McCLOUD was born on May 9, 1970, at Baptist Memorial Hospital, Memphis, TN, the daughter of Robert and Priscilla Whitehead McCloud. The family was living in Southaven, MS at the time of her birth.

Left photo, Jarrel David and Annette McCloud Jimmerson Right photo, Annette McCloud, Emma Reese and Jarrel David Jimmerson

Annette attended public school in Fayetteville, NC, graduating from Seventy-First High School in 1988. Annette later attended the University of North Carolina at Wilmington and then Pembroke University, Pembroke NC. She then attended Lamar University in Beaumont, TX; graduating from Lamar on December 21, 1996, with a B. S. in Communication with a concentration in corporate communication.

Annette married Jarrel David Jimmerson on March 29, 1997, at Mount Pleasant, SC. Jarrel was born at St. Mary Hospital, Port Arthur, TX, on March 6, 1971, the son of Mary Ann Richardson and James Jimmerson. Jarrel graduated from Nederland High School in 1989. He then enlisted in the U.S. Army for three years, serving in Desert Storm with the HHB XVII Airborne Corps Artillery.

Jarrel graduated from Lamar University on May 16, 1998, with a B. B. A. in Management Information Systems. Annette and Jarrel moved to Austin, TX in 1998.

Jarrel is employed by Charles Schwab.

Annette and Jarrel are the parents of one child.

   1. Emma Reese Jimmerson

<u>CHERYL ANN McCLOUD</u> was born on January 15, 1973, at Baptist Memorial Hospital, Memphis, TN, the daughter of Robert Davis and Priscilla Whitehead McCloud. The family was, at that time, living at Southaven, MS. Cheryl's father was then a student at Southern College of Optometry, Memphis, TN.

Cheryl attended public school in Fayetteville, NC, graduating from Seventy-First High School. She then attended the University of North Carolina at Charlotte for one year. Following her return from school, Cheryl went to work for a day care school.

Top photo, Cheryl McCloud and Mark James Lewis Helm Bottom photo, Christopher Adam, Noah Thomas, Mark James Lewis, Cheryl McCloud and Madison Nicole Helm

Cheryl Ann McCloud married Mark James Lewis Helm on October 30, 1993 in Dillon, SC. The couple repeated their vows to family and friends on March 26, 1994, at the Church of the Nazarene in Fayetteville. Mark was born on October 22, 1971, in Ann Arbor, MI the son of Gail Helm Kelsey and Dennis Lewis Helm of Ann Arbor MI. He graduated from Huron High School in 1989. After attending college for a while, Mark joined the U.S. Army in July 1991, taking basic training at Ft. Jackson, SC. Following basic, he took Jump School at Ft. Benning, GA and was then sent to FT. Bragg, NC where he joined the HHC 2/504th PIR, 82nd Airborne Division in 1992.

Mark attended the Fayetteville Nazarene Church which was where he and Cheryl met and eventually married.

It was while the couple was stationed at Ft. Bragg that their first child Christopher Adam Helm was born on April 13, 1995 at Womack Army Hospital. Following an accident during a night jump, Mark became an Army Recruiter. In 1997, they were transferred to FT. Belvoir, VA where Mark recruited in the Fairfax area. Cheryl worked for Bank of America as a teller and became Head Teller within a year and a half. The family was blessed with a second child when Madison Nicole Helm was born on June 23, 1998 at National Naval Medical Center, Bethesda, MD. Mark served in the Army for 8 ½ years attaining the rank of Sergeant. Following his discharge in January 2000, the family moved to Rantoul, IL so he could enter college.

Mark entered college at Parkland in Champaign, IL; eventually transferring to Illinois State University from where he graduated on December 13, 2003 with a B.S. in Management Information Systems.

While Mark attended school Cheryl worked as a Teller Supervisor with the Busey Bank where she stayed until April 2001. She then went to work for Champaign County as a Circuit Court Clerk. While there, she worked as the swing clerk going into the various courtrooms when the regular clerk was out. After six months she was assigned as clerk for Circuit Court Judge John D. La Mar until his retirement in 2002. Then she was assigned to work for Circuit Judge Michael Q. Jones. Within six months she was assigned to work for Presiding Judge J. G. Townsend until December 2003.

Following Mark's graduation, the family eventually moved to Round Lake Beach, IL. Cheryl is employed by Alight Solutions as an Operations Manager. Mark is a Director at Alight Solutions and is currently pursuing his MBA at Colorado Technical University.

Cheryl and Mark are the parents of two children.

1. Christopher Adam Helm
2. Madison Nicole Helm

CHRISTOPHER ADAM HELM was born on April 13, 1995, at Womack Army Hospital, Ft. Bragg, NC, the son of Mark James Lewis and Cheryl McCloud Helm.

Christopher married Kayla Patricia Konczal on September 19, 2015. Kayla Konczal is the daughter of Richard and Carey Konczal of Round Lake Beach, IL. They divorced in 2018.

Christopher currently attends technical school at Fayetteville Technical Community College.

Christopher Adam and Noah Thomas Helm

Christopher and Kayla are the parents of one son.

1. Noah Thomas Helm

MADISON NICOLE HELM was born on June 23, 1998, at National Naval Medical Center, Bethesda, MD. Madison graduated from the University of Minnesota on May 13, 2020 with a degree in Bachelor of Science in Chemistry.

She is currently pursuing her doctorate in Chemistry from Pennsylvania State University.

Madison Nicole Helm

LAWRENCE JOSEPH WHITEHEAD was born in Fayetteville, NC on March 26, 1945, the son of William Bray Whitehead and Winona Odell Whitehead. Lawrence, known as Larry, graduated from Fayetteville High School on June 2, 1964. He then attended Pembroke University for about two years. He joined the U. S. Navy at about 1968. He was on active duty for four years serving on a destroyer that was in action several times in Vietnam.

Lawrence Joseph Whitehead

Following his discharge from the Navy, Larry worked for his father as an optician and later for his brother-in-law. Eventually, he went to Sanford where he did the optical work for his brother Dr. William Odell Whitehead. Larry stayed with Bill until Bill decided to re-enter the Navy.

Top photo, Lawrence Joseph Whitehead
Bottom photo, Lawrence Joseph Whitehead and Elizabeth Young Whitehead

Larry married Elizabeth (Liz) A. Young on July 27, 1980, at the home of his sister Priscilla Whitehead McCloud. Liz was the mother of three children from a previous marriage. Liz died of cancer on August 11, 1985. She was buried in the Whitehead family section at Lafayette Memorial Gardens.

Larry became a security guard working at Pope Air Force Base. He died unexpectedly at his home on September 11, 1992 He was missed at his job and they called Larry's sister Priscilla. Priscilla sent her son Edward W. McCloud to Larry's home where he found the front door unlocked and Larry in the bathroom deceased. Larry was taken to Cape Fear Valley Hospital where he was pronounced dead. He was buried in the Whitehead family section of Lafayette Memorial Gardens in Fayetteville, NC.

MARIAN ELMA WHITEHEAD was born in Kansas City, MO on August 26, 1913, the daughter of Joseph W. Whitehead and Floribel Needles Whitehead.

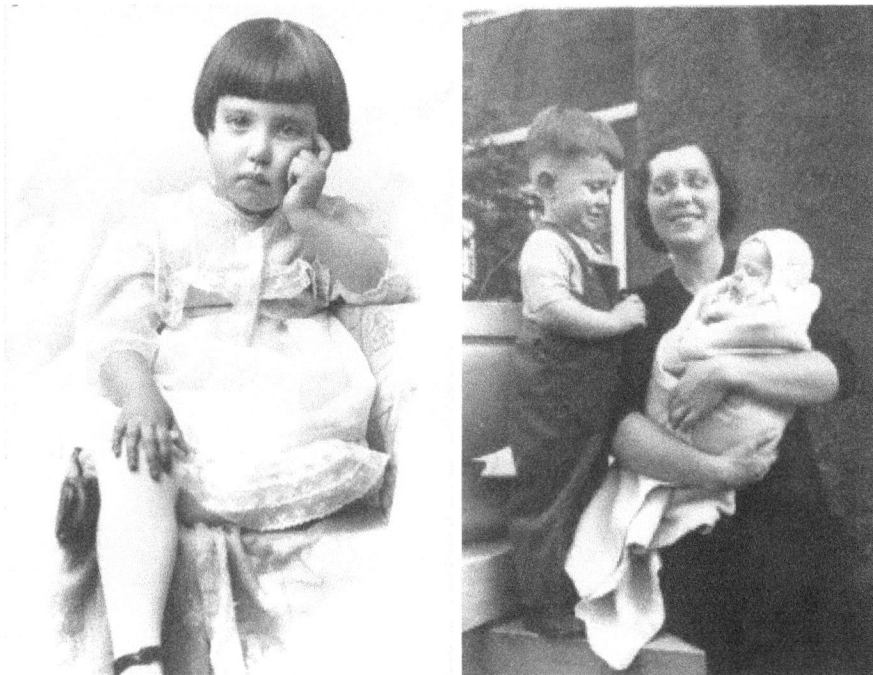

Left photo, Marian Elma Whitehead Right photo, David, Marian Whitehead and Daniel Eichenberger

Marian married Walter Otto Eichenberger on September 30, 1939. Walter was born August 23, 1915. They became the parents of three children. They were later divorced.

Elizabeth Needles Whitsel, Cynthia Whitsel, Margaret Needles Whitehead, Marian Elma Whitehead Eichenberger, Walter Otto Eichenberger, Benjamin Dwight Whitehead, William Odell Whitehead and Faye Whitsel

Marian W. Eichenberger died on May 2, 1999. She was buried in Kansas City.

Marian Elma Whitehead and Walter Otto Eichenberger are the parents of three children.

1. David Eichenberger
2. Daniel Eichenberger
3. Lida Jean Eichenberger

DAVID WILSON WHITEHEAD was born in Kansas City, MO on December 28, 1915, the son of Joseph Wilson Whitehead and Floribel Needles Whitehead. David graduated from Central High School in Kansas City.

David served as a Staff Sgt. with the 45th Field Artillery Division during World War II. He was in the Italian campaign and at the Battle of the Bulge. He received a head injury during one of the battles.

David Wilson Whitehead

Following his discharge from the military, David attended Northern Illinois College of Optometry, graduating on September 24, 1948. David was issued a license to practice Optometry in North Carolina on February 28, 1949.

David married Wilma Swanson in Chicago, IL on ____. Wilma was born on September 18, 1921, the daughter of Edwin E. Swanson and Olive Drummon Swanson of Manson, Iowa. Manson, Iowa is situated in the northwest corner of Calhoun County about 18 miles west of Fort Dodge. Wilma served as a WAC during WW II.

David and Wilma moved to North Carolina living for a short time with his brother Dr. William B. Whitehead in Fayetteville. David and his brother then worked together at the Fayetteville practice for a while. After serving at practices in Raeford, Southern Pines, and Greensboro, NC, David and family moved to Winston-Salem where he established a practice in 1961.

Wilma Swanson Whitehead and David Wilson Whitehead

David W. Whitehead died at Mercy Hospital in Charlotte, NC of a heart attack on February 3, 1980. Services were held at Vogler's Reynolds Road Chapel conducted by Dr. David Burr. Burial was at Forsyth Memorial Park in Winston-Salem.

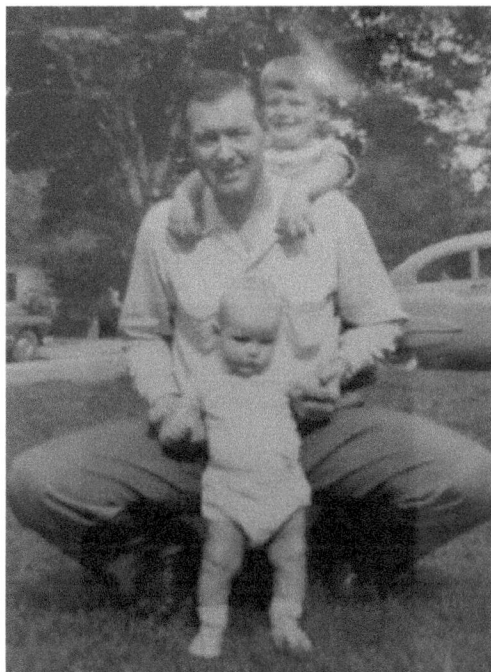

Top to Bottom, Donald E. Whitehead, David Wilson Whitehead and James W. Whitehead

Wilma Swanson Whitehead passed away on September 23, 2000 at Clemmons, NC. Wilma had worked for Triangle Broadcasting CO, later called Summit Communications, for 25 years as an administrative assistant. She had been in retirement for many years. The funeral was held at the Clemmons Moravian Church where she had been a member. Services were conducted by the Revs Q. Ray Burke and Jan Peterson under the care of Vogler's Chapel at Clemmons. Wilma was buried beside her husband in Forsyth Memorial Park.

The obituary that appeared in the September 24, 2000, issue of the *Winston–Salem Journal* recorded Wilma as having five grandchildren, Amy Whitehead of Cullowhea, Megan Whitehead of Clyde, Justin and Sarah Whitehead of Sherrills Ford and Daniel Beck of Lexington.

David and Wilma were the parents of two children.

1. Donald E. Whitehead
2. James W. Whitehead

BENJAMIN DWIGHT WHITEHEAD was born in Kansas City, MO on July 5, 1917, the son of Joseph W. Whitehead and Floribel Needles Whitehead. Benjamin, known as Ben, was named after his uncle Benjamin W. Dwight. In fact, the Whitehead family was living with the Dwight's when Ben was born.

Benjamin Dwight Whitehead

After graduating from high school, Ben attended Northern Illinois College of Optometry. Following graduation, he returned to Kansas City where he established his practice. Ben married the widow Kay Kristine Miller, who had one child Ralph Miller. Ben and Kay did not have any children. Kay died in 1994. Ralph still lived with his stepfather.

Benjamin Dwight Whitehead and Kay Miller Whitehead

Benjamin died on February 9, 2010, he was buried in Overland Park, Johnson County, Kansas.

PHILIP MAXWELL WHITEHEAD was born in Kansas City, MO on June 10, 1919, the son of Joseph W. Whitehead and Floribel Needles Whitehead. Following completion of high school, Philip attended Northern College of Optometry from where he graduated on August 1, 1942.

Philip Maxwell Whitehead after his first solo flight

Philip joined the Army Air Corps on 4 December 1943. He became a pilot, flying B 24's in the Pacific campaign. He left the service on December 12, 1945, with the rank of Captain. Philip returned to Chicago following his discharge from the military where he went to work at Illinois College of Optometry as an instructor.

Left photo, Philip Maxwell Whitehead Right photo, Sonja Greiner and Floribel Needles Whitehead

Philip was issued a license to practice Optometry in North Carolina on April 17, 1946. Philip then married Sonja Lee Greiner on August 31, 1946, at seven o'clock in the evening at Saint Peter Anglican Lutheran Church, Skokie, IL. She was born at Jersey City, NJ on June 3, 1922, the daughter of Otto and Lina Greiner. Sonja's parents were immigrants from Germany. Otto specialized in making artificial glass eyeballs.

Philip initially setup his first practice in Southern Pines, NC, but eventually settled in Rockingham, NC, where he practiced for many years.

Philip M. Whitehead died at Richmond Memorial Hospital on 1998. Services were held at First Presbyterian Church at Rockingham, NC, handled by Boles Funeral Home and Crematory of Laurinburg.

Sonja Lee Whitehead passed away on Tuesday, July 14, 2009, at the Forsyth Medical Center. She was a resident of Rockingham, NC for over 50 years and was a member of First Presbyterian Church. She loved lapidary and jewelry, selling handmade jewelry for many years.

She was preceded in death by her parents; her husband, Dr. Philip M. Maxwell; and a sister, Ellen Greiner Erde. She was survived by a son, Philip O. (Brenda) Whitehead; a daughter, Christie (Davor Graic) Whitehead; two grandchildren, James Maxwell Whitehead and Alece Christine Whitehead; and many nieces and nephews.

Memorial services were held on July 18, at the Frank Vogler and Sons Reynolda Road Chapel.

Philip and Sonja were the parents of two children.

1. Philip Otto Whitehead, October 7, 1956
2. Christine Anna Whitehead, born March 26, 1958

SAMUEL HOWARD WHITEHEAD was born in Kansas City, MO on November 21, 1921, the son of Joseph W. Whitehead and Floribel Needles Whitehead. Samuel, known as Sam, graduated from high school in 1939 and started working at the Commerce Trust Company that summer. It was while he was working at the bank that he met Betty Thomas in the Transit Department and they eventually started dating.

Left photo, Betty Thomas Whitehead and Samuel Howard Whitehead   Right Photo, Samuel Howard Whitehead

Sam joined the Army Air Corps in the Aviation Cadet program in the fall of 1942. He received his wings as 2nd Lieutenant on August 30, 1943, after which he continued his training as a B-17 bomber pilot. Before he shipped out to England, Sam married Betty Lou Thomas on February 5, 1944, in Alexandria, Louisiana. Betty was born in Kansas City, MO on March 31, 1924, the daughter of Harry and Lula Thomas, the youngest of four daughters.

Left photo, Samuel Howard Whitehead Right photo, Flying Fortress Sunday, March 19, 1944 Kansas City, MO

During the war, Sam flew 32 missions over France and Germany starting in the spring and summer of 1944 and including the D-Day invasion. He received the Distinguish Flying Cross and the Air Medal with three Oak Leaf Clusters. Sam finished his tour of duty as an instructor for B-29s until the end of the war.

Following his discharge from the Army, Sam and Betty moved to Chicago, IL where he attended Northern Illinois of Optometry. Sam graduated from Northern Illinois College of Optometry in February 2, 1949. He was licensed to practice Optometry in North Carolina on March 1, 1949. Sam moved to North Carolina where he practiced Optometry at Fayetteville, NC with his brother William B. Whitehead for a while. Sam established his practice in Whiteville, NC in the spring of 1953.

Sam has been a member of the Civitan Club and the American Legion for 50 years. He was a founding Board Member of the Boys and Girls Home of North Carolina.

Betty Thomas Whitehead passed away on July 14, 2008.   She was buried in Columbus Memorial Park. Sam Whitehead died March 22, 2017; he was buried beside his wife.

Sam was survived by daughters Linda Whitehead of Whiteville and Rita Whitehead of Griffin, GA; daughter and sons-in-law, Susan and Matt Henney of Charlotte and Kim and Gil Strader of Julian; grandchildren, Casey Strader of Dallas, TX, Matt Henney of Charlotte, Harrison Henney of Charleston, SC, Brett Strader of USMC Camp Lejune; and Samantha Strader of Annapolis, MD.

Betty Thomas Whitehead and Samuel Howard Whitehead

Sam and Betty were the parents of five children.

1. Thomas Howard Whitehead
2. Linda Lou Whitehead
3. Rita Anne Whitehead
4. Susan Needles Whitehead
5. Kimberly Jean Whitehead

THOMAS HOWARD WHITEHEAD was born in Kansas City, MO on June 14, 1946, the son of Samuel and Betty Thomas Whitehead. Thomas, known as Tommy and later Tom, graduated from Whiteville High in 1964. He then attended the University of North Carolina at Chapel Hill for three years. In 1968, he joined the Army in the Warrant Officer Flight program. He was trained to fly Cobra helicopters; serving two tours in Viet Nam from 1969-1971.

Betty Thomas Whitehead, Thomas Howard Whitehead and Samuel Howard Whitehead

After Vietnam, Tom moved to Denver, CO and later to Vail. He became a successful real estate agent in the Vail area. Tom's passion was all kinds of sports but his main one was golf. He played every year in the Jerry Ford Invitational Golf Tournament with golfing greats like Jack Nicklaus and movie stars like Clint Eastwood.

Back row, Thomas Howard and Lawrence Joseph Whitehead
Front row, Donald E. and James W. Whitehead

Tom died September 2, 1985, from head injuries from a horseback riding accident. He was returned home where he was buried in the family section of the Whiteville cemetery. Friends and co-workers of Tom started the Tom Whitehead Junior Golf Foundation of

Colorado. The Tom Whitehead Memorial Golf Tournament is a yearly event that raises funds to support the Tom Whitehead Junior Golf Foundation.

LINDA LOU WHITEHEAD was born in Chicago, IL on September 3, 1948, the daughter of Samuel and Betty Thomas Whitehead. She graduated from Whiteville High School in 1967 and attended East Carolina University. In 1969, Linda started with United Airlines as a flight attendant. She was stationed in Washington, DC for a few years and then was transferred to Denver, CO. She lived in Vail, CO for several years were she also worked for the Jimmie Huega Foundation, helping to organize their fundraising.

Left photo, Samuel Howard Whitehead and Linda Lou Whitehead
Right photo, Linda Lou Whitehead, Kimberly Whitehead Strader and sitting Susan Whitehead Henney

Linda, while living in Denver, was a Senior Flight Attendant flying out of Chicago on international flights to China, South America and Europe. In 2001, Linda began to design jewelry and had her designs made in China and South America. She has turned this passion into a successful business, LindaLu Designs. Linda has since retired and lives in North Carolina.

RITA ANNE WHITEHEAD was born in Fayetteville, NC on November 26, 1952, the daughter of Samuel and Betty Thomas Whitehead. Rita graduated from Whiteville High School in 1971 and then attended the University of North Carolina in Chapel Hill. She graduated in 1975 with a B.S. in Business Administration. In 1976, she moved to Griffin, GA to work for Nashville EMS, a fund-raising company. In 1978, Rita took a position with the Commercial Bank of Griffin, got married, got divorced and started her Computer career with the bank.

Left photo, Linda Lou Whitehead, Thomas Howard Whitehead, Rita Anne Whitehead and Samuel Howard Whitehead Right photo, Samuel Howard Whitehead and Rita Anne Whitehead

In 1982, Rita took a position in computer programming with Delta Airlines. In 1995, she was transferred to Worldspan, a Technology and Computer Reservation Company owned by Delta, NWA and TWA. Currently, she is a System Advisor with Worldspan in their Delta Center.

Rita is active with the First United Methodist Church in Griffin. As a Charter member of the Iris Charter Chapter of the American Business Women's Association, Rita has held many offices including President. As an Adult Volunteer with Girl Scouts of Pine Valley Council, Rita has been Treasurer of the Board of Directors and a Member at Large. She finished six years as President of the Council in 2000. She currently is Third Vice Chair of the Board of Directors. Rite loves to travel, particularly on cruises.

SUSAN NEEDLES WHITEHEAD was born in Whiteville, NC on June 16, 1956, the daughter of Samuel and Betty Thomas Whitehead. Susan graduated from Whiteville High School in 1974 and then attended the University of North Carolina-Chapel Hill. She graduated in 1978 with a Bachelor of Fine Arts Degree. After college, Susan worked at a restaurant where she met Matthew Elon Henney. They worked together and dated for six years until they were married in 1984.

Linda Lou Whitehead, Rita Anne Whitehead, Kimberly Jean Whitehead Strader,
Susan Needles Whitehead Henney and Samuel Howard Whitehead

Matthew Elon Henney was born on July 30, 1953 in White Plains, NY. His family moved to Charlotte, NC in 1954. In 1958 his family moved to Chapel Hill, NC where he grew up. He graduated from Chapel Hill High School in 1971 and then attended the University of North Carolina-Chapel Hill from 1971 to 1973. He then began a career in the restaurant industry at Raleigh. He attended the Culinary Institute of America from 1976 to 1978. Matthew went to work for Slugs Restaurant in Chapel Hill in 1978 where he stayed until 1993. Matthew became the owner of the 30th Edition restaurant in Charlotte for five years. Currently, he manages Mickey and Mooch Restaurant in Lake Norman. Susan is a stay at home mom; enjoying watching her children play various sports. Her other passions are art and interior design.

Susan and Matthew's first child Matthew Thomas Henney was born in Charlotte, NC on August 15, 1987. He was named after his father and his uncle Tommy (Thomas Howard Whitehead). Their second child Samuel Harrison Henney was born two months early in Charlotte, NC on March 19, 1987. He remained in the hospital for a month following his birth before he could go home. Samuel was named after his two grandfathers Samuel Howard Whitehead and Harrison Thomas Henney.

Susan and Matthew are the parents of two children.

1. Matthew Thomas Henney
2. Samuel Harrison Henney

KIMBERLY JEAN WHITEHEAD was born in Whiteville, NC on January 31, 1961, the daughter of Samuel and Betty Thomas Whitehead. Kimberly, known as Kim, graduated from Whiteville High School in 1979 and then attended North Carolina State University, graduating in 1983 with a B.S. in Biology with a teaching certificate.

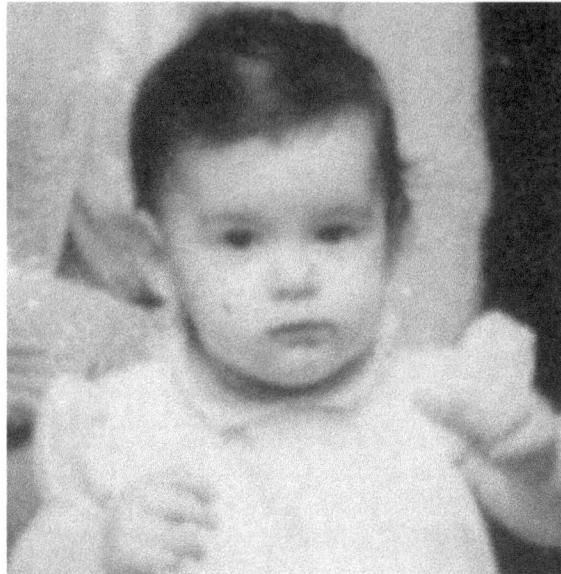

Kimberly Jean Strader

Kimberly Jean Whitehead married Raymond Gilbert Strader III of Pelham, NC on June 7, 1984. Raymond, known as Gil, was born April 1, 1961 in Danville, VA. Gil graduated from Bartlette Yancey High School, Yanceyville, NC in 1979 then attending North Carolina State University graduating in 1983 with a B.S. in Agricultural Economics.

Gil became a sales representative with Ciba Geigy residing in Washington, NC from 1983 to 1987. He became a Sales Trainer for the company in Greensboro, NC from 1987 to 1989. He became the District Manager for the company at Annapolis, MD from 1989 to 1994. He returned to Greensboro, NC in 1994 as Manager of Sales Training until 1996. In 1996 he returned to Annapolis, MD as the District Sales Manager, Ciba/Norartis/Syngenta where he currently remains.

Kim worked as a high school science teacher at Washington High School, Washington, NC from 1985 to 1987. She then worked at the Wesleyan Christian Academy, High Point, NC from 1988 to 1989. In 1989 Kim went to work at the Southern High School, Anne Arundel, MD where she stayed until 1992. In November 1999 Kim became the owner of Mail Boxes Etc./The UPS Store at Sevema Park, MD.

Brett Gilbert Strader, Casey Lou Strader, Kimberly Whitehead Strader, Samantha Jean Strader and Gilbert Strader III

Kim and Gil are members of the Broadneck Evangelical Presbyterian Church. They both belong to Bible Study Fellowship, International. Kim is a volunteer with youth programs at the church and at various activities at the children's schools. Gil is an assistant Sunday School Teacher; coaches at the local county recreation football, baseball, softball and basketball teams. He also finds time to run in local marathons.

Kim and Gil Strader are the parents of three children

1. Casey Lou Strader, born April 11, 1987, Washington, NC
2. Brett Gilbert Strader, born October 17, 1992, Annapolis, MD
3. Samantha Jean Strader, born May 4, 1994, Annapolis, MD

MARGARET NEEDLES WHITEHEAD was born in Kansas City, MO on December 17, 1925, the daughter of Joseph W. Whitehead and Floribel Needles Whitehead. Margaret was named after her aunt Margaret Needles who served as a missionary in China for many years.

Top left, Margaret Needles Whitehead Top right, Margaret Needles Whitehead
Bottom photo, standing, Scott Stephen, Karen, Donald Vincent and Gregory Merle Smith
sitting, Lucinda Rae, Margaret Whitehead and Julie Janean Smith

Margaret married Merle P. Smith in Phoenix, AZ on October 1, 1953. Witness to the marriage were Don Ramirez and Marjarie Duzenbury. The family moved to Scottsdale AZ.

Merle died on January 26, 1980. He was buried at Paradise Memorial Gardens, Scottsdale, AZ. Margaret lived in Scottsdale, AZ. She died on August 16, 2012; she was 86 years old.

Margaret and Merle Smith were the parents of five children.

1. Donald Vincent Smith
2. Gregory Merle Smith
3. Scott Stephen Smith
4. Julie Janean Smith
5. Lucinda Rae Smith

CHAPTER THREE

The Wilson Family and their Related Families, the Gaston and Maxwell

An early version of this name has been found written as Willson. As late as the 1890s certain members of this family were still using that variation of the name while others chose to use the 'Wilson' form. The Wilsons, a lowland Scottish clan, were historically staunch Presbyterians and like so many early Presbyterian settlers in the American colonies, the Wilsons found the frontier the best place to practice their religion. In the more settled areas of the thirteen colonies, the Church of England had a monopoly on both political power and control of taxation.

The Wilson family that Columbus Delano Whitehead married into has a Scot-Irish Presbyterian heritage and traces its history back to John Wilson. John Wilson was one of the defenders in the siege of Londonderry, Ireland. The Protestant forces loyal to William and Mary were shut up in the city by an army commanded by the deposed King James II. On April 13, 1689, King James II came to the gates of Londonderry expecting the walled city to surrender. Instead thirteen apprentice boys shut the gate in the face of the deposed king and his army.

The Siege of Londonderry began on April 20, 1689, when the city was shelled by the forces under the command of James II. There were then 20,000 people in the city, with a little over 7,000 able to fight. The siege lasted an incredible 105 days. Famine and pestilence threatened to wipe out the entire population within the city. The siege was broken on July 28, 1689, when the merchant ship, *The Mountjoy,* crashed the boom over the river Foyle that prevented ships from landing at the dock at Londonderry. The city was shelled for three more days until James II's army finally gave up and withdrew. The fighting force in the city had been reduced from 7,000 men to about 3,000 effectives.

This victory by the forces loyal to William and Mary at the Siege of Londonderry forever ended the rule by an absolute monarchy in the British Isles. The day the siege was lifted, Britain started on the road to a parliamentary democracy, a road well-traveled to this day. In British history this entire episode is considered one of the most important cornerstones in what has been called the 'Glorious Revolution' of 1688.

JOHN WILSON was the son of John Wilson, the defender of Londonderry, and the first known member of this family to come to America. He lived in what is now Letterkenny Township, Franklin County, in the Cumberland Valley of Pennsylvania. At a time and place yet unknown John Wilson married Nancy Brackenridge. Nancy came to America from Londonderry, Ireland when she was twelve years old. She traveled with her brother and their parents who unfortunately died on the voyage to America.

The first settlement in what was then known as Lancaster County and is now known as Franklin County, Pennsylvania was at Falling Spring in 1730. This community is now known as Chambersburg, PA. The early settlers lived on the land for a while before they could acquire any legal right to the property. The process for acquiring land in those early years started with what was termed a warrant for survey, the survey then was made and then a patent was issued for the property after the survey was recorded. The process from beginning to end could sometime take several years.

John Wilson's earliest warrant for survey was requested on June 5, 1746, in what was then known as Lancaster County. The survey was for "One Hundred Acres of Land ..." A second warrant for survey was issued to John Wilson on May 2, 1748, for land in Hopewell Township. A draught or survey for this and other property for John Wilson was made on September 11, 1767. The survey concerned two tracts of land; one tract was for 202 acres while the other tract was for a little over 150 acres. The east end of John Wilson's property was about 100 rods from the Rocky Spring Presbyterian Church. The county name by this 1767 date had been changed from Lancaster County to Cumberland County and this became the Wilson family home place. This area later became Franklin County in _____.

About four miles north and one mile west of Chambersburg, Pennsylvania stands the old Rocky Spring Presbyterian Church. The congregation was organized at about 1737. The present church was built in 1794. John Wilson was an elder in this church. The church no longer has services and is being preserved through the efforts of the DAR and others.

For many years after the defeat of General Braddock in 1755, the settlers of Cumberland County, later named Franklin County, were exposed to the merciless attacks of the Indians following Braddock's retreat. Many settlers were massacred, and others were driven from their homes. Public and private forts were built in various parts of the country. John Wilson was part of the militia raised in 1755 that was made up of people from the Rocky Spring neighborhood for the defense of the frontier. Many people from the Cumberland Valley area migrated to North Carolina in 1764 because of the unsettled nature of the Pennsylvania frontier at that time.

When John Wilson died on July 9, 1773, he had survived the death of his wife by at least seven years. It is believed he lies in an unmarked grave in the Rocky Springs Presbyterian cemetery as probably does his wife Nancy. Wilson's will which was dated August 23, 1768, list the names of five sons, no daughters or sons-in-law were mentioned. The John Wilson home place passed to John's son Samuel Wilson nineteen years after his father's death.

John Wilson and Nancy Brackenridge were the parents of five known sons.

1. John Wilson
2. Hugh Wilson
3. James Wilson
4. William Wilson
5. Samuel Wilson

JOHN WILSON was born in 1738 in what later became Franklin County, Pennsylvania, the son of John Wilson and Nancy Brackenridge. John married Mary Wray time and place unknown. She was also born in 1738. John Wilson and others from the Franklin County area moved to North Carolina in 1764.

John Wilson was a Revolutionary War soldier and fought either at Kings Mountain or Cowpens. In 1778, he bought 416 acres of land lying "on the So. Side of Catawba river on the Middle Fork of Crowders Creek" in Tryon County which was later renamed Gaston County. Gaston County was named after Judge William F. Gaston of New Bern, North Carolina. Judge Gaston was from the southern branch of the Gaston family that eventually married into another part of the Wilson family.

John and Mary Wilson had a son by the name of Robert G. Wilson who was a pastor of the Presbyterian faith. Rev. Wilson's first charge was in the Abbeville District, South Carolina, which was the place where the Gaston and Hutton families from New Jersey had settled. Robert G. Wilson later became the pastor of the First Presbyterian Church of Chillicothe, Ohio. Chillicothe is the county seat for Ross County, Ohio where Rev. Wilson's uncle James Wilson lived. Rev. Wilson later became the President of Ohio University at Athens.

John Wilson died on January 4, 1799. He lies buried in the Olney graveyard three and a half miles south of Gastonia, the county seat of Gaston County, North Carolina. Mary Wray Wilson died on April 3, 1830.

The Revolutionary War Plaque denoting John Wilson located in Olney Churchyard

John and Mary Wilson were the parents of eight known children.

1. Sarah Wilson, born June 17, 1763, died August 24, 1837
2. Mary Wilson, born February 25, 1765, married Jo. James Denny, moved to Ill.
3. John Wilson, born March 6, 1767

4. Robert G. Wilson, born December 30, 1768
5. James Wilson, born April 5, 1771, died April 20, 1803
6. William Joseph Wilson, born September 24, 1777
7. Isabella Wilson, born September 29, 1779
8. Samuel Blaine Wilson, born March 17, 1783

ROBERT G. WILSON was born in South Carolina on December 30, 1768, the son of John and Mary Wray Wilson. As a boy in South Carolina, he attended an academy with Andrew Jackson. Years later he would recall that Jackson was "the worse boy in the school." Robert graduated from Dickerson College in Carlisle, Pennsylvania where the future President James Buchanan also attended.

Following his graduation from seminary, Reverend Wilson returned to Abbeville, South Carolina, where he started his pastorate. He was a neighbor of Patrick Calhoun, the father of the celebrated statesman John C. Calhoun.

Robert G. Wilsom

From 1805 to 1824, Reverend Wilson was pastor of the First Presbyterian Church of Chillicothe, Ross County, Ohio. After that he was for many years President of Ohio University at Athens, Ohio. He served as president of the school from 1824 to 1839. Rev. Wilson was a Quaker and an abolitionist. He was found on the 1850 Ohio census living in Buckskin Township, Ross County in the home of Mary W. Irevin, presumably his daughter and her three children

Rev. Robert G. Wilson had a grandson James Wilson McDill who served in both the U. S. Senate and the House of Representatives from Iowa. On the 1850 Ohio census,

Buckskin Township, Ross County, McDill was living in the home of his mother and his two sisters.

SAMUEL BLAINE WILSON was born in South Carolina on March 17, 1783, the son of John Wilson and Mary Wray Wilson. He was a Presbyterian minister who married Elizabeth Hanna in 1806. He organized the Presbyterian Church of Fredericksburg, Virginia in 1805 and was its pastor until 1840. His parsonage was the Mary Washington House where George Washington's mother lived from 1775 until her death.

Under Rev. Wilson's leadership a church was built at the corners of George and Princess Ann Streets in 1835. The church served as a hospital during the Civil War. Rev. Samuel B. Wilson later became a professor at the Union Theological Seminary at Hamden-Sydney, Virginia.

HUGH WILSON was born at Letterkenny Township, Cumberland County, Pennsylvania in ___, the son of John and Nancy Breckenridge Wilson. He married Catherine _____ and moved to Savannah, GA and later to Louisville, GA. He was an elder in the Presbyterian Church.

JAMES WILSON was born in Letterkenny Township July 12, 1743, in an area that later became Franklin County, Green Township, PA, the son of John Wilson and Nancy Breckenridge. James Wilson married Agnes Henderson on June 27, 1769. Agnes was born February 14, 1746, the daughter of a neighbor James Henderson.

James Wilson served as a Revolutionary soldier in the Third Company of the Fourth Battalion of Cumberland County Militia in 1780 and 1781. These records are found in Pennsylvania Archives, 5th Series, volume 6, pages 280, 281 and 291.

James Wilson was an Elder in the Rocky Spring Presbyterian Church. He occupied pew number 38. He vacated this pew on June 12, 1797, at that time his family moved west to Ohio.

James Wilson moved his family to Derry Township, Westmoreland County, PA, for only a short while and later moved on to Ohio. The family arrived in Chillicothe, Ross County, Ohio on May 1, 1798. They then went up the Pickaway Plains and settled on the banks of Congo Creek, just above its junction with Sippo. Here James Wilson and William McCoy organized a church of fourteen members. This was the third Presbyterian Church organized in Ohio and it became known as the Mt. Pleasant Presbyterian Church.

Agnes Henderson Wilson died in Derry Township, Westmoreland County, PA on June 30, 1796. James Wilson died in Ross County, Ohio on June 8, 1799. His will dated 1797 was found in Ross County Will Book A, page 2, it gave his name as "... James Willson Late of Franklin County Green Township, now living in Derry Township Westmoreland County: Yeoman ..."

James Wilson and Agnes Henderson Wilson were the parents of nine known children.

1. Sarah Wilson, born Apr. 7, 1770, married John Swan
2. Mary Wilson, born Jan. 22, 1773, married James Shields
3. Martha Wilson, born Mar. 29, 1775, married Samuel Strain
4. Agnes Wilson, born Feb. 4, 1777, married Solomon Templin May 5, 1803
5. John Wilson, born Feb. 18, 1779, married Lucy Taylor, April 22, 1802
6. James Wilson, born May 16, 1781, married Sahale Horn
7. Esther Wilson, born Oct. 18, 1783, married Terah Templin May 29, 1804
8. William Wilson
9. Jane Wilson, born Aug. 28, 1789, married John Barr

WILLIAM WILSON was born on June 11, 1787, probably in Franklin County, Pennsylvania, the son of James and Agnes Henderson Wilson. William married Mary Gaston on February 14, 1811. Mary Gaston was born in Abbeville, County, South Carolina on September 23, 1792, the daughter of Joseph Gaston and Martha Hutton. The Gaston family had moved from South Carolina to Ohio because of the slavery issue. Mary Gaston and her brother made a trip of more than sixty miles from their home to attend church services and this was when Mary met William Wilson. He fell in love with her on first sight. Mary had a pleasant disposition although she was inclined to worry and look on the dark side of things.

William Wilson served in the War of 1812 as a teamster transporting supplies to the northern army on the Great Lakes.

William Wilson owned a 200-acre farm in Paint Township, Ross County, Ohio. The west boundary of his farm was on a north-south road known as Taylor Road, now known as Rocky Forge Pike. The Wilson home was partly frame and partly log. The log part of the house was covered with weather board. The chimney was constructed with the lower part stone and the upper part brick. Slightly west of the house there was a knoll covered with sugar maples from which the Wilson's made maple sugar and derived the name of their farm. They called the farm Sugar Knoll Farm and it was located about one mile east of Paint Creek and about six mile south of the public square in Greenfield.

William Wilson attended the Rocky Spring Presbyterian Church which is located across Paint Creek in Highland County. It was organized in 1810 and named at the suggestion of John Wilson, the son of James Wilson and William's brother, in memory of the church of the same name where the Wilson's had attended in Pennsylvania.

William Wilson got in trouble with the church leadership in July 1827, when he was helping finish a mill race for his brother "Big John Wilson." About sixty men were involved and they had split into two teams with each digging a section of the raceway. As dinner approached, neither team wanted to be the first to go to dinner. It was decided that they would wet one side of a chip and toss it to see which team went to dinner first. The church considered the tossing of that chip "as casting a lot."

When William Wilson appeared at the church session about the incident, he stated "he meant no harm, and of course (he thinks) did not intentionally make an appeal to heaven in the case." The session concluded that "he had been guilty,...,of profaning, in a most irreverent manner, a solemn appeal to Almighty God in the case... The session believed the cause of religion had suffered by his so doing. He would not confess sorrow for what he had done, as sinning against God. And we believe sin unrepentant of unfits the soul for holding communion with her maker. And his crime being that as ruling elder in the church, makes it more heinous in the sight of heaven." Wilson was found guilty and prohibited from receiving the sealing ordinances of the church until he confessed his sin. He appealed the decision to the Presbytery on July 26, 1827.

The situation with the church was concluded on October 12, 1827, when William Wilson came before the session and "acknowledged that casting lots was an appeal to the Almighty, which ought not be made, but in matters of importance. And that in the case for which he was suspended he had sinned." After the preaching of the following Sunday, he was to be restored to his former standing in the church.

In a letter written to his mother-in-law, Martha Gaston, dated March 31, 1834, William Wilson expressed his views about temperance and slavery saying, "Intemperance is certainly a very great sin, destructive both to the souls and bodies of men. And slavery is doubles still worse." "To hold men in involuntary servitude is unjust. It is unjust in the same sense and for the same reason as it is to steal, to rob, or to murder." The Wilson family served as a conductor on the "Underground Railroad," harboring run-a-way slaves and helping them move on to Canada. This act of helping slaves was full of peril and penalties if caught were severe. William Wilson finally came to believe that slavery would only end when there was a war to end it. William was a candidate for the legislature on the Liberty Party Ticket, but apparently was unsuccessful.

William Wilson was described as "even tempered, and social in his disposition. He did not lack much of being six feet in height and had light brown hair and blue eyes. His wife was above medium size, had blue eyes and an abundance of beautiful wavy light brown hair." The Wilson family was found on the 1850 Ross County, Ohio census living in Paint Township. William was a 63 years farmer, born in Pennsylvania. Mary was 59 and her place of birth was South Carolina. A 20-year-old Mary Wilson was in the listing as was a 14-year-old laborer by the name of John L. Wallace. The family enumerated on the census after the William Wilson family, was that of their son James A. Wilson.

William Wilson died on July 15, 1852. He was buried in the Rocky Springs graveyard, Highland County, Ohio. He was buried beside an infant daughter and his son Samuel Milton Wilson. Mary Gaston Wilson died at Lebanon, Boone County, Indiana on April 15, 1864, where she was buried.

William Wilson's daughter Martha Wilson Craven, the wife of John Gill Craven, wrote in 1876 about her last visit to her old family home. She wrote of the condition of her old home and the church she attended as a child. Traveling with her sister Lucinda and others, she wrote, "We went in a big wagon to our old home, now looking very much changed and dilapidated, I felt that I never would wish to see it again. From there we went to Rocky Spring- found the old church blown down- visited the graveyard, and the good old spring of whose waters I drank from childhood on Sabbaths in the old times when there were two sermons with thirty minutes between. I still hear the preacher say, 'After an interval of thirty minutes another discourse may be expected.' The young people ate their cookies and marched decorously to the spring, then back to their pews."

William Wilson and Mary Gaston Wilson were the parents of eight known children.

1. Joseph Gaston Wilson
2. James Alfred Wilson
3. John Newton Wilson, born Aug. 6, 1818, died Feb. 23, 1844
4. Lydia Jane Wilson
5. Lucinda Wilson
6. Samuel Milton Wilson, born Mar. 8, 1825, died Mar. 31, 1845
7. Martha Wilson
8. Mary Wilson

JOSEPH GASTON WILSON was born in Ross County, Ohio on March 15, 1812, the son of William Wilson and Mary Gaston Wilson. Joseph G. Wilson graduated from Western Reserve College and then studied theology at Lane Seminary under the direction of Dr. Lyman Beecher. Joseph became a friend and associate of Rev. Beecher's son Rev. Henry Ward Beecher when he began his ministry at Lawrenceburg, Indiana and later in Indianapolis, Indiana. Joseph married Maria Bradley on June 20, 1839. She was born in Salem, Indiana on April 30, 1819.

Joseph G. Wilson preached successfully for many years and during his pastorate in Lafayette, Indiana, he and wife work fearlessly and constantly during the cholera scourge that occurred there in 1849. For several weeks they kept themselves ready day or night to attend the calls of the sick and dying. Joseph said of his wife's effort during this time, "She was the Florence Nightingale of that day."

Compelled to give up preaching because of throat trouble, Joseph became the owner and editor of the Fort Madison, Iowa newspaper called the *Plain Dealer.* Wilson moved from West Point, Iowa to Fort Madison in May 1864, when he purchased the newspaper from a "Col." Caffrey. Rev. Wilson retained ownership of the paper until 1877 when he was appointed Consul to Jerusalem by President Rutherford B. Hayes.

Maria Wilson died on March 31, 1876 and was buried in the Fort Madison City Cemetery. The following year, 1877, the Rev. Joseph G. Wilson was appointed U. S. Consul at Jerusalem where he served for five years. Rev. Wilson lost his only child Mary Wilson when she died on November 14, 1877, while he was on duty in the Holy Land. Mary was also buried in the Fort Madison City Cemetery with her mother.

Rev. Wilson returned to the United States in 1882 in rather poor health, but he again purchased the *Plain Dealer* and edited it for only a short while. With his health in a continuing state of deterioration he again sold the newspaper and then moved to Kansas City where he lived with his niece Mary Wilson Whitehead in Kansas City, MO. He died there on January 24, 1886. Rev. Wilson's body was removed to Fort Madison, Iowa where he was buried beside his wife and daughter.

There is an interesting postscript to the Rev. Joseph G. Wilson family burial in the Fort Madison City Cemetery. The Wilsons are all buried under the name of Willson. The newspaper article that appeared in the April 5, 1876, issue of the Fort Madison *Weekly Democrat* telling about her death gave Mrs. Wilson's name as Mrs. Maria Bradley Willson. The January 27, 1886, issue of the Fort Madison *Weekly Democrat* telling of his death also gave Rev. Wilson's name as Willson. Finally, the three tall stones that mark their graves are all set on one cement footing with this inscription, "Reset by nephew Samuel N. Wilson, D. D. 1928." Rev. Samuel N. Wilson was the brother to Mary Maxwell Wilson Whitehead.

JAMES ALFRED WILSON was born on December 18, 1815, on the farm known as Sugar Knoll in Ross County, Ohio, the son of William Wilson and Mary Gaston Wilson. James entered Hanover College, Indiana in the fall of 1835, but broke down in health during his first year. He became ill and emaciated and was an invalid for many years. It was probably during his stay at Hanover College where he first met members of the Maxwell family who lived near the college and who also attended the Hanover Presbyterian Church.

Partially recovering his health, James taught school for a time at Crawfordsville, Indiana. His assistant at this position was Emily McCullough Maxwell. James Alfred Wilson married Emily Maxwell at Crawfordsville on July 24, 1845. Emily McCullough Maxwell was the daughter of Samuel Campbell Maxwell and Jenny Tilford Maxwell of Hanover, Jefferson County, Indiana. The Maxwell home was near the Hanover College campus where James A. Wilson had attended for a short while. Prior to her marriage Emily was a member of the Disciples of Christ.

The James A. Wilson family lived in the Crawfordsville area for a number of years. Two children were born during this time, William Harvey Wilson and Samuel Newton Wilson. However, by October 5, 1850, the family was living at South Salem, in Ross County Ohio. Their third child Mary Maxwell Wilson was born there on that October date. The 1850 Ross County, Ohio census that was taken on October 10, 1850, lists this family living next to or with his father William Wilson. James's occupation was given as an O L P Minister. The meaning of the initials is unknown but may mean "Ordained Licensed Presbyterian." Interestingly, Mary's name was recorded on the census as Mary P. Wilson and she was one month old at that time.

James Alfred Wilson cherished the purpose to be a minister. To this end he pursued a theological course under the direction of the Presbytery and was licensed to preach and assumed charge of a church at Covington, Indiana. He had preached only a few months when he was taken sick in the pulpit and died shortly thereafter. The *Maxwell History*, see page 103, gives his date of death as June 18, 1851. His funeral sermon was preached on the day he had expected to be ordained at his church. He was buried at Covington in a country graveyard about six miles from Crawfordsville, Indiana.

Emily Maxwell Wilson died on November 11, 1853, at the home of her sister Mrs. Preston Wiley near Kent, a few miles from Hanover, Indiana. She was buried at Mt. Carmel Church graveyard. Emily's untimely death left her family with two very young children to care for; one was five while the other was only three years old. The care of the children was eventually turned over to James' sister Mary Wilson Coyner, who lived at Waveland, Indiana. Waveland is located in the southern part of Montgomery County, a few miles from Crawfordsville. Mary Wilson Coyner and Professor John M. Coyner were both teachers.

James A. and Emily Maxwell Wilson were the parents of three known children with two surviving to adulthood.

1. William Harvey Wilson, born June 12, 1846, died July 28, 1846.
2. Samuel Newton Wilson
3. Mary Maxwell Wilson, born October 5, 1850, married Columbus Delano Whitehead. See page 15.

SAMUEL NEWTON WILSON was born at Crawfordsville, Indiana on November 18, 1847, the son of James Alfred Wilson and Emily McCollough Maxwell Wilson. Following the deaths of his parents, Samuel grew to maturity in the home of his aunt and uncle, Prof. John M. Coyner and Mary Wilson Coyner.

Samuel entered Hanover College at Hanover, Indiana in the fall of 1868 and graduated in the class of 1872. He then attended Lane Seminary at Cincinnati, Ohio, graduating in the class of 1875. Samuel married Eliza Jane Phillips on November 18, 1875. Eliza Jane Phillips was born on August 9, 1851, near Lexington, Indiana. That day was indeed Samuel's special day because it was also his birthday. The young couple was married in the old College Church at Hanover by the beloved Prof. J. W. Garrett.

Reverend Samuel Newton Wilson

Rev. Samuel N. Wilson's first call was to the Presbyterian Church of Lawrenceburg, Indiana. This was the same church and building where Henry Ward Beecher had started his ministry. The Wilsons stayed at this church for nine and a half years, seeing the construction of a new church. From there they were called to Valparasio where he served for seven and a half years. After Valparasio, Samuel served in Anderson, Indiana for four years until he was called by the Walnut Street Presbyterian Church in Evansville, Indiana.

In June 1900, Samuel received the degree of D. D. from Hanover College. That same year he was called to the Presbyterian Church of Wausau, Wisconsin. He stayed at this position until 1908 until he was called to a church in Reedsburg, Wisconsin. Dr. Wilson had the joy of uniting his daughter Mary Margaret Wilson in marriage to Dr. Harry A. Vedder at the Wausau Presbyterian Church on June 27, 1906. The occasion was marked by the appearance of Dr. Wilson's sister Mary Maxwell Wilson Whitehead of Kansas City for the wedding. To share a special family event with one's sibling is always a special celebration.

Dr. Samuel N. Wilson retired from active ministry in 1916 because of impaired health. After living in Stevens Point, Wisconsin and Detroit, Michigan, Samuel and Eliza moved into their own home in Marshfield, Wisconsin.

The 1920 Michigan, Wayne County census shows Samuel and his wife Eliza and their son Alfred G. Wilson living in the home of Nathan J. Newman. Samuel's occupation was stated as 'Minister, Church' while Alfred's was listed as 'Dealer, Lumber.' It was during 1920 that Rev. Samuel N. Wilson had three stones set on one cement footing that covered the graves of his uncle the Rev. Joseph G. Wilson and his wife and daughter in

Fort Madison, Iowa, City Cemetery. An inscription on one of the stones reads, "Reset by nephew Samuel N. Wilson D. D. 1928." See page 90.

Samuel N. Wilson, writing in 1925, made this comment, "Near Hanover was the old Maxwell home of my mother's family, and in the cemetery near by lies buried its Revolutionary representative, Bezaleel Maxwell."

The 1930 Wisconsin, Wood County census located this family living in Marshfield. Samuel was 82 years old while Mrs. Wilson was 78. There was no occupation listed for Samuel on this census. Marshfield was also the home of the Wilson's daughter Mary Wilson Vedder, wife of Dr. Harry A. Vedder.

The Rev. Samuel N. Wilson died at St. Joseph's hospital in Marshfield, WI on March 3, 1931. Services were held at his home at 210 South Vine Street and then at the First Presbyterian Church in Marshfield. His body was then removed to Pine Grove Cemetery, Wausau, WI where he was buried. Lovely obituaries for Dr. Wilson appeared in both the *Marshfield News Herald* and the Wausau newspaper. Both articles concluded with this information, "Dr. Wilson pursued two hobbies during his lifetime. In earlier years he delighted casting the fly for trout. His other hobby was writing poetry. At a celebration last November in observance of the fifty-fifth wedding anniversary of Dr. and Mrs. Wilson, the aged couple were honored with an original poem written by Edgar A. Guest."

Eliza Phillips Wilson died of heart disease at her home in Marshfield, WI on January 30, 1933. She was 81 years old. Services were held in the privacy of her late home on 210 South Vine Street. She was then removed to Pine Grove Cemetery in Wausau, WI where she was buried. Mrs. Wilson was survived by two sons, Alfred G. and Donald C. Wilson of Detroit and one daughter, Mrs. H. A. Vedder of Marshfield.

Samuel Newton and Eliza Phillips Wilson were the parents of six children

1. Edgar Stonehouse Wilson, born November 3, 1876, died November 28, 1901
2. Mary Margaret Wilson
3. Gertrude Comstock Wilson, born October 6, 1880, died June 22, 1887
4. Alfred Gaston Wilson
5. Donald Coyner Wilson
6. Alla Jeanette Wilson

MARY MARGARET WILSON was born in Lawrence burg, Indiana on August 13, 1878, the daughter of Samuel Newton Wilson and Eliza Phillips Wilson.

Mary M. Wilson married Dr. Harry A. Vedder in Wausau, Wisconsin on June 27, 1906. The ceremony was held at the Presbyterian Church where Mary's father Dr. Samuel N. Wilson served as pastor. The father of the bride was the officiating clergyman. One of the guests from out of the city was Mrs. Whitehead of Kansas City. This was Mary's aunt Mary Maxwell Wilson Whitehead, wife of Columbus Delano Whitehead.

Dr. Harry A. Vedder was born on November 1, 1879, the son of Sidney H. Vedder and Eliza Stoddert Veddrer. Dr. Vedder practiced medicine at Edgar, WI until he came to Marshfield in 1916 where he and his bother Dr. James Vedder formed the Marshfield Clinic.

Dr. Harry A. Vedder died on March 12, 1943. He was buried in the Marshfield Hillside Cemetery. Mary Wilson Vedder died at a hospital in Hollywood, Calif. on July 20, 1948. Mrs. Vedder had been living for the past five years in home of her daughter Mrs. Stanley Morner at La Canada, CA. Mrs. Stanley Morner, Lillian Mae Vedder, was married to the actor Dennis Morgan, aka Stanley Morner.

Mary Wilson and Harry Vedder were the parents of four children.

1. Mary Jeanette Vedder, born March 17, 1907, married Frank J. Deckert Jr., 16 Feb 1931
2. Lillian Mae Vedder, born February 21, 1909
3. Harry Alfred Vedder, born January 18, 1911, died February 18, 1914
4. Virginia Emily Vedder, born February 13, 1915, married Roy C. Rhyner, 18 Nov 1939

LILLIAN MAE VEDDER was born on February 21, 1909, probably in Marshfield, WI, the daughter of Mary Wilson Vedder and Dr. Harry Vedder. Lillian married Stanley Morner on September 5, 1933. Stanley was born on December 20, 1908. Stanley later became the actor known as Dennis Morgan. Dennis had a fine voice and appeared in many movies with some of the top actors of his day.

Lillian Vedder Morner attended the wedding of Dr. William B. Whitehead and Winona R. Odell in Chicago on January 1, 1934. Stanley was not remembered as being at the wedding.

Dennis Morgan, aka, Stanley Morner, died at Alwahoee, Madera, CA on September 7, 1994. Lillian Vedder Morner died in Madera, CA on April 7, 2003.

ALFRED GASTON WILSON was born in Lawrenceburg, Indiana on March 31, 1883, the son of Samuel Newton Wilson and Eliza Phillips Wilson. Alfred graduated from Beloit College in 1906. In 1919, he and his brother Donald Wilson formed the Wilson Lumber Company in Detroit. Alfred was deeply involved with the Presbyterian Church in Detroit where he met the widow Mrs. Matilda Rausch Dodge.

Alfred married Mrs. Matilda Rausch Dodge on June 29, 1925, in Detroit, Michigan. She was born on October 19, 1883, in Walkerton, Ontario, Canada, the daughter of George and Margaret Rausch. Matilda was the widow of John Francis Dodge, co-founder with his brother Horace Dodge of Dodge Motor Company. John Dodge died on January 14, 1920.

Alfred Gaston Wilson and Matilda Rausch Dodge Wilson

Matilda was the parent of three children with John Dodge; Francis Dodge, born November 27, 1914, Daniel George Dodge, born July 23, 1917, and Anna Margaret Dodge, born in 1919.

Following their marriage, the family moved to a farm called Meadowbrook, a collection of farms that by the start of W. W. II totaled some 2,600 acres. Alfred and Matilda Wilson adopted two children in 1930. Their names are recorded below.

In 1957, Alfred and Matilda Wilson donated 1,500 acres that also included the Meadowbrook mansion and $2 million to Michigan State University to create what eventually became Oakland University.

Alfred G. Wilson died in Phoenix, Ariz. on April 6, 1962. Services were held at the First Presbyterian Church located at Woodward Avenue at Edmund Place. The place of burial was not mentioned.

Matilda died while on a trip to Brussels, Belgium on September 19, 1967. She was returned to the United States where funeral services were held at the First Presbyterian Church, Woodward Avenue, Edmund Place. Memorial tributes were asked to be sent to either the Salvation Army Auxiliary or Oakland University Scholarship Fund. There was no mention of the burial place.

1. Richard Wilson, adopted at 18 months of age in 1930
2. Barbara Wilson, adopted at 3 months of age in 1930

DONALD COYNER WILSON was born in Valparaiso, Indiana on December 26, 1885, the son of Samuel Newton Wilson and Eliza Phillips Wilson. Donald married Mabel Powell Slane in Peoria, Illinois in 1914.

Donald along with his brother Alfred G. Wilson formed the Wilson Lumber Company in Detroit, MI in 1919. Donald and his family with two children were found on the 1920 Michigan, Wayne County census living on Commonwealth Ave., Detroit, MI. Donald's occupation was given as 'Exruary(?)-Wh. Lumber.'

The 1930 Michigan Oakland County, Avon, census enumerates this family. At this date the family was living on Dodge Road and there were still only two children in the home. Donald did not give an occupation.

1. Oliver Slane Wilson, born August 29, 1916
2. Donald Coyner Wilson Jr., born November 28, 1919

ALLA JEANETTE WILSON was born in Valparaiso, Indiana on June 12, 1888, the daughter of Samuel Newton Wilson and Eliza Phillips Wilson. Jeanette married Clinton W. Copps in Reedsville, Indiana on June 25, 1913. In 1920, Jeanette died leaving a son five years old. The family was then living at Steven Point, WI.

The 1930 Wisconsin, Portage County census show this family living at Stevens Point. Clinton Copps was listed on the census as "wholesale merchant, grocery." Clinton had remarried and his wife was named Sadie. There was one child in the home, Donald Copps, who was recorded as 15 years old.

1. Donald William Copps, born May 10, 1914

MARY MAXWELL WILSON was born according to the *Maxwell History* at South Salem, Ohio on October 5, 1850, the daughter of James Alfred Wilson and Emily McCollough Maxwell Wilson. It has been assumed by Wilson family sources that Mary was born at Crawfordsville, Indiana like her brother. Following the death of her parents, Mary went to live was her aunt and uncle, Prof. John M Coyner and Mary Wilson Coyner at Waveland, IN. Mary Maxwell Wilson married Columbus Delano Whitehead. Her biography may be found on page 15.

LUCINDA WILSON was born in Ross County, Ohio on January 1, 1823, the daughter of William Wilson and Mary Gaston Wilson. Lucinda married Dr. John Baxter Evans on May 26, 1842. They made their home in Frankfort, Ohio. Dr. Evans died in 1877 after which Lucinda made her home in Chillicothe where she was a member of the First Presbyterian Church. She died at the home of her daughter near Frankfort on February 28, 1897. Lucinda and John Evans were the parents of three children.

1. Marcus Gaston Evans, married Stella Nelson
2. William Edgar Evans, married Julia B. Sanford
3. Mary Evans, married John W. Jenkins

MARTHA WILSON was born in Ross County, Ohio on June 8, 1827, the daughter of William Wilson and Mary Gaston Wilson. Martha married John Gill Craven on August 30, 1849. At the time of her marriage, her husband who was a preacher and his father were conducting Eleutherian College at College Hill near the village of Lancaster, Jefferson County, Indiana. Lancaster was about ten miles north of Madison, the county seat of Jefferson County. Eleutherian College was an "abolition school" that was open to all no matter their color. While at the college, sometime before 1861, there were several slave families that were building cottages near the school. But prejudice against the colored people was so strong by some of the local people that the cottages were burned to the ground. People at the school also received threats and many nights the staff would worry about being burned out themselves. Martha and John were part of the abolitionist movement, hiding run-away slaves during the day and taking them from place to place at night to help them escape slavery. Helping run-away slaves at this time was against the law because of the passage of the "Fugitive Slave Law."

In 1861 John G. Craven moved his family to High Forest, Olmstead, Minnesota where he preached and taught. The family later moved to Hamilton, Minn. and in 1867, the family moved to Pella, Iowa. In 1869, they moved again, this time to Independence Township, Jasper County, Iowa. In 1872, the family moved to Irving, Benton County, Iowa and in 1879 they returned again to College Hill in Indiana where John attempted to revive Eleutherian College. In 1887, the family again moved, this time to Beloit, Kansas where John engaged in Biblical studies and began a work-study on the subject of baptism, and he would occasionally preach.

John Gill Craven died at his home of neuralgia of the heart on January 19, 1893. Martha Wilson Craven died on January 7, 1895, of acute bronchitis at the home of her daughter Mary near Beloit, Kansas. John and Martha Wilson Craven are buried side by side in Elmwood Cemetery in Beloit, Kansas.

John Gill Craven and Martha Wilson Craven were the parents of seven children.

1. Edwin William Craven, born April 25, 1851
2. Mary Craven, born October 29, 1855
3. Arthur John Craven, born December 12, 1857
4. Hermon Wilson Craven, born December 25, 1860
5. Roger Carey Craven, born September 29, 1863
6. Alfred Milton Craven, born October 11, 1865
7. Anna Viva Craven, born August 26, 1868, died June 4, 1871

MARY WILSON was born in Ross County, Ohio on October 25, 1829, the daughter of William Wilson and Mary Gaston Wilson. Mary married John M. Coyner on April 7, 1853. Mary and Professor John M. Coyner were both teachers who at the time lived at Waveland, Indiana. After her brother James Alfred Wilson and his wife Emily Maxwell Wilson died, Mary and John took in their children Samuel and Mary and raised them.

After teaching for many years in Indiana and Illinois, John and Mary were sent as teachers and missionaries to the Nez Perces Indians at Lapwai in northwestern Idaho. The next year John founded the Salt Lake Collegiate Institute which he conducted for ten years. Mary Wilson Coyner died on January 20, 1888, at the home of her sister Lucinda in Chillicothe, Ohio.

WILLIAM WILSON was born at Letterkenny Township, Cumberland County, Pennsylvania on____, the son of John and Nancy Breckenridge Wilson. He never married and was a soldier in the American Revolution. He contracted camp fever and came home and died in 1778. He is believed buried in the Rocky Springs graveyard.

SAMUEL WILSON was born in 1754 at Letterkenny Township, Cumberland County, Pennsylvania, the son of John and Nancy Breckenridge Wilson. When his brother William returned home sick with camp fever, Samuel attended his brother and caught the fever also and nearly died. During his sickness he resolved that if he survived, he was going to devote his life to God. Accordingly, on his recovery he quit farming and went to Princeton College where he graduated in 1782.

Rev. Samuel Wilson became pastor of the Big Spring Presbyterian Church in 1787. This church was located about 15 miles east of the Rocky Spring Presbyterian Church. Samuel Wilson married Jane Mahon.

Rev. Samuel Wilson died on March 4, 1799. He was buried under a large marble slab in the Big Spring Presbyterian Church graveyard. He was the parent of two children, John Wilson who died at the age of sixteen and a daughter, Jane Wilson, who married Dr. William Sharpe.

THE GASTON FAMILY

JEAN GASTON was born in France, probably about the year 1600. He was a Huguenot who was banished from France for religious reasons and had his property confiscated. He found refuge in Scotland and during this time his family in France, although they were Catholic, sent him financial support. He was believed to be forty years of age and unmarried when he went to Scotland. Between 1662 and 1668, during a season of persecution, Jean and his sons John, William, and Alexander migrated to the Northern Ireland to live, seeking safety and religious freedom.

John Gaston and his brother Alexander immigrated to America and started the Gaston family in New England.

The third brother William Gaston remained in County Antrim, Ireland, however several of his children came to South Carolina and started the southern branch of the family.

HUGH GASTON was born in County Antrim, Ireland. He was a direct descendant of Jean Gaston who married Jennet ___ and came to America at about 1720. It was said that he, his bother Joseph, John and Alexander came to America at the same time.

Hugh Gaston lived in Bedminster Township, Somerset County, New Jersey and was an attendant at the Lamington Presbyterian Church from 1740 to 1766. He took up land in Mt. Bethal Township, Bucks County (later Northampton), Pennsylvania on February 10, 1746, possibly for his son William Gaston. On June 20, 1751, Hugh and his son William took up land in the same township.

Hugh Gaston died on December 23, 1772, "in his 85th year," as his tombstone in the Lamington graveyard indicates. Jennet Gaston died August 1, 1777, in her 80th year and was also buried in Lamington graveyard.

Hugh Gaston was the parent of at least three sons.

WILLIAM GASTON was born about 1720, the son of Hugh and Jennet Gaston. He lived in Northampton, Pennsylvania. William Gaston was killed by Indians in December of 1755 leaving a widow and five children. The Delaware and Shawnee Indians went on the war path massacring settlers on both side of Blue Mountain from the Hudson River to the Susquehanna River.

It is thought that the children made their home with their Uncle John Gaston, the miller. In 1762, 182 acres of land in Bethel Township belonging to the estate of William Gaston was ordered sold for the benefit of the five children. The petition was signed by John Gaston who was then the only heir of William Gaston of legal age.

HUGH GASTON was born in 1734, the son of Hugh and Jennet Gaston. He succeeded to his father's estate and lived at Peapack, Bedminister Township in a stone house. He was married three times. He died June 25, 1808, in his 75th year.

JOHN GASTON was born May 1740, the son of Hugh and Jennet Gaston. John married Charity Cheeseman on February 4, 1760. Charity was the daughter of Joseph Cheeseman of Upper Freehold (now Millstone) Township, Monmouth County, NJ. She is believed to have been the granddaughter of William and Charity Cheeseman who took up 100 acres of land in Monmouth in 1688 and who left two sons, Joseph and William Cheeseman.

At Tennent, Monmouth County, New Jersey is a Presbyterian Church organized in about 1692 and was known as the Old Scots Church. It was later known as the Freehold Church and was still later called the Old Tennent Church which is the current name. John Gaston belonged to this church for a number of years and church records give dates of baptism for his first five children. The present church was erected in 1751 and the Battle of Monmouth during the American Revolution took place about a mile and a quarter from the church.

On about 1767, John Gaston moved to Mt. Bethel Township, Northumberton County, Pennsylvania. This move appears to have been on the heels of the settlement of his father's estate in 1762. He took up 275 acres of land in February 1772. The name of John Gaston and that of William Cheeseman appear as Revolutionary soldiers in a list of the Mt. Bethel Company of Col. Jacob Stroud's Battalion in 1776. John Gaston was designated as "Major John Gaston of Mt. Bethel Township."

About 1783, John Gaston moved to Rostraver Township, Westmoreland County, PA where he remained for several years. In 1790, he moved to Washington County, PA where he bought about 300 acres of land. On this property was established a village called Gastonville located near the Monongahela River.

In 1791, John Gaston and a group a farmer's took part in the "Whiskey Rebellion" opposing the whiskey tax on distillers. Under the law, big producers would pay six cents per gallon annually and the more they produced the more tax breaks they incurred. Whereas, small producers paid nine cents a gallon which was further compounded in that only cash would be accepted for the tax payment. In 1795, the "Whiskey Rebellion" was defeated by federal troops who were dispatched by President George Washington. Located in the Mingo Presbyterian Church graveyard is a plaque outlining the location of the men who took part in the rebellion. John Gaston is noted on this plaque as "a Revolutionary War Veteran, delivered "Tom the Tinker" letters to the Pittsburgh "Gazette" for all to read and be forewarned."

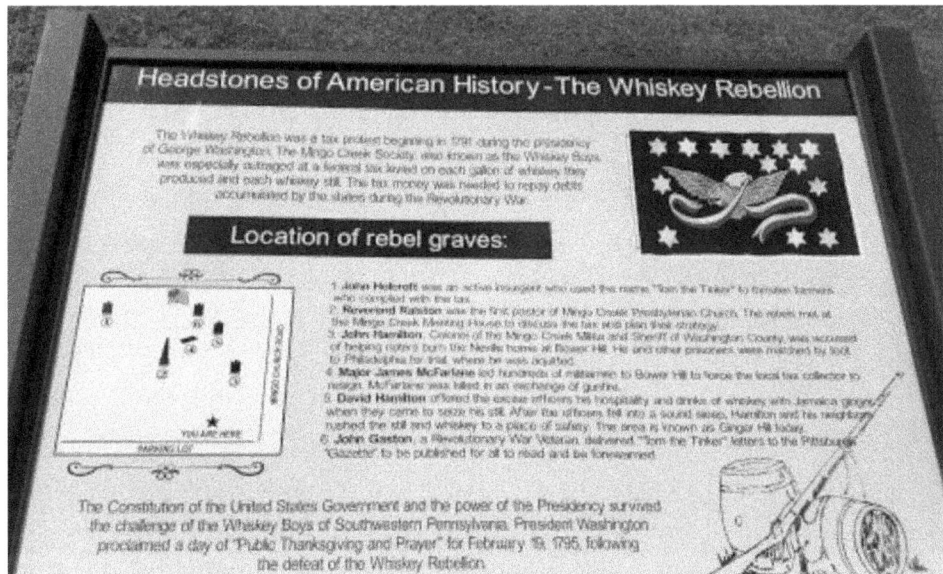

Plaque in Mingo Presbyterian Church graveyard

Charity Cheeseman died on February 15, 1821, and John Gaston died on September 10, 1823. John and Chasity Gaston are buried in Mingo Presbyterian Church graveyard, in Union Township, Washington County, Pennsylvania.

John Gaston and Charity Cheeseman were the parents of eight known children.

1. William Gaston, born July 15, 1761
2. Joseph Gaston
3. John Gaston, born January 7, 1765
4. Samuel Gaston, born February 18, 1767
5. James Gaston, born February 18, 1767
6. Samuel Gaston, born October 10, 1772
7. Elizabeth Gaston, born May 8, 1778
8. Margaret Gaston, married Samuel McClain.

JOSEPH GASTON was born April 25, 1763, the son of John and Charity Cheeseman Gaston. Joseph married Martha Hutton in South Carolina on April 17, 1783. She was born probably in Somerset County, New Jersey on January 12, 1766, the daughter of William Hutton and Rebecca Craig. The Old Tennent Church has an early connection to the Hutton family.

William Hutton moved from New Jersey to South Carolina it is believed by way of Pennsylvania. He settled on a large 800 acres plantation near Abbeville, South Carolina. William Hutton died sometime in 1809 and his will was probated on September 4, 1809, Abbeville County Will Book 1, page 378. He left his estate to his widow Rebecca and his four children, Martha, Joseph, Rebecca and Mary.

Captain William Hutton had a "sorrel gelding" shot out from under him at the Battle of Kettle Creek on February 14, 1779. This battle lasted about one hour and forty-five minutes between a Tory force of 700 men and a patriot force of some 400 men. Of the Tories captured five were executed while the others were pardoned.

Martha Hutton Gaston's brother Joseph Hutton married Nancy Calhoun, first cousin to John C. Calhoun on August 30, 1823.

On July 4,1794, Joseph Gaston was commissioned "Captain of Militia in the Savannah Regiment in Abbeville County' by Governor William Moultrie. In 1804, he was commissioned Major in the militia. Owing to his strong opposition to slavery, Joseph moved his family to Hamilton, Butler County, Ohio in 1807. A large number of Scotch-Irish and Huguenot-Irish moved from Abbeville County, South Carolina to Ohio about this time.

Joseph Gaston was an ingenious man, a man who could turn his hand to almost any kind of work. His health was not always good, and he had times of despondency. Yet, he was fond of jokes and enjoyed society.

Joseph Gaston died November 21, 1821. Martha Hutton Gaston died on July 9, 1844.

Joseph Gaston and Martha Hutton Gaston were the parents of eleven known children.

1. Rebecca Gaston, born Feb. 20, 1784, married John Kerr
2. Ann Gaston, born Dec. 16, 1785
3. Margaret Gaston, born Mar. 7, 1788
4. John Gaston
5. Mary Gaston, married William Wilson February 14, 1811
6. William Gaston
7. Joseph Smith Gaston, born October 9, 1796
8. Matta Ann Gaston
9. Lydia Gaston
10. Lucinda Gaston
11. Eliza Gaston

MARY GASTON was born on September 23, 1792, in South Carolina, the daughter of Joseph and Martha Hutton Gaston. Mary and her family left South Carolina and moved to Ohio. On one fateful trip, Mary and her brother made a sixty-mile trip where at the local church she met William Wilson. He fell in love with her on first sight. Mary married William Wilson on February 14, 1811.

Mary died April 15, 1864, at Lebanon, IN. See page 87.

The Maxwell Family

The Maxwell name in Scotland is believed to have been derived from Maccus, son of Undweyn a Saxon Lord, who lived in the 12th century and is said to have given his name to Maccuwell, a pool of the Tweed River located near Kelso Bridge. Some authorities say the name is of Norse or Anglo-Scots origin while others claim the name is of Anglo-Norman descent. Whatever the origin of the name, the Maxwell's have played an integral role in the history of Scotland. Titles and dignities bestowed on the Maxwells by various kings are many, there have been four Earldoms, five Lords, six Baronets and there are twenty-eight castles associated with the Maxwells. There are two great branches of the Maxwells recognized by historians today, the Maxwell's of Pollok and, the Maxwell's associated with the great border castle of Caerlaverock, located about seven miles from Dumfries, and now in ruins. The Maxwell clan members played a large and significant role in the history of Scotland and later in the early evolving history of the United States. However, it must also be noted there were great Maxwell families of England and Ireland.

Much of what has been researched on this particular Maxwell family was found in the 1916 publication of the *Maxwell History and Genealogy* by Florence Wilson Houston, Laura Cowan Blaine and Ella Dunn Mellette, hereafter referred to as the *Maxwell History*. These three ladies were all descendants of Bezaleel Maxwell. Public records have been searched to verify or augment what was written in that Maxwell family history. When research has proven the Maxwell book to be in conflict with the public records, the conflict has been noted and the public records than become the primary source of information and is recorded here.

It must be noted at this time that there is reference to a coat of arms in the *Maxwell History* attributed to John Maxwell that does not correspond with the current Maxwell Clan crest or to any Maxwell crest found in Burke's book of heraldry. All attempts to reconcile the crest mentioned in the *Maxwell History* with what is found published today have been unsuccessful.

The *Maxwell History* notes that there was a John Maxwell who appeared at the Orange County, Virginia Court on July 24, 1740 with the court records recording the following comments. "John Maxwell came into Court and made oath that he imported himself, Margaret, John Jr., Thomas, Mary, Alexander Maxwell from Ireland to Philadelphia and from thence to this colony at his own charges, and this is the first time of his proving his rights in order to obtain land. Which is ordered to be certified." Receiving land for the importation of people was a common act in the Virginia Colony.

While a connection of this John Maxwell family to our Maxwell family has not been established, the course of how this family arrived in the British Colony appears to have been the source used for this family in the *Maxwell History*.

BEZALEEL MAXWELL was born in Scotland and is said by family tradition to be the son of John Maxwell. Bezaleel's grandfather was, by the same source, believed to have been James Maxwell. There has been no date of birth given for this Bezaleel Maxwell, but it had to have been either late 1600 or early 1700. Bezaleel is a Hebrew name which means "God protects him." Unverified family research sources state that at a time and place yet unknown, Bezaleel Maxwell married Rebecca Boyd, but it appears most likely the marriage was in Scotland. This same source states the family emigrated from Scotland to Philadelphia and then settled in Lancaster County, Pennsylvania. They later removed to Augusta County, Virginia and then into Albemarle County, Virginia.

The assertion of the arrival in Philadelphia, the settlement in Lancaster County, PA and then a settlement in Augusta County, VA has yet to be documented. However, it is documented that a Bezaleel Maxwell purchased 400 acres of land in Albemarle County, Virginia from Charles Lewis and his wife Mary of Goochland County on May 14, 1751, Albemarle County Deed Book 1, page 268. The land was described as being situated in Rich Cove.

On December 27, 1758, Bezaleel Maxwell of St Ann Parish, Albemarle County sold 200 acres of this land to his son John Maxwell, Albemarle County Deed Book 2, page 86. This land was purchased from Charles Lewis Sr. and was "a part of the tract on which said Bazeleel lives." This deed was witnessed by Thomas and James Maxwell and Roger Kilpatrick.

Bezaleel Maxwell and Rebecca his wife on February 11, 1761, sold to Thomas Maxwell sixty acres for 10 Pounds. The land was part of the 400 acres purchased of Charles Lewis Sr., Albemarle County Deed Book 3, page 2.

William Maxwell and Anne his wife on April 12, 1769, sold 50 acres to Bezaleel Maxwell that had been granted to William Maxwell on February 14, 1761. The land was described as adjoining that of said Bezaleel Maxwell. Albemarle County Deed Book 5, page 450.

John Maxwell and his father Bezaleel Maxwell sold a portion of the Lewis tract to George Bline on August 26, 1771, in Albemarle County, Virginia, Albemarle County Deed Book 5, page 450. The amount of land was not stipulated but the property was said to be part of tract that Bezaleel Maxwell had deeded to his son John. This was the last known land transaction in this county involving Bezaleel Maxwell with his son John Maxwell. This, also, appears to be at about the time that the John Maxwell family moved to the Virginia frontier.

William Maxwell on August 13, 1783 sold to Bezaleel Maxwell 100 acres for L150. The land was where William lived at on Green Creek, commonly called Cove Creek, that was purchased of George Douglas, Albemarle County Deed Book 8, page 109.

On September 4, 1783, Bezaleel Maxwell Sr., "for the love and good will, to his son Bezaleel Maxwell Jr., 250 acres, "on which I live and have lived for many years," in Rich Cove, "without any consideration whatever." Albemarle County Deed Book 8, page 109.

There is a census dated from 1785 found in the book *First Census of the United States* where there was only one Bezalel (sic) Maxwell listed in the enumeration. Recorded after Maxwell's name was one dwelling with 13 white people in that dwelling and there were six other buildings on the property. This Bezaleel had to be the junior Bezaleel Maxwell. The elder Bezaleel Maxwell was most likely a member of the 13 people noted as living in the house.

On November 22, 1808, the county court ordered the Bezaleel Maxwell estate inventoried, the estate was appraised on October 3, 1808, by Samuel W. Anderson, Samuel Harmer and William Sudderth, Albemarle County Will Book 4, page 353. The value of the estate was L 109.2.4. Bezaleel Maxwell Sr. apparently lived to a considerable age and was most likely buried on the Rich Cove property he had purchased from Charles Lewis in 1751.

Bezaleel Maxwell was the parent of five known sons. The order of their births is unknown. There may have been daughters but no reference to them has been found.

1. Bezaleel Maxwell Jr., wife named Jean
2. Thomas Maxwell
3. John Maxwell
4. James Maxwell, wife named Jane
5. William Maxwell, wife named Anne

JOHN MAXWELL was born apparently in Scotland or Ireland about the year 1738 and came to America with his family headed by his father Bezaleel Maxwell. John Maxwell was said to have been married to Fannie Garner, time and place yet unknown.

John Maxwell was given 200 acres of land in Albemarle County, VA by his father Bezaleel Maxwell of St. Ann Parish on December 27, 1758, Albemarle County Deed Book 2, page 86. The land was described as bought from Charles Lewis Sr. and "part of the tract on which said Bezaleel lives."

On March 12, 1767, John Maxwell purchased from Samuel Woods of Amherst County, 264 acres of land for L27 Pounds, land described as beginning at Captain Charles Lewis' line, Albemarle County Deed Book 4, page 534. This land had to be very close to the property that John's father had purchased from Captain Lewis in 1751.

On August 26, 1771, John and Bezaleel Maxwell sold 68 acres to George Bline, Albemarle County Deed Book 2, page 86. This was part of the two hundred acres Bezaleel Maxwell had given John. The deed did not mention a wife for either John or Bezaleel Maxwell. John Maxwell sold 264 acres to Richard Lawrence on March 9, 1772, Albemarle County Deed Book 7, page 435. It appears that John Maxwell sold off all his land in Albemarle County at this time and moved to southwest Virginia.

Fincastle County, Virginia was created from Botetourt County in 1772. John Maxwell entered the deed book of this newly formed county on January 4, 1773, and again on the following day, January 5, when he purchased 160 acres for 65 Pounds "current money of Virginia" from the estate of John Buchanan of Augusta County through the executors William Preston and William Campbell, Montgomery County Deed Book A, pages 4-5. This new county at this time included what is now all of Kentucky and part of West Virginia. It is in the Fincastle County Militia records where John Maxwell and his sons Bezaleel and David next appeared together.

John Maxwell and his son's David and Bezaleel Maxwell were recorded as members of Robert Doack's Company of Fincastle Militia on June 2, 1774. According to militia pay records Bezaleel Maxwell served in this company for four days, while David Maxwell served for six days. The pay records do not record John Maxwell's name at all which could only mean he was unable to serve after his name was recorded. John Maxwell and his sons Bezaleel and David Maxwell are credited by various sources as being at the Battle of Point Pleasant which occurred on October 10, 1774. Militia pay records, however, indicate only Bezaleel Maxwell was at this famous battle. The Battle was located at the confluence of the Kanawha River and the Ohio River in what in now Mason County, West Virginia. The fight was a bloody affair that lasted for about six hours and ranged over a heavily forested area covering about one mile. The battle, which saw the defeat of the Indian forces led by Chief Cornstalk, has been credited by some historians as both the conclusion of Lord Dunmore's War and the first battle of the American Revolution.

On January 4, 1775, John Maxwell leased an additional 310 acres of the John Buchanan estate from the executors William Preston and William Campbell. One day later, January 5, John Maxwell purchased the 310 acres for L65 Pounds from Preston and Campbell. The land was described as "being in the County of Fincastle on a branch of Reed Creek, a branch of Woods River."

During the struggle for American independence, the period from 1774 to 1781, the settlers in Kentucky and western Virginia were virtually ignored by the nascent Virginia government. Conflict with native Indian tribes, British intrigue with those tribes and a virtual lack of military assistance from the eastern portion of Virginia, who were having their own unique problems, created a need for self-reliance among the settlers. As early as 1784, Kentucky asked to become a state separate from Virginia. The problem of the transference of legal affairs or public records from county to new county during this period has created a great research problem for those trying to follow family members from one set of public records to another. The reader must be aware of these problems when one reads this account of the family's progressive movements from one location to another.

In 1777, the Virginia government divided Fincastle County into three new counties, Montgomery County, Washington County and Kentucky County. The area where the Maxwells had purchased land was now in Montgomery County. Kentucky County lasted but three years when it was further divided in 1780 into three additional counties, Lincoln County, Fayette County and Jefferson County. It was in the Lincoln County records that the Maxwells were found posting land grants or patents in what later became the state of Kentucky.

Exactly how long the John Maxwell family lived in Fincastle, i.e. Montgomery County is not known, but it is known with certainty that John Maxwell and his sons were living in Lincoln County in April 1780 because of information found in a deposition given by John Maxwell at a session of the County Court of Madison County, Kentucky on March 24, 1801. The concern of the Court was over a drain of a spring believed to be on Maxwell's property. John Maxwell stated that "he and his sons, Bazel(sic) and David had killed some Buffalo at this place in April of 1780. They had chosen to locate land here and knew of no other claim in the area at that time other than the Elk Garden and Locus Bent claims." As it would have taken many months for John Maxwell and his sons to travel to this spring, it can only be concluded they had already been in the area many months if not years before this time.

John Maxwell was issued a land warrant for 200 acres on Paint Lick Creek on March 10, 1780. On June 24, 1780, he received an additional warrant for 400 acres at the same location. John Maxwell and Joseph Wray were credited with the establishment of Maxwell's Station in 1780. At that time Maxwell's Station was the northern outpost of the settlement. The station was used as a base to locate unclaimed land to the north of the white settlement. The Maxwells were said by local custom in this part of Kentucky to be of the group known as the early Scotch-Irish hunters and militiamen who came to Kentucky following the Battle of Point Pleasant.

Several published sources state that in April 1781, a party of northern Indians came into the settlement on the Clinch River murdered and scalped two of John Maxwells' daughters and took nine prisoners. Captain John Martin led an expedition against the Cherokee Indians. There are several variations of this story, even one in which Captain Maxwell was killed in the pursuit, which story could not have been our John Maxwell.

On August 2, 1783, John Maxwell of Lincoln County VA sold the 310 acres he owned in Montgomery County to Thomas Copeheifer for 5,000 Pounds of current money of Virginia. Two days later, August 4, 1783, John Maxwell sold the 160 acres to Robert Black for 80 Pounds. Both properties were described as being on the "south branch of Reed Creek, a part of a tract known by the name of Radliff Marsh." The reader must be aware that Montgomery County was divided many times into other counties and the actual area where the Maxwells lived could now be in West Virginia.

John Maxwell patent of 400 acres of land in Lincoln County, Virginia was approved on November 18, 1783. This land was situated on Paint Lick Creek. He received approval for the other 200 acres on Paint Lick Creek on November 22, 1784. This made the total land patented to John Maxwell on Paint Lick Creek to be 600 acres. This part of Lincoln County became Madison County, Virginia in 1786.

The 1787 personal property tax rolls for Madison County, Virginia, later part of Kentucky, records the names of Bazel(sic) Maxwell, David Maxwell and John Maxwell in Michael McNeely's District. Bazel(sic) had 14 horses and 35 head of cattle; David had 10 horses and 17 head of cattle and John had one horse and 11 cattle.

The State of Kentucky was established on June 1, 1792. The portion of Madison County where the Maxwells lived and along with portions from Lincoln and Mercer Counties became Gerrard County on December 17, 1796.

John Maxwell Sr. sold 200 acres of land located on the waters of Paint Lick Creek to Bezaleel Maxwell on November 10, 1801, for $1,000.00, Gerrard County Deed Book A, page 476. The deed for this property was posted to the court on June 26, 1802. It appears that Bezaleel Maxwell may have taken possession of the property long before this time as he was taxed for the land in 1797. At this time Bazel(sic) Maxwell was the only Maxwell who still paid tax on land in Garrard County. The 200 acres had been part of the original John Maxwell survey and was probably the old home place for John Maxwell.

On August 11, 1803, Bezaleel Maxwell and John Maxwell Sr. sold 400 acres to Thomas Kennedy for 200 Pounds, Gerrard County Deed Book D, page 532. The property was not described by this source. John and Samuel Maxwell witnessed the signing of the deed. The fact that the property was sold for Pounds instead of Dollars suggest the deed agreement was made long before the deed was posted at court. This assertion is further reinforced with the fact that the 1797 tax records do not show the Maxwells paying tax on this property. This transaction also appears to be the last in which John Maxwell Sr. took part.

John Maxwell, according to family tradition, loved to entertain his children and grandchildren with stories of the comforts of the old family homes in Scotland and Ireland. He told of the family coach with its quartered arms and boar's head crest, of the great house with its beamed ceilings and spacious halls, of the walls hung with claymores, spears and trophies of past wars and of the family coat of mail which occupied the same corned of the fireplace. These stories were a never-ending source of awe and mystery and the inspiration of many bloody tales to the young children. The date of John Maxwell's death is unknown. However, the property on Paint Lick Creek in Gerrard County, Kentucky where he was last known to have lived appears to be the likely place of his death and burial.

John Maxwell was known to have four surviving sons. He was also believed to have had two daughters who were murdered and scalped by the Indians.

1. Bezaleel Maxwell
2. David Maxwell, married Mary Stephenson* and died in Wayne County, KY
3. Samuel Maxwell
4. John Maxwell

BEZALEEL MAXWELL was born December 20, 1751, in Albemarle County, Virginia, the son of John Maxwell and Fannie Garner. Family sources state Bezaleel grew up near the home of Thomas Jefferson, having at times the same school masters for teachers. He is believed to have studied medicine and law and was intensely patriotic although an advocate of peace. Albemarle County deed records suggest Bezaleel Maxwell probably moved in 1772 with other members of his family into a frontier area of western Virginia that became known as Fincastle County. Fincastle County was created in 1772 and embodied an area of what is now West Virginia and Kentucky. Bezaleel's father John Maxwell purchased property in Fincastle County on January 4, 1773. The original deed records of Fincastle County are now found in Montgomery County, VA.

Bezaleel Maxwell entered military service as a militia private on June 2, 1774, as a member of Captain Doack's Company. Militia pay records record Bezaleel Maxwell serving only four days in this company. On August 25, 1774, there was a draft call for 30 men from Captain Herbert's Company and Bezaleel Maxwell was a member of that company who answered the call. This company, along with three other companies of "Fincastle Troops", was stationed at Fort Union under the command of Colonel Fleming. Fort Union was located at what is now Lewisburg, Greenbrier County, WV. Militia pay records state that Bezaleel Maxwell served in Herbert's command for 104 days. During this time the 22-year old Basileal (sic) Maxwell was found listed as a volunteer in Captain Evan Shelby's Company of Volunteers from Fincastle under the command of Colonel Andrew Lewis.

Colonel Andrew Lewis led 800 hundred men from Fort Union to the banks of the Ohio River at the mouth of the Great Kanawha River at a place now known as Point Pleasant, Mason County WV. Numbered among Lewis' command was Captain Evan Shelby's Company that included Bezaleel Maxwell. The troops arrived on the south banks of the Ohio River on October 7, after a long difficult march from Fort Union and awaited a body of men to arrive from Pittsburg led by the Virginia Governor Lord Dunmore. The pending assemblage of men was gathered to halt Indian attacks on the settlers.

On the other side of the Ohio River from where Lewis' troops were encamped was a body of about 1,000 Indians led by the Shawnee Chief Cornstalk. This group was made up of warriors not only from the Shawnee tribe but from the Mingo, Delaware and Wyandot tribes as well. Chief Cornstalk was aware of the expected arrival of Lord Dunmore's troops and decided to attack the smaller body of troops led by Colonel Lewis. The Indians stealthily crossed the Ohio River and attacked Lewis's forces on the morning of October 10, 1774. The battle was a vicious conflict that lasted over six hours and raged over an area of over a mile of heavy forested terrain. There was, at times, bloody hand to hand combat as both sides considered this a battle to the death. By early afternoon and fearing the arrival of Dunmore's troops, the Indians withdrew back across the Ohio River.

Of the 800 men who had arrived for battle, a little over 200 of them were killed during the fight. The number of Indian warriors killed was never established. Bezaleel Maxwell was numbered among those who survived the Battle of Point Pleasant on October 10, 1774. Chief Cornstalk and his forces were eventually defeated and signed a peace treaty with Lord Dunmore and that is why this battle has become known as Lord Dunmore's

War. This battle is also now believed by many historians to be the first battle of the American Revolution.

At the conclusion of Dunmore's War there were auditor records that showed Bezaleel Maxwell was paid for 104 days of service as a member of Captain Herbert's Company. There have been assertions by certain later family members that Bezaleel Maxwell saw military service up to the end of Revolutionary War and was at the final battle at Yorktown. However, there are no records that support this assertion. The fact was that living on the Virginia frontier during the struggle for American Independence and fighting almost daily battles with the British and their Indian allies, was more than enough test for Bezaleel's patriotism and his family's survival. It is also a known fact, stated by John Maxwell in a court deposition, that he and his sons Bezaleel and David Maxwell were hunting buffalo in April 1780 on the Kentucky frontier in an area that later became Madison County, Kentucky.

Bezaleel Maxwell returned to Albemarle County, VA following the Battle of Point Pleasant and married Margaret Anderson there on February 6, 1775. Margaret Anderson was born September 4, 1755, the daughter of Col. John Anderson and Anne Irvine. Col Anderson was said to be one of the founders of "The Old Stone Presbyterian Church." This church is located in what is now Lewisburg, Greenbriar County, West Virginia, which was the location of the original Fort Union. This fact seems to suggest that the Maxwells and the Andersons lived in this area then known as Fincastle County for a time before they moved further west. It appears the Andersons and the Maxwells moved to what is now Kentucky at the same time and settled in the same area.

Bezaleel Maxwell requested a warrant for 100 acres of land on Silver Creek in Lincoln County, Virginia on April 25, 1780. On May 25, 1780, he requested a warrant for 200 acres on Paint Lick Creek. On August 20, 1786, he received patents for both parcels of land. The property on Paint Lick Creek appears to have been where Bezaleel and Margaret Anderson Maxwell reared their family.

Between the years 1787 to 1792, while Madison County was still part of Virginia, there were personal property tax records listed that are available to researchers today. A review of those records will be helpful for us to understand more about the family during this time. In 1787, Bezaleel Maxwell listed 14 horses and 13 cattle and no slaves. In 1788, he listed 13 horses and no cattle and no slaves. In 1789, he had 13 horses, no cattle and no slaves. 1790 is missing, so in 1791, he listed 12 horses, no cattle and no slaves. In 1792, Bezaleel listed 13 horses, 32 cattle and 2 slaves, both salves were young females. The 1792 tax listing was also found published in the book *Early Kentucky Tax Records.*

As incomprehensible as slavery is for us today some of its practices must be understood. Just because a slave may have been listed under one's personal property tax listing did not necessarily mean you owned that slave. Many slaves had their labor rented out by the year by their owner. If one was renting the slave for the year when tax time came around, you had to pay the tax on that slave. That is most likely why slaves were reported one year and not others. Since the slaves appear so irregularly in the Maxwell household during this time this was likely the situation here. This is not to say that the Maxwells never owned slaves because they did, but to explain why slaves could move out of a tax list so quickly.

The state of Kentucky was created on June 1, 1792. The area where the Maxwells lived in Madison County on Paint Lick Creek became Gerrard County four years later on December 17, 1796.

On December 20, 1797, Bezaleel Maxwell purchased from Edward Russell for $100.00, a bay horse, a still and a negro wench, Gerrard County Deed Book A, page 108. This is the first evidence of Bezaleel Maxwell actually owning a slave. The use of a still was a common thing on the frontier as alcohol was often used as a medicine or as trade goods.

There are no 1800 census records because those records were destroyed when the British burned Washington during the War of 1812. However, 1800 was an important year in the life of Bezaleel and his wife Margaret Maxwell because it was the year that their eleventh and last child was born. This fact may also help explain Bezaleel's need for more help to care for a large family when he purchased the Negro wench from Russell in 1797.

On August 6, 1801, Alexander Carnes sold 200 acres to Bezaleel Maxwell for L20 Pounds. Location of land was not stated. The sale was witnessed by John and Samuel Maxwell and John and Ralph Carnes, Gerrard County Deed Book B, page 261.

John Maxwell Sr. on November 10, 1801, sold 200 acres of land located on the waters of Paint Lick Creek to Bezaleel Maxwell for $1,000.00. The deed was posted on June 26, 1802, Gerrard County Deed Book A, page 476. This property was most likely the old home place of John Maxwell.

Bezaleel Maxwell and John Maxwell Sr. of Gerrard County on August 11, 1803, sold 400 acres for L200 Pounds to Thomas Kennedy. John and Samuel Maxwell witnessed the deed, Gerrard County Deed Book D, page 532.

There was a document found among the family archives of Dr. David H. Maxwell that was an interesting bill of sale signed by his father Bezaleel Maxwell.

> "Know all men by these present that I, Bezaleel Maxwell, Gerrard
> County and State of Kentucky, do sell and by these present have bar-
> gained and sold to David H. Maxwell, of the county and State afore-
> said, one negro woman named Sal, of 18 years of age, for the sum of
> $350.00 current money of Kentucky, the receipt whereof I acknowledge
> myself fully satisfied. Which negro I do warrant and defend to him, the
> said David H. Maxwell, his heirs and assigns forever, and from me and
> my heirs and assigns forever and further from all manner of persons
> whatever. In witness whereof I have hereunto set my hand and seal this
> 25th day of September, 1809.

The above document firmly fixes the fact that Bezaleel Maxwell was still living in Gerrard County, Kentucky in 1809. The 1810 Gerrard County census further confirms Bezaleel Maxwell was still living in that county at that time. The 1810 census enumerations only list the head of household and everyone else by sex and age. In the Maxwell home there were still three boys and four girls noted. There were also five slaves listed in the household.

Bezaleel Maxwell appears to have stayed on the property purchased from his father until March 15, 1810, when he sold the 200 acres on the waters of Paint Lick Creek to David M. Maxwell for $1,200.00. This land was described as the property where "the said Bezaleel now lives." It is not known who this David M. Maxwell was, Bezaleel's brother, his son or his nephew. The 1810 Kentucky census shows that the only Maxwells living in Gerrard County at that time were Bezaleel Maxwell, Daviss(sic, probably David) Maxwell and James M. Maxwell.

On April 21, 1810, Bezaleel Maxwell of Gerrard County and Davis (David) M. Maxwell sold 250 acres to Jeremiah Turpin for $1,800.00. This deed transaction appears to be the last that Bezaleel was involved with in Gerrard County.

There has been considerable confusion over the later years of Bezaleel Maxwell's life. One source in the *Maxwell Book* claims he came from Scott County, with his family and several of his colored servants, some of whom he had previously manumitted. There are no records to support any of these claims. What is known, however, is found in the 1820 census records for Jefferson County that should help clarify some of the facts about the last few years of Bezaleel Maxwell's life. The area previously known as the Indiana Territory became the State of Indiana on December 11, 1816. The first census for the newly formed state occurred in 1820 and the census records for Jefferson County, Indiana recorded the names of Edward Maxwell, John Maxwell, Samuel C. Maxwell and William Maxwell as heads of household. These four men are all believed to be the sons of Bezaleel Maxwell. David H. Maxwell, another known son of Bezaleel Maxwell, was living in Monroe County, Indiana at the time of the 1820 census enumeration. Bezaleel Maxwell's name was not found in Jefferson County, Indiana. These facts are important to understand because of an old mansion located near Hanover, Indiana that through time has become known as the Bezaleel Maxwell Home.

A Maxwell family mansion was built near Hanover, Indiana in 1817. How the date of the construction has been established is unknown. This house, a well-known historic structure in the area today, has, over time, come down believed to have been built by Bezaleel Maxwell. The Maxwell house was built of brick made of native clay and fired on the property. The structure was built in a Colonial style with two stories and an attic. A hall runs through the house which gives entrances to all rooms on both floors. The house has ten rooms and at the time it was built, it was considered to be one of the finest homes north of the Ohio River. The house and its large surrounding farmlands were famous for its fine orchards and sugar maples.

There is no doubt that Bezaleel Maxwell lived out his final days at this home, however, the house appears to have belonged to and was probably built by his son Edward R. Maxwell. Bezaleel Maxwell's granddaughter, Mrs. Mary Maxwell Sheyer, speaking in 1913 at a gathering to honor her grandfather, said in a speech given for the occasion that, "...he (Bezaleel Maxwell) and his wife made their home with their youngest son- Edward (Maxwell)..." This assertion by Mrs. Sheyer is given credence when the 1820 census record of Edward R. Maxwell's family was viewed more closely, because listed within the family are two individuals, one male and one female, and both over 45 years old, who were most likely Edward's parents. It must also be noted that Bezaleel Maxwell's name appeared on only one deed in Jefferson County, Indiana. The content of that deed is found below.

> I Bezaleel Maxwell of the County of Jefferson &
> State of Indiana do certify that I was the proper and
> lawful owner of a woman of Colour by the name of
> Eve Maxwell and that she has served me until she
> was of age or eighteen years old and that I have no
> further claim or demand on or of her service and
> that she is free from me my heirs executors & adminis-
> trators forever or from the claim or claims of all other
> persons whatsoever. Given under my hand and seal
> this ____ day of October A. D. 1819.
> Witness   *Bezaleel Maxwell* Seal
> *John Maxwell*
> *William Maxwell*
>   Recorded Jany. 27th 1821

The contents of this deed are very important. The date of the signing of this document in October 1819, suggest this would have been close to the time Bezaleel Maxwell and his wife moved to Indiana from Kentucky. Had the move occurred any earlier it would have been unlawful for Bezaleel Maxwell to have maintained ownership of the slave Eve Maxwell. Slavery had been outlawed in Indiana when it became a state in 1816.

After their arrival at Hanover, Bezaleel and Margaret Maxwell became members of the Hanover Presbyterian Church. The church was started in 1819 by Rev. Thomas C. Searle who died shortly thereafter in October of 1821. It took nearly two years for the new church to find a replacement. A call was given to the Rev. John Finley Crowe who was a dedicated abolitionist. The vote in the affirmative to accept Crowe was taken on January 16, 1823. Basallel (sic.) Maxwell was the fifth name listed for the vote, while Margaret Maxwell was the twenty-fifth name listed of the 34-member congregation. Interestingly, none of Bezaleel's sons were members of this church. In fact, Edward R. Maxwell, the son with whom Bezaleel and Margaret lived, was a member of the Disciples of Christ or Christian Church.

The Hanover Presbyterian Church was headed by Williamson Dunn who was related to Bezaleel Maxwell by marriage. Two of Bezaleel's sons, John and David, were married to two of Dunn's sisters; two more of his sons, Samuel and Edward, were married to two of Dunn's wife's sisters. Dunn was a justice of the peace and a judge of the court of common pleas for the Indiana Territory. He was a representative in the first three legislatures in the newly formed state of Indiana, serving as Speaker of the House twice. Dunn was appointed in 1823 by President Monroe as the register of the land office, probably one of the most important posts in the government. He issued patents for all the free government lands in the state. He along with an Army officer laid out the town of Crawfordsville where the land office was located. The village of Hanover was created from his farm. He gave land for the creation of Hanover College, and he, also, gave land for the creation of Wabash College in Crawfordsville.

It was while Bezaleel and Margaret were living at the Edward R. Maxwell home that lasting impressions, especially about Mrs. Maxwell, were left on several of her very young grandchildren. Years later when the *Maxwell History* was being researched, comments were made by three of these grandchildren for the book, who were by that time all well pass the age of 80. One granddaughter remembers her grandmother as always wearing on the Sabbath when communion was held a heavy black silk dress- an offering of the very best she had for the service. She was further remembered as saying, "A woman's hair was her glory" and "A beautiful skin was the gift of the Lord, and it was wrong not to take care of it." She encouraged the use of sunbonnets and gloves.

In her slight person, Margaret Anderson Maxwell was quiet, austere and, forcefully consecrated to what she felt was her duty. One grandchild vividly remembered one Sabbath morning when she was sitting in her swing. The child was noticed by her grandmother and admonished with threats of dire punishment, that any child should seek pleasure on a Sabbath day was a mortal sin and not to be condoned.

Bazeleel Maxwell died on January 9, 1828, at the age of 77 years. He was buried near Hanover, Indiana on the brow of a hill just south of where the Presbyterian Church now stands. Margaret Anderson Maxwell died on March 16, 1834 and was believed to have been buried beside her husband. It is not known if their bodies were removed to the new cemetery when the old cemetery was abandoned. It is still believed by some family members that Bezaleel and Margaret are both buried side by side in the "Old Church Yard."

On October 14, 1913, there was an event in the little cemetery at Hanover, Indiana that was called "A Patriotic Function Celebrated." There was the unveiling of a marker to the memory of Bezaleel Maxwell, a Revolutionary War Soldier, by the John Paul Chapter of the Daughter of the American Revolution of Madison, Indiana. President Millis of Hanover College presided at the ceremony. Speaking that day was the granddaughter of Bezaleel Maxwell, Mrs. Mary Maxwell Sheyer. Also speaking were Judge U. Z. Wiley, Dr. Harvey W. Wiley and Dr. Allison Maxwell, all great-grandsons of Bezaleel Maxwell.

Several of the comments made that day by Mrs. Mary Maxwell Sheyer about her grandfather Bezaleel Maxwell were: "Preaching was held in their homes and their groves, and Bezaleel's home was headquarters for the preachers who went through the country. He was always opposed to slavery and thought it morally wrong. And it was only when they had a large family of eleven children to rear, and the work of the house and the care of the children became a burden for his wife that it was impossible for her to do that he consented to have slaves-there was no other way of having help."

Mrs. Sheyer continued, "He was among the first to predict a war over slavery; and he advised the young men of Kentucky to leave there on that account and go to Indiana which would be a free state. When his own children were leaving Kentucky on account of slavery, although he was fast nearing the sunset of life, he freed his slaves, sold his property, and again faced the wilderness, where the Indian with his tomahawk and scalping knife in hand, roamed over the territory. Many of his slaves followed him. They worked for themselves, but when they were "out of a job" they went back to the home of their old master, always sure of maintenance until they could find work again."

It is important to note that a letter for the DAR Library dated November 6, 2000, offers the following sentence. "The DAR credits Maxwell (Bezaleel) with military service as a private under Captain Evan Shelby at the Battle of Point Pleasant in Virginia (now West Virginia) on 10 October 1774." One final comment about Bezaleel Maxwell's military service needs to be stated here. There were land bounty claims for those who served in Revolutionary War after the war, Bezaleel Maxwell never made claim for these bounties.

Perhaps one paragraph found in the comments made by the Honorable Judge U. Z. Wiley at the 1913 gathering to honor Bezaleel Maxwell best sums up the truth about what the family at that time knew about his great-grandfather.

> The present descendants of Bezaleel Maxwell are in possession of
> very little data in regard to the latter years of his life, but it is known
> that he died in Jefferson County, Indiana, near what is now the town
> of Hanover, on January 9th, 1828, at the age of seventy-seven years.
> The best information that we have leads us to believe that he was buried
> on the brow of the hill immediately south of where the Presbyterian
> Church now stands, at a point very near, if not immediately beneath the
> present town school building. Whether or not his remains were re-
> moved to this cemetery when the old burial ground was abandon, with
> other bodies that have been laid at rest there, is not definitely known.

The truth of the matter was that there were no stones placed over the graves of Bezaleel Maxwell and Margaret Anderson Maxwell at the time of their deaths. Over time even the exact locations of the graves were lost. It was left to the grandchildren and the great-grandchildren to try to remember what they could recall of these two people. Some of what they remembered was accurate, some of it was a blending of the stories from their grandfather and their great-grandfather and some of it was fantasy. However, it does not matter what percentage of each of these three variables make up Bezaleel Maxwell's life for us today because the sum of his life is told in the lives of his descendants and for that he would have had every reason to be justly proud.

Bezaleel Maxwell and Margaret Anderson Maxwell were the parents of eleven known children. The names and dates of birth listed below came from a transcribed copy of a bible that was published by Mathew Carey in Philadelphia in the year 1813. The bible was transcribed by a Maxwell family member Charles M. Robertson (1872-1961). He stated the bible was that of his grandfather who would have been Edward Franklin Maxwell. However, Edward Franklin Maxwell, who was born on February 16, 1816, appears to have been too young to have been the original owner of the book. The date of the book's publication, 1813, and the family information found therein suggest that part of the information found in the bible was probably recorded during the lifetime of Bezaleel Maxwell, who could have vouched for the accuracy of the information. The book appears to have been originally the property of Edward Franklin Maxwell's father Samuel Campbell Maxwell, who was a son of Bezaleel Maxwell.

1. John Maxwell, born Dec. 25, 1775, married Sarah Dunn, February 4, 1802, died November 12, 1824
2. Samuel Campbell Maxwell
3. James Anderson Maxwell, born September 25, 1779, married Ann B. Blanton on June 27, 1801, died December 9, 1823
4. Ann Maxwell, born June 30, 1781
5. Elizabeth Maxwell, born June 30, 1784, married Joseph Reid, Spring of 1801
6. David Hervey Maxwell
7. William Maxwell, born October 6, 1788, married Rachel Stevens, October 8, 1812
8. Edward R. Maxwell
9. Fannie Maxwell, born March 26, 1791, died November 1795
10. Margaret Maxwell, born August 2, 1795, married James McCullough, August 16, 1813, died March 16, 1834
11. Matilda Maxwell, born January 1, 1800, married Peter Batterton, 1820

SAMUEL CAMPBELL MAXWELL was born on the Virginia frontier on September 6, 1777, probably in Fincastle County, Virginia, the son of Bezaleel Maxwell and Margaret Anderson Maxwell.

Samuel married Jenny Tilford in April 1807. Jenny was the parent of eight children. She died at 4:00 PM on Saturday, January 15, 1820 of cramps and colic. She was 32 years old.

Samuel then married Rebecca Marcus on August 16, 1820. She died on November 10, 1823, at the age of 34. She left one child, Rebecca Ellen Maxwell, born November 10, 1823.

Samuel then married Sarah (Sally) C. Stevens on September 17, 1824 and they had four children. Sarah died November 30, 1868, age of 79 years. She was buried at Harrisonville, MO.

Samuel C. Maxwell died of pleurisy at the age of 59 on January April 27, 1837. His estate was probated in 1841, Jefferson County Will Book B and listed these heirs, Joseph M. Tilford and Mary Ann Maxwell, his wife, Preston P. Wiley and Lucinda Maxwell, his wife, James A. (Maxwell), Lucinda and Nancy Jane Batterton, children of Eliza Maxwell Batterton and David Batterton; Edward F. Maxwell, Harvey H. Maxwell, Emily Maxwell, Maria Maxwell, Julia Maxwell. Julia C. Maxwell, age 11 and Maria A., age 7, infant heirs of Samuel C. Maxwell.

1. Eliza Reid Maxwell
2. Lucinda Wier Maxwell
3. William Tilford Maxwell
4. James Anderson Maxwell
5. Mary Ann Maxwell
6. Edward Franklin Maxwell
7. Harvey Henderson Maxwell
8. Emily McCullough Maxwell
9. Rebecca Ellen Maxwell, born November 10, 1823, died July 14, 1830
10. Margaret Jane Maxwell, born August 12, 1825, died June 20, 1826
11. Julia Chitwood Maxwell
12. Nancy Malvina Maxwell, born November 22, 1828, died July 16, 1830
13. Maria Araminta Maxwell

ELIZA REID MAXWELL was born near Hanover, Jefferson County, Indiana on January 18, 1808, the daughter of Samuel C. Maxwell and Jenny Tilford Maxwell. Eliza married David Batterton on September 12, 1826.

Eliza Maxwell Batterton died in September 1833, leaving two small children. Their names were noted in the settlement of the Samuel C. Maxwell estate, Lucinda and Nancy Jane Batterton.

LUCINDA WIER MAXWELL was born near Hanover, Jefferson County, Indiana on June 25, 1809, the daughter of Samuel C. Maxwell and Jenny Tilford Maxwell. Lucinda married Preston P. Wiley on March 1, 1832.

WILLIAM TILFORD MAXWELL was born near Hanover, Jefferson County, Indiana on December 24, 1810, the son of Samuel C. Maxwell and Jenny Tilford Maxwell. William married Maria Chitwood on December 26, 1832.

William later married the widow of Harvey Maxwell, Isaphena McCullough Maxwell in October 1854. William died April 21, 1872, at the age of 62 years.

JAMES ANDERSON MAXWELL near Hanover, Jefferson County, Indiana on July 24, 1812, the son of Samuel C. Maxwell and Jenny Tilford Maxwell. James Maxwell married Isibella Tilford in June 1833.

(James) Anderson Maxwell died in California. It is believed he had seven sons.

MARY ANN MAXWELL was born near Hanover, Jefferson County, Indiana on February 18, 1814, the daughter of Samuel C. Maxwell and Jenny Tilford Maxwell. Mary Ann Maxwell married McCullough Tilford on September 3, 1833.

Mary Maxwell Tilford died in Indianapolis, IN on September 3, 1883.

EDWARD FRANKLIN MAXWELL was born near Hanover, Jefferson County, Indiana on February 16, 1816, the son of Samuel Campbell Maxwell and Jenny Tilford Maxwell. Edward married Melissa Wiley in 1838. It is Edward Franklin Maxwell's bible through the transcription by his grandson Charles Maxwell Robertson, that much of this information is stated.

Edward F. Maxwell died of pneumonia on January 15, 1849, at the age of 34 years.

HARVEY HENDERSON MAXWELL was born near Hanover, Jefferson County, Indiana on September 16, 1817, the son of Samuel C. Maxwell and Jenny Tilford Maxwell. Harvey married Isaphena McCullough on December 29, 1839. Harvey H. Maxwell died on March 2, 1845, at the age of 29 years. He was buried at Crawfordsville, IN.

Isaphena McCullough Maxwell married her brother-in-law William T. Maxwell in October 1854.

EMILY McCULLOUGH MAXWELL was born near Hanover, Jefferson County, Indiana on July 25, 1819, the daughter of Samuel Campbell and Jenny Tilford Maxwell. Emily married James Alfred Wilson on July 24, 1845. (See page 90)

JULIA CHITWOOD MAXWELL was born near Hanover, Jefferson County, Indiana on November 26, 1826, the daughter of Samuel C. Maxwell and Sarah (Sallie) Stevens Maxwell. Julia married Henry G. Berry on October 24, 1844.

Julia Maxwell Berry died August 15, 1849.

MARIA ARAMINTA MAXWELL was born June 21, 1831 near Hanover, Jefferson County, Indiana on June 21, 1831, the daughter of Samuel C. Maxwell and Sarah (Sallie) Steven Maxwell. Maria married William J. McGowen on June 26, 1851.

Maria Araminta Maxwell McGowen Deane

Maria Maxwell McGowen later married Rev. A. H. Deane on June 3, 1863.

DAVID HERVEY MAXWELL was born in what is now Gerrard County, Kentucky on September 17, 1786, the son of Bezaleel Maxwell and Margaret Anderson Maxwell. David helped his father clear the forest, till the ground, hunt game and be on the watch for Indians. At the age of eighteen he was sent to school in Danville, Kentucky. After his primary education he studied medicine under Dr. Ephraim McDowell. He entered medical practice in 1809. That year he also married Mary E. Dunn of Danville, Kentucky on September 21, 1809. Mary was the daughter of Samuel Dunn who was originally from County Down, Ireland.

In 1810, Dr. Maxwell moved to the Indiana Territory near the town of Hanover. He practiced medicine there and at Madison until the spring of 1819. During the War of 1812, he was a surgeon in the company of his brother-in-law Captain Williamson Dunn.

DAVID HERVEY MAXWELL

David Hervey Maxwell

In 1816, Congress passed an enabling act authorizing the creation of a state government for the Indiana Territory. Dr. Maxwell was elected delegate from Jefferson County to attend the constitutional convention. Dr. Maxwell worked to abolish slavery from the new state and to create a system of education within the state open and equal to all.

Dr. Maxwell bough a lot in the new town of Bloomington, Indiana in 1818 and move his family there in 1819. In September 1819, the First Presbyterian Church was established in Bloomington and Dr. Maxwell and his wife were charter members. During the winter of 1819-1820, Dr. Maxwell worked to establish a school or seminary in Bloomington. On January 20, 1820, an act was passed to establish the State Seminary at Bloomington. Dr. Maxwell and five other men were named as the board of trustee of the State Seminary with Dr. Maxwell presiding as President of the Board. On January 24, 1828, the name of the school was changed to Indiana College. It was because of the work of Dr. Maxwell and later his son Dr. James Darwin Maxwell for education in Indiana that Indiana University named one of its university buildings "Maxwell Hall."

EDWARD R. MAXWELL was born in what is now Gerrard County, Kentucky on October 6, 1788, the son of Bezaleel Maxwell and Margaret Anderson Maxwell. Edward married Jane C. Tilford in Jefferson County, KY on December 2, 1817.

In 1838, Jane Maxwell, widow of Edward R. Maxwell, stated to the Jefferson County Court that "Edward moved to Illinois, died soon after." Edward was buried in Hanover. Court records state Jane Maxwell asked the court if she could buy the "house in Hanover." Presumably this was the house now associated with Edward's father Bezaleel Maxwell. The answer of the court was not recorded.

118

Edward R. Maxwell's heirs listed for the estate of Edward R. Maxwell were recorded and are listed below with their ages at the time.

1. Susan Weir Maxwell, age 18
2. Samuel Davis Maxwell, age 16
3. Mary Adeline Maxwell, age 14
4. John Milton Maxwell, age 12
5. Julia Ann Maxwell, age 11
6. Sarah Eliza Maxwell, age 9
7. Gabriella Tilford Maxwell, age 2

THE ANDERSON FAMILY

JAMES ANDERSON was born in Scotland on November 17, 1678. He settled near New Castle, Pennsylvania and later moved to Lancaster County where he became a well-known Presbyterian minister. He was pastor of the Donegal Presbyterian Church which was established in 1722.

James Anderson
Star Member of Donegal Presbytery
1732-1740

James Anderson married Sudt Garland. She was daughter of Sylvester Garland, who was the son John Garland and Susan Ver Planck. John Garland was one the "Twelve Men" of New Amsterdam.

James Anderson and Sudt Garland Anderson were the parents of eleven children. The seventh child of this marriage was John Anderson.

James Anderson died in Lancaster County, PA on July 16, 1740.

JOHN ANDERSON was born January 13, 1724, in Lancaster PA, the son of James Anderson and Sudt Garland. John moved to Virginia where he spent most of his life. He married Anna Irvine (Irvin) about 1750.

John Anderson's history is tied with the Old Augusta Stone Church, he was an elder in the church. The church was often used as a fort against the Indians during the bloody French and Indian wars after 1750.

Toward the end of the Revolutionary War, John Anderson moved to Garrard County, Kentucky. He served with Gen. George Rogers Clark in the taking of Forts Vincenns and Kaskaskia in February 1779. In 1783, John had 400 acres of land in Lincoln County, KY surveyed for him. This area later became Madison County. John and his son Samuel were surveyors.

John Anderson died in 1796 in Madison County, KY. John and Anna Irvine Anderson are buried on a hill overlooking Silver Creek near Richmond.

John and Anna were the parents of ten children with Margaret Anderson being the oldest. Margaret Anderson married Bezaleel Maxwell.

CHAPTER FOUR

The Needles and Bray Family

WILLIAM J. NEEDLES was born about 1792 probably in Kent County, Delaware the son of _____. William married Mary Clements about the year 1822. Mary Clements was born about 1794 in Maryland. The family moved from Delaware to Franklin County, Ohio in 1841.

The Needles family was located on the 1850 Franklin County, Ohio census, in Madison Township. William J. Needles was a farmer. There were, at that time, eleven children in the family, three of them with occupations. Enoch Needles was noted as a farmer, John Needles was a 'Book Pedler' and William Needles was also a farmer.

William Needles died on August 30, 1864 and is buried in the Woodland Cemetery and Arboretum in Dayton, Ohio.

William and Mary Clements Needles were the parents of eleven known children, all information taken from the 1850 census.

1. Sarah Needles, born 1823
2. Enoch Needles
3. Eliza Needles, born 1828
4. John Needles, born 1829, book peddler
5. Malvina Needles, born 1831
6. William Needels, born 1833, farmer
7. James Needles, born 1836
8. Rueben Needles, born 1838
9. Margaret Needles, born 1840
10. Sims (Simgessmer) G. Needles
11. Joel Needles, born 1844.

ENOCH NEEDLES was born on September 24, 1824, in Kent County, Delaware the son of William and Mary Clements Needles. He moved with his parents to Franklin County, Ohio in 1841 when he was seventeen years old. Enoch was located with his family on the 1850 Franklin County census, Madison Township. He was a farmer. Enoch married Margaret M. Knapp on May 22, 1850, in Columbus, Ohio. Margaret was born in Sandusky County, Ohio on August 14, 1831.

Enoch Needles came to Missouri in 1859 and made his home in Grand Pass country in Saline County just as a storm of civil war was starting to fragment the people of Missouri. Being an intense lover of the Union, he took a strong and open stand for the Union. The area where he lived, however, believed it was time for the southern states to set up a nation of their own. As the smoldering embers of dissatisfaction fanned into the blaze of war, Enoch Needles in September 1861, as leader of the pro-Union people in his community had them load their belonging into wagons, herded the stock they could not sell and took up a line of march for Brookfield. They had heard that there were Union troops encamped there.

The night before they reached Brookfield then encamped nearby and their camp fires set off concern in the town of Brookfield. The people in the town had heard the news that there were confederate forces moving in the direction of Brookfield and so they sent out scouts to see who was at the encampment. The scouts were much relieved when it was discovered that the encampment was of Union refugees. Many of those who had traveled with Needles to Brookfield moved on to other communities in the state and elsewhere in other states like Illinois and Iowa. Enoch Needles, however, stayed and made the little community his home.

After Enoch Needles made Brookfield his home he engaged in the mercantile business and then built Central Hotel, one of the first hotels in Brookfield which was built alongside the tracks of the Burlington Railroad. Enoch was a familiar figure on the streets of Brookfield for many years. The 1876 Platt Book of Linn County, Mo. has an add about the hotel, "Central Hotel, E. Needles, Proprietor, livery, Feed and Salt Stable attached on Livingston Street, near Brook Street. Traveling men and others wishing Livery Rigs for business or pleasure, will find superior accommodations at this stable. Horse boarded any length of time. Terms reasonable in all cases."

At one point Enoch, who had no children, brought his brother Simgessmer G. Needles and his large family to Brookfield to let his brother manage the hotel. Simgessmer's two youngest children, Enoch R. Needles and Margaret M. Needles were born at the Central Hotel. Enoch was born there on 1889 and Margaret was born there on July 26, 1891. Margaret many years later could still remember the happy days of her early years at what she termed "the rail way hotel."

Margaret Knapp Needles died on Tuesday, August 26, 1902. Services were held at the Christian Church with burial in the Rose Hill Cemetery. After his wife's death, Enoch Needles' health gradually declined over the years and on November 24, 1911, he moved to Kansas City to live with his brother. Enoch died in Kansas City at the home of his brother Simgessmer G. Needles on Tuesday, December 26, 1912. His body was returned to Brookfield where he was buried beside his faithful and beloved wife Margaret in Rose Hill Cemetery. Services were conducted by Rev. Ben F. Hill, pastor of the Christian Church.

The Saturday, January 6, 1912, issue of *The Brookfield Gazette* said of Enoch Needles that after nearly a half century he had "passes off the stage and takes up his abode in Rose Hill cemetery, Brookfield's city of the dead, in which sleep so many of the men and woman who in that early day were part and parcel of the Brookfield pioneer days and who helped lay the foundation of the substantial structure that the goodly city of Brookfield is today and is to be in the future." The is a sign along the tracks of the old

Burlington Railroad which lie slightly southwest of the town of Brookfield which says 'Needles," marking the site where the Central Hotel use to stand.

The will of Enoch Needles was recorded in Linn County, MO and dated May 8, 1911, with Walter Brownlee as trustee. A sister named Malvina Algeo and two children of Simgessmer Needles, Enoch and Margaret Needles, were named as heirs. The will was probated on February 12, 1912. The death certificate gave his occupation as "Hotel Keeper" and stated he died of "Chronic Interstitial Nephritis." He was a little over 87 years of age at his death.

MALVINA NEEDLES was born on February 5, 1831, probably in Kent County Delaware, the daughter of William and Mary Clements Needles. Malvina married ____ Alego.

Malvina Needles Alego was mentioned in the will of her brother Enoch Needles which was dated May 8, 1911 and probated on February 12, 1912. Malvina died on May 13, 1914, and was buried in Rose Hill Cemetery, Brookfield MO.

SIMGESSMER G. NEEDLES was born in Franklin County, Ohio on December 1, 1841, the son of William and Mary Clements Needles. The 1850 Franklin County census has his name as Sims Needles.

Simgessmer married Elma Florence Bray on October 16, 1871, in Saline County, MO. They were married by A. P. Sallaway, MG (Minister of the Gospel). Elma was born on August 13, 1853, in Millersburg, Holmes County, Ohio, the daughter of William and Maria Yates Bray.

*Top row, Elma Eliza Needles, William Bray Needles, Mary Leonard Needles Arbuthnot,
Enoch Ray Needles and Genevieve Needles Grout
Front row, Lucy Bray Needles, Simgessmer G. Needles, Floribel Elma Needles
Whitehead, Elma Bray Whitehead and Margaret Marie Needles Williams*

Simgessmer Needles was living in Sedalia, Pettis County in 1879. He appeared for the first time in the city directory for that year. His occupation was given as clerk and he resided at 213 E. 6th Street. Interestingly, the 1880 Pettis County census, city of Sedalia, has the family, but the head of the household is E. F. (Elma Florence) Needles. Where Sims was is not known, but he was not on the 1880 Missouri Soundex. He was probably out of state learning a new occupation. The children listed on the census in 1880 were, Lennie, 7, Lida, 5, Jennie, 3 and Willie, age one year. It appears the children early on picked up nicknames.

A new occupation for Sims showed up in the *Sadalia/Pettis County Directory* for the years 1883-84 which had the following advertisement, "Needles, S G, dealer in sewing machines, 205 Ohio, res 213 e 6th." The 1886/1887 city directory gave his occupation as mechanic residing at 16th & Ohio St. This was the last time Simgessmer was listed in the Sedalia directory.

The family left Sedalia about 1886 and moved to Brookfield, MO where Simgessmer took over management of the Central Hotel owned by his brother Enoch Needles. This hotel has come down through the Needles family known as the Rail Way Hotel because it was located next to the railroad tracks, but that was not the name of the hotel. It was while the family was living in Brookfield that the two youngest children were born into the family. The family moved to Kansas City MO about the year 1896.

Elma Florence Bray Needles

The Simgessmer Needles family was located on the 1900 census in Kansas City, MO. His occupation at that time was given as machinist. The 1900 Kansas City directory listed him as Sim Needles and his occupation was given as machinist. The 1900 census for Kansas City, MO shows the family was living at 3227 Garner Ave. In 1910, Sim Needles was listed in the city directory as an optician which was probably the result of his son Dr. William B. Needles opening the Needles Institute of Optometry in Kansas City in 1907. The Needles family was then living at 1021 Askew.

Simgessmer G. Needles died at his home on 3841 East 68th Street Terrace on the evening of July 30, 1921. Services were held at the home on Tuesday at 2:30 in the afternoon. He was buried at Mt. Washington Cemetery. The death certificate for Simgessmer noted he was retired from the hotel business and had died of "Carcinoma of Stomach." The informant on the death certificate was W. B. Needles. Mr. Needles was nearly 80 years of age at the time of his death.

Left to right, Floribel Needles Whitehead, Margaret Needles Williams, Genevieve Needles Grout, Elma Eliza Needles, Mary Needles Arbuthnot and Lucy Bray Needles

Elma Bray Needles died in Chicago, IL on Wednesday, December 12, 1928, as a result of being struck by a car after she got off a streetcar. She never regained consciousness and died several days after the accident. The driver who struck her was the one who carried her to the hospital. Mrs. Needles, who was 75 years old, was apparently living with her daughters Lida and Lucy Needles in Chicago and she had been attending a church missionary meeting. She carried a letter from her daughter Margaret telling the good news that she was soon coming home from her missionary work in China. Mrs. Needles was so happy, she told one of the ladies in the vestibule as she was leaving the church, "Margaret is coming home." Sadly, she never got to see her youngest child home from China. Tragically, Elma's father William Bray had also died as the result of being struck by an automobile. He died in Kansas City on September 26, 1910.

The surviving children mentioned in the obituary for Mrs. Needles found in the *Kansas City Times* were, two sons, Dr. W. B. Needles of 3327 Bellefontaine and Enoch R. Needles of Elizabeth, NJ. There were six daughters mentioned, Mrs. J. B. Arbuthnot, Joplin, MO, Mrs. J. H. Grout, 3841 E. 68th St. Terrace, Mrs. J. W. Whitehead, 3215 E.

32nd, Miss Lida Needles and Miss Lucy Needles, Chicago, IL and Mrs. Margaret Needles Williams of China.

Mrs. Needles' body was returned to Kansas City were services were held on Saturday at 2:30 in the afternoon at the Nazarene Church on 24th and Troost Ave. Interment was at Mt. Washington Cemetery in the family section where her husband was buried.

Simgessmer and Elma Bray Needles were the parents of nine children.

1. Mary Leonard Needles
2. Elma Eliza Needles
3. Genevieve Needles
4. William Bray Needles
5. Sadie M. Needles, born July 1881 and died December 10, 1916
6. Lucy Bray Needles
7. Floribel Elma Needles
8. Enoch Ray Needles
9. Margaret Marie Needles

MARY LEONARD NEEDLES was born near Malta Bend, Saline County, MO on 1873 the daughter of Simgessmer G. and Elma Bray Needles. Mary, known as Lennie, married James B. Arbuthnot.

On June 4, 1913, Mary Leonard Needles Arbuthnot was accepted as a member of the Daughters of the American Revolution under the name of her ancestor Captain Asa Bray of Connecticut. At that time, she and her family were living at 12th and Madison Street, Webb City, MO.

The family lived in Joplin, MO. Lennie died in Chicago, IL.

There were four children of this family

1. Sarah Elma Arbuthnot, born 1907, married Roy Watson, Topeka, KS
2. Harold Arbuthnot
3. Walter Arbuthnot
4. Alfred Arbuthnot, died in flu epidemic of 1919

ELMA ELIZA NEEDLES was born in Sedalia, MO, on December 22, 1874, the daughter of Simgessmer G. and Elma Bray Needles. When her brother Dr. William Bray Needles purchased the optometry school in Chicago, Elma better known as Lida served as secretary and registrar to the school. Lida and her sister Lucy never married and were known as the aunts or the sisters. They were virtually inseparable. Priscilla Whitehead McCloud remembers that Lida and Lucy had the most wonderful apartment in Chicago.

Lida Alma Needles died of a coronary thrombosis on March 21, 1965. She was 90 years old. She was buried in the Needles section of Mt. Washington Cemetery.

GENEVIEVE NEEDLES was born in Sedalia, MO on January 10, 1877, the daughter of Simgessmer and Elma Bray Needles. On the 1880 Pettis County census, City of Sedalia, shows this family and Genevieve was listed as Jennie, age three.

Genevieve, later known as Ve, married James Hugh Grout on September 7, 1904.

James H. Grout died on November 6, 1933. Ve died on March 20, 1976.

Ve and Jim were the parents of two children.

1. Helen Grout
2. James H. Grout

HELEN GROUT was born in Kansas City, MO on August 25, 1906, the daughter of Ve Needles and James Grout. Helen married Earl B. Taylor. He was the owner and president of H. F. Anderson Engraving Company. Earl Taylor died in January 1984. Helen Grout died on November 21, 1984.

JAMES H. GROUT was born September 2, 1914, the son of Ve Needles and James H. Grout. Jim graduated from Northern Illinois College of Optometry in December 1938. James married Dorothy Wilson in ___.

James was issued a license to practice Optometry in North Carolina on August 9, 1949.

He moved to North Carolina in and established his practice in Charlotte, North Carolina.

James and Dorothy were the parents of two children.

1. James W. Grout
2. Stephen Grout

WILLIAM BRAY NEEDLES was born in Sedalia, MO on May 17, 1879, the son of Simgessmer G. and Elma Bray Needles. William was named after his grandfather William Bray. William moved with his family to Brookfield, MO in about 1886 and then to Kansas City, MO in 1895. Married Alva S.

As a teenager growing up in Sedalia, MO, William worked in a jewelry shop that sold spectacles. Following an interest in the optical profession he attended Chicago's McCormick Optical Colleges in 1899. Following graduation, Dr. Needles returned to Kansas City and open an optometric practice. Troubled by the lack of professional education found in his local colleagues, he turned his attention toward optometric education. He began a series of lectures and workshops which proved so successful that he eventually accepted a teaching position with the Kansas City School of Optometry. His courses were so popular that he finally started his own school called the Needles Institution of Optometry in Kansas City in 1907.

William Bray Needles

Dr. Needles' reputation, gained through his popular lectures, spread throughout the United States. In 1921, Dr. Needles was offered the opportunity to purchase the Northern Illinois College of Ophthalmology and Otology of Chicago, which he accepted. After purchasing the school, he moved his family and practice to Chicago and left the Needles Institute in Kansas City under the leadership of an associate Dr. Ernest Occhiene. Dr. Needles merged the two schools in 1926 under a new charter and renamed the school the Northern Illinois College of Optometry. Dr. Needles established himself as president-dean of the school and his sister Lida Needles served as its secretary and registrar.

Dr. William Bray Needles died in Chicago, IL on June 5, 1948, at the age of 69 years. Services for Dr. Needles were held at the college auditorium in Chicago and then later at Newcomer Chapel in Kansas City. He was buried in Mt. Washington Cemetery in Kansas City. The Sunday, June 6, 1948, issued of the *Kansas City Star* stated that he had been president of "one of the largest colleges of its kind in the world. Dr, Needles held honorary memberships in the American Optometric Association and other groups."

Following Dr. Needles death, the school was administered by his son Dr. Richard Needles for about a year after which the school passed out of the control of the Needles family. The school was eventually renamed and is now known as the Illinois College of Optometry.

William Bray Needles and Alva S. Needles were the parents of three children.

1. John W. Needles
2. Richard A. Needles

3. Elizabeth Needles

JOHN W. NEEDLES was born the son of William B. Needles and Alva Needles. John married Mary Salisbury. There were two children of the marriage.

1. William Needles
2. John Needles

RICHARD A. NEEDLES was born on October 31, 1911 the son of William B. Needles and Alva Needles. Richard married Maxine Butterfield.

William Bray Whitehead, Winona Odell Whitehead, Maxine Butterfield Needles and Richard A. Needles

Richard graduated from Northern College of Optometry on June 9, 1933. Richard became president of the college after his father died in 1948. He stayed with the school until it was sold by the Needles family. Richard received a license to practice Optometry in North Carolina on March 30, 1950. He moved to Fayetteville where he practiced with his cousin Dr. William B. Whitehead for a short time.

Richard A. Needles died in Hickory, NC on September 30, 1997.

There were three children of this marriage.

1. Beth Needles
2. Phillip Needles
3. Jennifer(?) Needles

ELIZABETH NEEDLES was born ---- the daughter of William B. Needles and Alva Needles. Elizabeth, known as Betty, married Dr. Faye M. Whitsell.

They had four children.

1. David Whitsell
2. Cynthia Whitsell
3. Debbie Whitsell
4. Richard Whitsell

LUCY BRAY NEEDLES was born in Sedalia, MO on November 1, 1883. Lucy was hard of hearing and that may have been the reason she never married. She and her sister Lida were lifelong companions. In 1910, the Kansas City directory gave Lucy's occupation as stenographer working at the Missouri Can Company.

Lucy died of cancer on December 13, 1965. She was buried in the Needles family section of Mt. Washington Cemetery.

FLORIBEL ELMA NEEDLES was born in Sedalia, MO on November 8, 1885, the daughter of Simgessmer G. and Elma Bray Needles. Floribel married Joseph W. Whitehead on January 1, 1907. See Joseph W. Whitehead, page 30.

Foribel Elma Needles

ENOCH RAY NEEDLES was born on October 28, 1888, in the Central Hotel of Brookfield, Linn, County, MO, the son of Simgessmer and Elma Bray Needles. Simgessmer Needles was at this time working for his brother Enoch Needles who owned the hotel. It appears rather obvious that young Enoch was named after his uncle Enoch Needles. The family moved to Kansas City, MO in about 1896. Enoch attended classical high school in Kansas City where he developed an interest in engineering. While in high school he played baseball and one of his teammates was Casey Stengel who later became famous as the Manager of the New York Yankees.

Enoch Ray Needles

In 1909, Enoch enrolled in the University of Missouri School of Mines and Metallurgy in Rolla, MO. He graduated in 1914. During his senior year he served as class president and editor of *The Rollamon Boards*, the school newspaper. He was also a member of the Pi Kappa Alpha, the Tau Beta Pi and the Quo Vadis societies. Following graduation, he took a job with the Kansas City Southern Railway. He later took a job in the track department of the Kansas City Terminal Railroad and a year later was transferred to the bridge department. Enoch married Ethel Shuman on ___, at ____.

In 1917, Enoch took a 'temporary' job with the company, Harrington, Howard and Ash. The temporary job later turned into one of the owners of the company. One of Enoch's first projects for the company was helping design the bridge over the Red River in Texarkana, Texas. From this he moved on to Jacksonville, FL where he was resident engineer on the St Johns River Bridge. From there he moved on to New York for the Chesapeake and Delaware Canal project where he was part of the bridge designing effort. Enoch moved his family to Elizabeth, New Jersey in 1922. They later moved to Summit, NJ and then on to New Vernon, New Jersey. Enoch was made one of the partners to the company in 1928.

During World War II Enoch entered service in the Corps of Engineers as a Lieutenant Colonel and was promoted to Colonel in 1944. His work on redistribution of construction equipment and materials earned him the Legion of Merit. Following the end of the war his first project was the Delaware Memorial Bridge. Since that time the Firm of Howard, Needles, Tammen and Bergendoff has handled many of the largest bridge and turnpike projects in the country.

Enoch was featured in the September 1960 issue of *Consulting Engineer* magazine. The article noted he had just recently dedicated a new civil engineering building at his alma mater, the Missouri School of Mines and Metallurgy, where he gave a speech on the problems confronting the civil engineer. He spoke of the problems of new materials and equipment utilized in the design and construction of new structures. And how to plan cities and the movement of materials and people to them. He concluded his speech with the statement, "If we assume we already know the answers to such questions, we are being false to the trust which is ours as professional men." The Missouri School of Mines and Metallurgy gave Enoch the silver centennial medal of honor in 1971.

Enoch died on January 5, 1972, at the Morristown (NJ) Memorial Hospital. An obituary found in the January 7, 1972, issued of the *New York Times* stated Enoch R. Needles had retired as the principle partner of the consulting engineer firm of Howard, Needles, Tammen & Bergendoff in 1963. The firm was one of the largest in its field with more than 1,100 employees and office in 20 cities. At the time of his death Enoch was 83 years old and was living in New Vernon, NJ.

The obituary did not state where Enoch was to be buried, but it did state services were scheduled to be held at the United Methodist Church in Summit, New Jersey. The article also listed his surviving family members, Ethel, his wife and one son Thomas E. Needles. There were five daughters listed, Mrs. John W. Wight, Mrs. H. Philip Williams, Mrs. Howard P. McJunkin, Mrs. Chester E. Homer Jr., Mrs. H. James Toffey Jr. There were also two siblings mentioned, Mrs. Hugh Grout and Mrs. Horace Williams.

Enoch and Needles were the parents of six children.

1. Elma Needles
2. Margaret Needles
3. Mary Needles
4. Tom Needles
5. Carolyn Needles
6. Sally Needles

MARGARET MARIE NEEDLES was born in the Central Hotel of Brookfield, Linn County, MO on July 21, 1891, the daughter of Simgessmer and Elma Bray Needles. Margaret's father was at that time the manager of what Margaret later termed the "Rail Way Hotel" that was owned by her uncle Enoch Needles. Margaret appears to have been name after her uncle Enoch's wife Margaret Knapp Needles.

Although the Needles family normally attended the Methodist Church, Margaret's mother attended the Kansas City First Church of the Nazarene. On April 13, 1919, during a revival and having only recently recover from a near fatal illness, Margaret accepted Christ as her Lord. She resigned her position at the Kansas City Chamber of

Commerce and went to work in the missionary office of the National Headquarters of the Church of the Nazarene.

After much prayer and days of uncertainty, Margaret decided to become a missionary to China and after a review by the missionary board she was accepted. On September 1, 1924, at Vancouver, British Columbia, Canada, she sailed on the ship Empress of Australia to Shanghai, China. The Empress had been built by the German Kaiser that fell into the hands of the British following the end of World War I and was later made part of the Canadian Pacific Lines. The trip took about two weeks. While on board she met another young missionary named Horace S. Williams.

After arriving in China Margaret was sent to language school in Peking which also included Horace Williams. While in Peking she visited the Forbidden City and the Temple of Heaven with its blue glazed tile roof. In February 1925, Margaret was sent to do secretarial work at Tamingfo, Hopie Province where she continued her language studies.

Margaret's relationship with Horace grew over the months and she was troubled between what God wanted her to do with her life and her affection for Horace. After months of soul searching, she accepted Horace's proposal of marriage. Margaret Needles married Horace Williams on July 11, 1928, in Tientsin, China. They were married by the Rev. Leon Osborn. Horace Starr Williams was born in Bellefontaine, Ohio on October 29, 1903, the son of John Clark Williams and Nina Maye Starr Williams. The young couple honeymooned in Peking on their way to Horace's station in Kalgan, China.

During World War II Horace taught Chinese to American soldiers at the University of Chicago for one year. He was then assigned to Chungking, West China where he was employed by the Chinese government to train Chinese students as interpreters for the American military forces. While Horace was in China, Margaret stayed behind in the U. S. because of concerns about her safety. But perhaps one of the most touching stories of the relationship between Margaret and Horace occurred at the conclusion of the war.

Margaret, anxious to rejoin Horace to continue their ministry in China, took it on herself to go to him rather than for him to come back to the U.S. to get her. She sent him word that she was coming after requesting a passport to Shanghai and then she left Chicago for Los Angeles. A travel agent in Los Angeles booked her passage on a Dutch freighter to Manila but left her with no assurances she could get passage to Shanghai. As she was waiting in Los Angeles word came that her passport had been refused. Undaunted she called the State Department and after some wrangling, she was able to secure a passport to Shanghai. While in Los Angeles she stayed with her old friends from China, the Sonderboms.

As Margaret left Los Angeles, she found the freighter also contained other missionaries, but she found herself in rather unusual circumstances. She had no reservations in Manila, and she had no bookings for the next leg of her journey from Manila to Shanghai. While on board she met a kind Methodist doctor who agreed to take her luggage on to Shanghai with him. When they docked in Manila the doctor also arranged for her to go the Methodist Mission with him. Manila was still a city in shambles from the devastation from the war. The harbor was half full of sunken ships. Thanks to her new friend she was able to find an accommodation at the Methodist Mission for the first night and the next day she found other accommodations at the local YMCA.

Pressing on, Margaret talked her way on to a military airplane going from Manila to Shanghai. Moving from her room at the YMCA to a Quonset hut to await the airplane, she found the hut to be stifling hot. It was in February, a very hot time of the year in Manila. After several days, word came that they would be leaving, but she would need some warm clothing as it was cold in Shanghai. Having no extra clothing and little money to buy any with, Margaret went the way she was. Thanks to a young soldier on board who offer her his jacket, she able to stand the long cold airplane trip

At 2:30 in the morning the airplane arrived in Shanghai, Margaret was taken with others to the Cathay Mission, a hotel reserved for military and government personnel. Standing in alone in the street by her baggage in the middle of the night, forced her to ask the hotel if they could give her a room. They finally gave her a room and the next morning she got some Shanghai money and went in search of the YMCA where she hoped she could get a room. The awareness that she had not let Horace know she was coming to Shanghai at this particular time surfaced in her anxious mind.

The morning was cold and dark when she left the mission in search of a room. Locating a ricksha driver, she first went to the Mission Building where various missions' societies had their offices. As she approached the mission's building, she met two gentlemen and asked direction to the YMCA. They gave her directions and assured her it was only a few blocks away. Unable to locate the YMCA, she returned to the mission and found the same two gentlemen and told them she could not find the building. They then gave her the same instructions which added to her frustration.

Feeling a sense of despair, Margaret became frightened and desperate. The dark cold street and the stone wall which surrounded the mission compound added to her growing feeling of anxious desolation. Then suddenly she noticed a man walking toward her from a distance. As he got closer to her she noticed he had on a military uniform. As he got even closer, she saw it was Horace. Margaret's heart was overjoyed with gratitude, love and happiness. Horace had been in Peking when he received a letter from Mr. Soderbom's telling of Margaret's departure from Los Angeles. Horace calculated it was about time for Margaret to be in Shanghai and then asked permission to fly to Shanghai to meet her. He then was on his way to the Mission Building to ask about her when they met. Needless to say, they were both extremely happy for their reunion and thankful to God for their safety.

Margaret and Horace did return to their mission field in China but when the Communist took over the country they had to go to Taiwan where they continued their ministry.

In 1970, Margaret and Horace Williams moved to the headquarter of the Worldwide Evangelization Crusade (the W. E. C.) at Camp Hill, Fort Washington, Pennsylvania. After sixteen crossings of the Pacific Ocean by steamers and nearly fifty years of work in the fields, it was time to retire. Retire yes but inactive no. They attended conferences in Korea, Switzerland, Israel and the Philippines. They also started a magazine geared to the Chinese students then receiving access to an education in the United States.

Margaret Needles Williams was a favorite child in her family. Perhaps it was because she was the baby of the family or maybe it was because of the astonishment that she would select such an arduous life because of her faith. Every time she came home from the field there was a great celebration in her family. All of her siblings were so proud of their little sister. She became a favorite to her nephews and nieces and then later to their children. To hear her stories and to be in her warm company was a thrill and joy to all in her beloved family. Her rewards were many and the love of her family highest of all.

Margaret Needles Williams died on January 14, 1988, in Fort Washington, PA. She was 96 1/2 years old at her death. Horace Williams died on December 29, 1999, at the age of 96 years. Margaret and Horace are buried in George Washington Memorial Park at Plymouth Meeting, PA near Fort Washington.

THE BRAY FAMILY

ASA BRAY was born in Branford, Connecticut on June 22, 1741. Asa married Lydia Andrews on May 12, 1763, at or near Branford, Connecticut.

Asa Bray served in the Connecticut Militia rising to the rank of Captain. He commanded a company of militia in defense of the Hudson River in 1777. He served in the Burgeyon Campaign and opposed the invasion of the colony by Gov. Tryon in 1779.

Lydia died on December 1, 1775. Asa then married Hannah Hull. Asa died on October 21, 1815, at North Haven, CT.

Asa Bray was the father of five children with his first wife Lydia Andrews and two with his second wife Hannah Hull.

1, Florinda Bray, married Daniel Pardee
2. John Bray
3. Lydia Bray
4. Hoadley Bray
5. Abigail Bray

JOHN BRAY was born on June 7, 1768, the son of Asa Bray and Lydia Andrews Bray. John married Mercy Fields at Southington, Connecticut on November 26, 1789.

At some point John and Mercy Fields Bray moved to Steubenville, Jefferson County, Ohio.

John Bray and Mercy Fields were the parents of eight known children.

1. Sally Bray
2. Sylvester Bray
3. Perline Bray
4. John Bray, lived in Stuebenville, Ohio
5. Alfred Bray
6. Horace Bray
7. Anson Bray
8. James Bray, lived in Steubenville, Ohio

JOHN BRAY was born in Hartford, Connecticut at about 1806, the son of John Bray and Mercy Fields Bray. John Bray moved to Steubenville, Jefferson County, Ohio.

John Bray died of dropsy at Sloan's Station, Island Creek Township, on May 11, 1872, at the age of 76 years.

JAMES BRAY was born about 1808 in Hartford, Connecticut the son of John and Mercy Fields Bray. James Bray at some time moved to Steubenville, Jefferson County, Ohio.

James Bray was a minister and started the Island Creek M. E. church in 1837. A church was erected in 1838 on land donated by William Findley. One of the other first members of the church was a John Bray who could have been James brother or his father.

Rev. James Bray died at Toronto on September 11, 1903. He was 9 months over 95 years of age.

SYLVESTER BRAY was born on April 2, 1792, the son of John Bray and Mercy Fields Bray. Sylvester Bray married Sarah Brown.

Sylvester Bray died at Hartford (Berlin) Conn. on April 7, 1824. The family remained in the area following Sylvester's death until 1831 when Sarah and her son William moved to Little Rock, Arkansas. Sarah moved there to be near her son John Bray. John Bray joined in the fight between Texas and Mexico and was killed in battle.

Sarah Brown Bray died in Little Rock, Arkansas in 1832, leaving an eight-year-old orphaned child, William Bray. Friends of the family sent William to school in Marietta, Ohio where he learned he had family living in Steubenville, Ohio where he went to live.

Sylvester and Sarah Brown Bray were the parents of three children.

1. John Bray, died in the war between Texas and Mexico.
2. William Bray
3. Eunice Bray, died about April 1824.

WILLIAM BRAY was born at Hartford, Connecticut on July 15, 1823, the son of Sylvester Bray and Sarah Ellen Brown Bray. William's father and a younger sister Eunice died within nine months of William's birth. William and his mother moved to Little Rock, Arkansas in 1831 to be near William's older brother John Bray. Shortly after they arrived at Little Rock, John Bray was killed in the fighting between Texas and Mexico. William's mother died in 1832, leaving William an eight-year-old orphan.

Kind friends arranged for William to go to Marietta, Ohio to attend school. However, William's health made it impossible for him to keep up his schoolwork. While at school William learned that he had relatives in Steubenville, Ohio. When his family discovered he was in Marietta, they sent for him. He found his grandparents Bray there and his uncles John and James Bray. Here he made his home and tried to go to school but found due to his health this was impossible. Since his health was so poor it was decided he would learn tin and copper-smithing. At the age of 15 he became a lifelong member of the Methodist Church.

William's first work was in Wooster, Wayne County, Ohio. It was here that he met and later married Maria J. Yates in 1847. Maria was born in Wayne County, Ohio on January 15, 1827, the daughter of Samuel Yates and Maria Jane Yarnell. Mrs. Yates was of a

Quaker background. William was at that time employed by W. S. Johnson to establish a retail trade in stoves and stove trimmings.

In 1949, William moved to Millersburg, Holmes County, Ohio where started his own business in the stoves and stove trimmings trade. In 1850, Maria joined the Methodist Episcopal Church. William also became active in the church being a class leader, superintendent of the Sunday School and other duties in the church. The family was located on the 1850 Holmes County census, Hardy Township. William Bray's occupation at that time was noted as Tin and Copper Smith. There was only one child in the household, James L. Bray who was one year old. Maria's name on this census was written as Mariah. There was a Jane Yates in the household who was probably the mother to Maria. She was 50 years old and was born in New York. Samuel Yates, age 20 and also a Tin and Copper Smith and Ellen Yates, age 16, were also in the family enumeration. Jane Yates died in 1864.

In 1864, William's son James Leonard Bray wanted to move to a farm. So, they moved to a farm in Iowa. However, they did not find this place satisfactory, and looked for another farm to live on. They moved to a farm in Malta Bend, Grand Pass Township in Saline County, Missouri in 1865. This was just at the close of the Civil War and political feelings were still strong. William Bray was elected County Judge in 1868 and served as judge in Saline County for six years.

Churches and schools were scarce at this time and the Bray home was open for religious services. During a camp meeting held by Rev. Frank Oechsli and two other ministers, William and Maria received the experience of sanctification.

The 1870 Saline County census, Elmwood Township shows this family. William Bray was then a farmer with over $12,800 of real estate and $1,500 of personal property. Considering the time, this was a considerable estate. Mariah(sic) Bray was listed as 'keeps House.' There were seven children in the home at that time, James, Elma, Sarah, Emma, William, Lucy and Frank. A Jennie Brandon, age 19 from Ohio, was also in the family listing.

The family moved to Sedalia, Pettis County, Missouri in 1874, where William Bray established a hardware store located at 214 Ohio Street. A year later Mr. Branden(sic) was associated with the store and the firm became known as Wm. Bray & Co., Hardware, Stoves, and Tinware. This Mr. Branden(sic) who was in business with William Bray was actually Anderson C. Brandon who was Judge Bray's son-in-law.

The 1880 *Hawley's Sedalia City Directory* noted that William Bray came to Sedalia in 1874 from Saline County where he had been "a judge for six years." William Bray was known as 'Judge Bray' in the community. The directory had these words to say about the firm and their business.

> ... Both of these gentleman are among the most enterprising and
> liberal business men in Sadelia. In their store can be found all that
> is kept in a first-class establishment of the kind, such as hardware,

stoves, and tinware, shelf hardware, house furnishing goods, manu-
facturers of galvanized iron cornices, roofers, house-spouting goods,
etc. It is said that this firm does the largest portion of the roofing
work in Sedalia, and the reason is because they put in the best material
and do the work at the lowest possible figures...

Maria (Mariah) J. Yates Bray died on May 3, 1882, after suffering for one year with
cancer. Her obituary found in the Sadalia *Bazoo* stated she was the mother of eight
children, all of whom survived her. The article concluded with these words, "Her chief
labors in the church consisted in inducing the lady members to live more consecrated
lives, and her influence on the acts, habits, and lives of many ladies of this city will be
felt for a good long time after her form shall have mouldered back to dust." Services
were held on May 5th at the Ohio Street Methodist Episcopal Church. Burial was in
Crown Hill Cemetery.

Some years later William Bray moved to Springfield, MO where he was engaged in the
insurance business. While in Springfield William Bray married Ellen Mylar. When
Lucy and her husband Harry Hammond moved to California, William and his new bride
went to California to live also. In California, William was engaged in the grocery
business and became a postmaster. In August 1893, William and Ellen made a visit the
World's Fair in Chicago and after this settled in New Sharon, Iowa.

William Bray was run down by a motor car in Kansas City on Sunday, September 25,
1910. He was on his way home from attending evening services at Linwood Boulevard
Methodist church. It was late, 9:30 P.M., and it had just started raining in a down pore.
At the corner of Olive and Linwood Avenue he stopped and raised his umbrella which
apparently obstructed his view of the traffic. He then stepped into the intersection just as
a car was passing. The car was driven by Dr. F. M. Planck who stopped and
administered aid. Mr. Bray was taken to the home of his son-in-law, A. C. Brandon,
which was only a short distance away from the accident. William Bray died a few hours
later at 1:30 a.m., early in the morning of September 26, 1910. His death certificate
stated he died of a fractured skull, a broken left leg and fractured ribs and other injuries.
The informant for the death certificate was A. C. Brandon.

William Bray was 87 years old and been living with his daughter Mrs. A. C. Brandon of
336 Olive Street in Kansas City for eleven years. Funeral services were held at the
Brandon home and then the body was shipped by Missouri Pacific train back to Sedalia.
Services were held at the First Methodist Episcopal Church in Sedalia with the Rev. W.
F. Jones, superintendent of the church, officiating. William Bray was buried with wife in
Crown Hill Cemetery.

The *Kansas City Journal* dated Tuesday September 27, 1910, listed the following
children for William Bray; Mrs. A. C. Brandon, Kansas City, Mo., James Bray, Baldwin,
Kas, Frank Bray, San Diego, Cal., Mrs. S. Needles, Kansas City, Mo., Mrs. C. O. Green,
Sedalia, Mo. and Mrs. Frank Oechsley, Baldwin, Kas.

William and Maria J. Yates Bray were the parents of eight known children.

1. James Leonard Bray
2. Maria Jane Bray
3. Elma Florence Bray, married Simgessmer Needles
4. Sarah Ellen Bray, born about 1856
5. Emily Eliza (Emma) Bray, born about 1858
6. William Bray, born about 1860
7. Lucy Bray, born about 1863
8. Frank Fletcher Bray, born about 1868

JAMES LEONARD BRAY was born in Wooster, Ohio in 1848, the son of William Bray and Maria Yates Bray. James married Emily Gosline in Sedalia, MO on March 13, 1877. She lived but three years after her marriage, passing away on May 25, 1880. She was buried in the Crown Hill Cemetery in Sedalia, MO. James later married Anna Ditmar.

At the time of his father's death in 1910, James Bray was living in Bladwin, Kansas.

MARIA JANE BRAY was born in Millersburg, Ohio about 1850, the daughter of William Bray and Maria Yates Bray. Maria Jane, called Jennie, married Anderson Brandon in Saline County, Mo. on November 10, 1869. They were married by D. Landon, Judge Saline Court of Common Pleas.

Anderson Brandon was in business with his father-in-law in Sedalia, MO where they operated a hardware store. The Anderson Brandon family later moved to Kansas City.

ELMA FLORANCE BRAY was born in Millersburg, Ohio. Elma married Simgessmer Needles, see page 126.

SARAH ELLEN BRAY was born in Millersburg, Ohio on November 12, 1855, the daughter of William Bray and Maria Yates Bray. Sarah Ellen, called Sadie, married Rev. Frank Oechsli in Saline County, Missouri. He was a minister of the St. Louis Conference of the Methodist Episcopal Church. Frank Oechsli was born March 11, 1849, in Fraubrunner, Switzerland. He came to the U.S. when he was six years old.

In 1885, the family was living in Springhill, MO. In 1910, the family was living in Baldwin, Kansas.

Frank Oechsli died in Lawerence, Kansas in 1913. Sadie died in 1939. Frank and Sadie were the parents of seven children.

1. William Oechsli
2. Jennie Oechsli
3. Edythe Oechsli
4. Arthur Oechsli
5. Leonard Oechsli, born June 5, 1885, Springhill, MO

6. Earl Oechsli
7. Waldo Oechsli

EMILY ELIZA BRAY was born in Millersburg, Ohio on 1858, the daughter of William Bray and Maria Yates Bray. Emily, called Emma, married C. Omer Green in Sedalia, MO on November 24, 1881, at the home of her father Judge Bray. Omer was a young businessman in Sedalia.

In 1910, the family was living in Sedalia, MO.

WILLIAM BRAY was born in Millersburg, Ohio on 1860, the son of William Bray and Maria Yates Bray. William Bray died of consumption at the home of his sister Lucy in Springfield, MO.

LUCY BRAY was born in Millersburg, Ohio on 1863, the daughter of William Bray and Maria Yates Bray. Lucy married Harry H. Hammond in Sedalia, Pettis County, MO on March 18, 1885. This family lived for a while in Springfield, Mo. They later moved to San Diego, CA.

Early in 1893, Harry Hammond moved his family to New Sharon, Iowa where his brothers owned a bank. They wanted him to become a cashier in the bank. In 1897, Harry Hammond passed away from typhoid fever. Lucy was also in very poor health at the time of her husband's death. After his death she traveled some trying to regain her health but this was unsuccessful. She came home to her sister Jennie Bray Anderson in Kansas City, MO where she passed away.

Harry Hammond and Lucy Bray Hammond had one surviving child.

1. Clarence Hammond

FRANK FLETCHER BRAY was born in Saline County, Missouri in 1868. In 1910, Frank was living in San Diego, CA.

CHAPTER FIVE

The Odell Family and Schultz Family

The Odell Family

The surname Odell is not of Irish origin but is English. The name appears to have been derived from an estate located deep in the north Bedfordshire countryside located between the villages of Harrold and Sharnbrook and situated about 8 miles from Bedford and 10 miles from Wellingborough. The present-day village of Odell, England is one of the smallest villages in the Ouse Valley with about two hundred households.

The Odell village origins are traced back to Saxon days where the lands of Levenot, a wealthy thane of King Edward the Confessor, included Wahall, modern day Odell. The lands of Levenot became spoils of war after the Battles of Hastings and the title of Baron of Odell and the lands passed to Walter the Fleming at about A.D. 1068. Odell was originally called Woad-hill, named after a plant in the area used as a dye during Saxon times. The name of the village alternated between the spelling of Wodell and Odell until the 16th century when the W was finally dropped.

There was a baronage at one time associated with the estate and there was an Odell Castle, the remains of which may still be seen today. The All Saints Church in Odell was completed in the fifteenth century. The area was primarily farming, but lace making became a later popular source of income and still later the leather industry came to Odell.

It appears that it was through dissident members of the All Saint's Church in the Odell village under the leadership of the Rev. Peter Baulkley that left Odell, England to come to America. A group of them came to the American colonies and founded the town of Concord, Massachusetts in 1635. A close relationship between Concord and the village of Odell is maintained to this day as families from Concord still return to Odell to discover their roots.

Whether the Odells of our particular family were associated with the early founders of Concord, MA is not yet possible to say. The names recorded below are the results of various genealogical research efforts, primarily the work of William F. O'Dell in his book *"Twelve Families- An American Experience."* There are problems with this research effort because of the use of questionable sources and the extended influence of speculation and assumptions. The serious researcher must be aware of these short comings associated with the early information recorded below. Where our own personal research has influenced what is recorded will be stated as such.

CAPTAIN AUGUSTINE ODELL JR. was born about the year 1740, place of birth unknown. It is believed that Captain Odell served in both the Vermont and New York militia during the Revolutionary War.

The William F. O'Dell book, *Twelve Families – An American Experience*, states Augustine Odell Jr. and Jacob Odell became captains in the New York militia. They participated in several engagements in 1781 being called out for an alarm in Col. John Abbots Regiment. In 1784, Captain Augustine Odle served in Henry K. Van Rensselaer's Regiment. This author assumes the names Odle and Odell are interchangeable. The American Revolutionary War ended in 1781 and the year 1784 was certainly well after the war was over.

The DAR, *Daughters of the American Revolution*, have been very generous with their records and this is what their records show. The DAR has not found the application for membership of any ancestor of Augustine Odell who served in the Revolutionary War. This means that no woman has applied to join the society using the name of Augustine Odell. That does not mean there was not an Augustine Odell, who may have been a captain and served in the American Revolution, but no one using that name has applied to become a member of the DAR.

The military records of the DAR do show there was an Augustine Odell in Vermont, who served for four days in 1781(*Vermont Rolls of Soldiers*). However, the 1790 and 1800 census records for Vermont do not record an Augustine Odell.

An Augustine Odell served over a long period of time in the New York, Albany County Militia. There were five other Odells who served in this same Regiment, all as privates. The rank of this Augustine Odell was not stated. Albany County, New York at one time covered most of the state of New York. The county has been cut up many times since with the off springs themselves cut up many times as well. Covering the divisions of the New York counties is an art form in itself.

There was an Augustus Odle listed in the 1790 New York, Washington County census. In 1800 there were two Augustin Odles listed in Chenango County. The DAR reviewed books they have on Chenango County, NY and found that there was no Augustine Odell found in the index of county wills or recognized as a revolutionary War veteran. A mention of Augustin Odel living in Sherburne, Chenango County in 1798 was found in the publication *History of Chenango and Madison Counties NY*. The publication *1810 Census for Part of Chenango County NY* records no Augustin/e Odells, but there were three other Odells living in the greater Sherburne area.

Captain Augustine Odell is believed to have died before 1810, time and place unknown and is believed to have been the parent of seven children.

1. Jacob Odell
2. Nathaniel Odell
3. Benajah Odell

4. Lucy Odell
5. Samuel Odell
6. Austin Odell
7. Augustine Odell- this is believed to be our line

AUGUSTINE ODELL (Jr) was born about the year 1776, place unknown. It is believed he was married to Lydia Newman. He died date and place unknown.

Augustine Odell is believed to have been the parent of nine children with the names of only three known. These three known names have clear association to our family and are recorded below. The only doubt is whether they were truly the sons of this Augustine Odell, since no source gives proof of this assertion.

The reader is further cautioned that the three men associated to our family, because of their age, would not have been recorded individually on the 1820 or 1830 census. All U. S. census before the 1850 census recorded only the heads of household or individuals of taxable age. Others in the household were recorded simply by age and sex. Therefore, the only individual associated with this family who could have been recorded on census would have been Augustine Odell.

Our own review of New York census records for the most part agrees with the information supplied by the DAR. The 1790 Washington County census, Queensbury District records three men, one after the other; Augustin Odle, Jacob Odle, and Nath. Odle. The 1800 Chenango County census, Sherburn district lists Augustin Odle and Augustin Odle Jr. The younger Odle had only three individuals on the census suggesting a very young family. The older Odle had six individuals listed. It's easy to see Odle is not Odell, but it may have been the same family because spellings were at the mercy of the recorder.

Chenango County, NY is located near the center of the state. Sherburne is situated in the north-central part of the county on the Chenango River. Chenango County is only about one hundred miles due east of Seneca County where our Odell family was known with certainty to have lived at one time.

One of the few extant Odell documents from Seneca County, NY concerns the sale of land. Johnathan Tripp sold Lot number 20 containing 50 acres in the town of Junius to David Odell on January 22, 1817. The sale was witnessed by Benajah Odell and Augustin Odell. Fifty acres in a small community could have housed quite a few families. This is especially true if their income was from industrial work like building the Erie Canal and not from working the land.

The 1820 Seneca County census lists the following individuals; Austin Odell, James Odell and Nathaniel Odell of Galen and Allen Odell, Benajah Odell and David Odell of Junius. Austin Odell and Nathaniel Odell are names given to later descendants in our Odell family. There was only one listing for the Odle name on this census and that was

Zakia Odle of Junius. The community of Galen eventually ended up in Warren County and while the name of Junius was changed to Tyre; it still belongs to Seneca County.

The 1830 Seneca County census, Tyre district is important because of its time proximity to our proven family members. Our family members would have been part of a family somewhere and the two names that follow seem to fit that criterion nicely. Augustin Odell and Aeha. Odell were listed one after the other. Augustin Odell, obvious head of household, was between the age of 50 and 60. There were five boys listed between the ages of 10 and 30. There was one female in the family of the same age category as Augustin, probably his wife, and one female between the ages of 5 and 10. Aeha. Odell was between the ages of 20 to 30 with one male child under five. The oldest female in this family was between the ages of 20 to 30 with two females between the ages of 5 to 10, suggesting a very young family.

It must be noted that there was a noticeable pattern of westward movement of the Augustine Odell name from Washington County on the Vermont boarder, to Chenango County in the center of the state and finally to Seneca County in the west. Question easily arises if these are all the same man, sadly no clear answer to that question.

The event that may have propelled the Odells to the western part of New York was the construction of the Erie Canal. The canal was started on July 4, 1817, to connect Lake Erie to the Hudson River. There was a Benajah Odell who was a foreman of a gang who worked on the canal. Benajah Odell and Augustin Odell witnessed the signature of David Odell's deed at Junius, NY, (later named Tyre), on January 22, 1817, was one of the major ports along the canal. The canal was completed on October 26, 1825, effectively leaving those who built the canal out of a job.

It is also known that western New York was suffering under poor economic conditions by the 1830's. Land was cheap out west, so it was time to go. Finally, there are no land or probate records for an Augustine Odell of any spelling in Onondaga, Cayuga, Seneca or Wayne Counties in New York from 1794 to 1870.

The three names listed below are definitely our family members, but there is a fourth name that needs to be included because this family took the same route to Michigan from New York as did our family members. The names associated with this family show familial naming traits common to our early Odell family members. This would be the family of Augustin Odell of Livingston County Michigan. All these men except Austin M. Odell were living in Michigan by the time of the 1840 census.

1. Isaac Odell, born 1813, New York
2. Austin M. Odell, born 1814, New York
3. Nathaniel Alvin Odell, born 1816, NY - our line

AUGUSTIN ODELL was born in New York about the year 1799. This man's wife was named Lydia. She was also born in New York.

This family was located on the 1850 Michigan, Livingston County census. Augustin Odell was 51 years old while his wife Lydia was 52. There were eight children in the home who ranged from age 28 to 8. The oldest six children were born in New York while the two youngest were born in Michigan. The oldest of the two youngest was 12 which means he was born in Michigan in 1838 which gives an approximate date of when the family arrived in Michigan. This date, incidentally, was about the same time Isaac and Nathaniel Odell also arrived in Michigan.

The names of the first eight children of Augustin Odell recorded below come from the 1850 Livingston County census. The next two children listed are from the 1860 census.

1. George Odell, born NY, age 28
2. James Odell, born NY, age 23
3. Sarah Odell, born NY, age 21
4. Augustin Odell, born NY, age 19
5. Jacob Odell, born NY, age 17
6. Mary Odell, born NY, age 15
7. Samuel Odell, born Mich., age 12
8. Reuben Odell, born Mich., age 7
9. Rosada Odell, born Mich., age 9 in 1860
10. Charles A. Odell, born Mich., age 7 in 1860

ISAAC HENRY ODELL was born in New York, possibly Seneca County, on August 31, 1813 and is believed to be the son of Augustine Odell. Isaac appears to have immigrated to Michigan in 1835 or 1836 with his brother Nathaniel. Isaac and Nathaniel Odell were both listed in Comstock District on the 1837 Kalamazoo County, MI census; neither of the men were married at that time. Isaac Odell married Mary (Polly) Shoemaker on March 19, 1838, in Kalamazoo, Michigan. They were married by a local Justice of the Peace. Mary Shoemaker was a native of Pennsylvania.

Court records show Nathaniel Odell sold the property he received from the United States government on May 13, 1837, while he was still living in Kalamazoo County. After the sale of his property, Nathaniel moved to Calhoun County where he married and raised his family.

A review of the 1850 Michigan census shows there were only two men with the name of Isaac Odell found living in the state at that time and one of them was a sixteen-year-old boy.

The Isaac Odell family was also found on the 1860 and 1870 Michigan census living in Comstock Township, Kalamazoo County. The 1880 Kalamazoo, MI census also shows this family. Isaac was a sixty-six-year-old farmer, born in New York. His father was noted on the census as born in Ireland and his mother's birthplace was given as England.

The 1880 publication of the *History of Kalamazoo County, Michigan* carried a brief paragraph about Isaac Odell. "Isaac Odell came to the frontier in 1836, and after living in

Galesburg a year or two, settled on the north part of the southwest quarter of section 11. He is now on his old farm, and is one of our good farmers and worthy citizens."

Isaac Odell died at Comstock, MI on August 24, 1880. Burial was in the Old Galesburg Cemetery. There was a short article about Isaac that appeared in the September 3, 1880 issue of the *Kalamazoo Weekly Gazette* that stated "Isaac Odell reached the *terminus a quo* of his earthly pilgrimage on the 24th day of August, aged 67 years. He was one of the early settlers of the town of Comstock, where he resided up to the time of his death. He, with ax in hand, has caused the towering forest monarchs to fall and well cultivated field to take their places; and through his industry and frugality, he acquired much property for the comfort of his family."

Mary Odell died at Comstock, MI on March 28, 1895. She was also buried in the Old Galesburg Cemetery. Isaac and Mary Shoemaker Odell were the parents of eight known children, all born at Comstock, Michigan.

1. Austin Henry Odell, born 1839
2. Susan A. Odell, born 1841
3. Angeline Odell, born September 10, 1844
4. Jane A. Odell, born March 9, 1846
5. Sarah Odell, born November 3, 1848
6. Ellen Odell, born August 12, 1851
7. Azor Odell, born February 26, 1853
8. Isaac Henry Odell Jr., born 1857

AUSTIN M. ODELL was born in New York, possibly Seneca County, in 1814 and believed to be the son of Augustine Odell. This family was found on the 1850 Michigan, Calhoun County census, Newton. The family's enumeration was recorded just after that of his brother Nathaniel A. Odell and his family. Austin was noted as a 'Blacksmith,' his wife was Mary, who was also from NY, was born about 1818. There was no property value for this family suggesting they were living with Austin's brother Nathaniel. There were three small children in the home, the names are recorded below, all born in New York. The fact that all the children had been born in New York suggest the family was a recent arrival in the state of Michigan.

The family was found on the 1860 Michigan, Calhoun County census, Newton Township. There were then two additional children in the home, their names are recorded below. Austin Odell's occupation was blacksmith. Both his real estate value and personal property value were recorded as $500.00.

A. M. Odell and his wife Mary were found on the 1870 Iowa census, Delaware County, Colony District, living within the home of his brother Nathaniel Odell. No children were recorded for the family at this time.

Information from the 1850 and 1860 census shows Austin and Mary were the parents of five known children.

1. John L. Odell, born NY about 1842
2. Jane A. Odell, born NY about 1844
3. Lydia A. Odell, born NY about 1846
4. Stephen Odell, born MI about 1850
5. William Odell, born MI, about 1852

NATHANIEL ALVIN ODELL was born in Wayne County, New York on June 4, 1816. He is believed to be the son of Augustine Odell and Lydia Newman. Nathaniel and his brother Isaac Odell are believed to have emigrated from Seneca County, New York to Michigan in 1835. Nathaniel Odell entered the Michigan Tract Book on November 9, 1835 taking up 80 acres by survey identified as "Sec. 22, 1S, 8W, E ½, NE ¼." He was nineteen years old.

On May 13, 1837, Nathaniel Odell of Kalamazoo County, MI sold 80 acres of land to Caleb D. Ferris for $110.00. This land was described as "the east half of the northeast quarter of tract 22 in township No. 1 South Range No. 8 west." On The same day Nathaniel purchased two tracts of 80 acres each from the same Caleb D. Ferris for land in Calhoun County, Michigan. This property was described as "the east half of the southeast quarter of Section No five and also the west half of the southwest quarter of section four all in township No. three South of Range No 7 west containing each 80 acres." He paid the same $110.00 for this property as Ferris originally paid him which suggest this was nothing more than a land swap. Interestingly, Nathaniel received title from the United States Government on May 1, 1839, for the land he already sold to Ferris. President Martin Van Buren's name was affixed to the deed.

Nathaniel Odell married Mahala Brace at Battle Creek, Calhoun County, Michigan in 1838. Mahala was born in New York on November 26, 1816, the daughter of Chester Brace and Acenith Strong. Information compiled from several census states Mahala was born in New York while both her parents were born in Pennsylvania. Nathaniel's oldest child Elisha Brace Odell was born in Calhoun County, Michigan in 1838.

The 1850 Michigan, Calhoun County census shows the family living in Newton. Nathaniel Odell was a thirty-four-year-old farmer with seven children. Mahala his wife was also thirty-four years old. The family enumeration was found recorded just before the family listing of Austin Odell and his wife Mary. Austin Odell, undoubtedly Nathaniel's brother, was a thirty-six-year-old 'Blacksmith' and there were three young children in his family; John L., age 8, Jane A., age 6 and Lydia A., age 4. All members of this family were born in New York.

Nathaniel Alvin Odell

It was while he was living in Calhoun County that Nathaniel professed religion and subsequently started holding meetings to improve his gift as a preacher. The family moved to Delaware County, Iowa in 1854, and settled near the town of Colesburg after residing in Michigan for over fourteen years. Delaware County is located on the eastern portion of the state one county removed from the Mississippi River. The last deed transacted in Calhoun County, Michigan for Nathaniel Odell was recorded on March 25, 1854, when he sold 80 acres to Hugh S. Snedeker of Ontario County, NY for $3,300.00. Nathaniel appears to have turned a tidy profit from his original $110.00 investment.

On March 31, 1855, Nathaniel Odell purchased 40 acres in Delaware County, Iowa from Perry Perkins and his wife Charlotte Perkins. The land was described as "the SE ¼ of NW ¼ of Section eleven (11) in township Ninety (90) of Range 4 west of 5th principal meridian containing forty acres more or less." Nathaniel paid $350.00 for the land. The deed was filed on January 14, 1856.

Answering a request by the Free Baptist Church of Delhl, Iowa, Nathaniel A. Odell was ordained at a Quarterly Meeting, May 25, 1856. This was the start of his ministry. Although, every census record shows Nathaniel to be a farmer, his life's calling was the work of a Minister of the Gospel.

Nathaniel Odell's family was found on the 1860 Iowa census living in Colony Township, Delaware County. At that time there were nine children in the home and all except the youngest, Orville Odell, were born in Michigan. Orville Odell was only two at the time of the census.

The family was found for the 1870 Iowa, Delaware County census still living in Colony Township. Three children were recorded in the home, Amelia, Elanora and Orville B. Also listed within the family were Effie Edwards, age six, John Foot, age 21, and A. M. Odell, age sixty-two, and his wife Mary, age sixty. A. M Odell was undoubtedly Austin Odell and his wife Mary. Curiously, little Effie, who was recorded as born in Ohio, had $200.00 of personal property listed after her name.

Nathaniel and Mahala Odell's son Jeremiah Odell died on January 9, 1874 and was buried in the Oak Hill Cemetery located east of the Colesburg community. Jeremiah, who was about 29 years when he died, was buried beside his brother Tilinghast S. Odell who died on March 7, 1856, at the age of 3 months and 18 days. Jeremiah Odell was not living within his parent's home for the 1870 census.

On December 4, 1975, Nathaniel and Mahala Odell sold 1,200 acres of land to P.S. Malvin for $10,000.00, Delaware County records. The record of when this property was acquired and how much it cost has not been found. According to the 1869 county plat map, this land had a creek running through it and was heavily forested making the property quite valuable. The sale of the property appears to have been in anticipation of the family leaving the county.

Nathaniel Odell acquired 160 acres of land from Edwin Gilmore in Montgomery County on December 14, 1875. This property was located clear across the state in the western part of Iowa with the family moving into a home near the community of Elliott. The family had lived in Delaware County for over twenty-one years; so, it must have been difficult for the family to pull up roots and start over in a new community. It is not certain if the Edwin Gilmore selling this property was Nathaniel's son-in-law, Mary's husband, but it probably was. Part of this land was located in Cass County while the other part was in Montgomery County.

The 1880 Iowa, Cass County census shows this family living in Pleasant Township. There were two boarders also living in the home. One boarder was the child Effie M. Edwards age seventeen who was now listed as a granddaughter born in Iowa, not Ohio as noted on the 1870 census. Effie was the daughter of Aurilla Odell and Sam Edwards. The other boarder was Emma Sprague, age 19, who was also born in Iowa. The listing following Nathaniel's on the census was that of his son Orville B. Odell. Also recorded in Orville's home was his wife Rhoda and one child, Scott S. Odell.

Nathaniel and wife sold about 80 acres of land in Cass County to their son Orville B. Odell on September 29, 1880. The deed was found in the Montgomery County records and the value of the property was stated as $3,500.00.

Nathaniel A. Odell died on August 19, 1882. He was an ordained preacher; his tombstone gives his name as ELDER N. ODELL. The death records of Cass County, however, state he was a farmer and he was born in New York. Information attributed to Rev. N. W. Bixby appeared in the October 22, 1882, issue of the *Manchester Press,* Manchester, Iowa giving notice of the death of Rev. Nathaniel Odell in Montgomery

County where he had lived for several years. The article also stated, "He leaves the wife of his youth and six children to mourn their loss."

Orville B. Odell served as administrator of his father's estate which was probated in Montgomery County, Iowa on June 11, 1883. There were six children mentioned as heirs to their father's estate at that time. The children not mentioned in the estate settlement are noted as such below. When and where some of them died is unknown as is their place of burial.

On June 12, 1883, Mahala Odell signed a Quit Claim to Orville B. Odell for the same land his parents previously sold him on September 29, 1880. The price of the property was now only $800.00, which was probably the remainder of what Orville owed on the property. On June 15, 1883, Orville sold this same property to Augusta Johnson for $3,500.00. These transactions appear to be nothing more than a gift of money to Orville from his mother. Interestingly, Orville was noticed on the deed as already living in Nuckolls County, Nebraska.

Mahala Odell died on April 8, 1884, at the age of 68 years and 2 months, but apparently not in Cass County as her death was not recorded in the county records. Her tombstone states she was the wife of REV. N. ODELL. Nathaniel and Mahala Odell are buried in Waveland Township Cemetery, which was formerly located in Cass County, but due to a shift in county lines is now in Pottawattomie County, Iowa. Within this same cemetery section there is another tombstone that states; Grandson: Edward G., son of O. B. and R., who died Sept. 8, 1882. This young child was a little over one year old.

Nathaniel and Mahala Odell were the parents of eleven known children, all born in Michigan except the last two children who were born in Iowa. The listing below is compiled from the 1850 and 1860 census.

1. Elisha Brace Odell
2. Lydia O. Odell, born 1840, missing from 1883 estate settlement
3. Emily E. Odell, born 1842, missing from 1883 estate settlement
4. Julia Ann M. Odell, born 1843, missing from 1883 estate settlement
5. Jeremiah N. Odell, born 1845, missing from 1883 estate settlement
6. Aurilla U. Odell
7. Mary E. Odell
8. Amelia G. Odell
9. Elanora Odell
10. Tilinghast S. Odell, died March 7, 1856, age 3mo, 18ds
11. Orville Birt Odell

ELISHA BRACE ODELL was born in Calhoun County, Michigan on November 23, 1838, the son of Nathaniel A. Odell and Mahala Brace Odell. Elisha B. Odell married Marion Smith on October 7, 1861 at Lodomville, Clayton County, Iowa. They were married by the Rev. N W. Bixby. The marriage license was, however, issued from Delaware County, Iowa. Marion Smith Odell was born in 1841 in Scotland.

This family was not found on any 1870 census. The family was, however, found on the 1880 Minnesota, Polk County census. There were seven children in the home at that time, all born in Iowa. The names are listed below.

1. Nathaniel A. Odell, age 17
2. Wallace S. Odell, age 15
3. Robert L. Odell, age 11
4. John C. Odell, age 9
5. Minne L. Odell, age 6
6. Charles E. Odell, age 4
7. Astor May Odell, age 2

EMILY E. ODELL was born about the year 1842 in Calhoun County, Michigan, the daughter of Nathaniel A. Odell and Mahala Brace Odell. Emily E. Odell married Josiah B. Chapin on October 7, 1861, at Lodomville, Clayton County Iowa. They were married by N. W. Bixby, Minister of the Gospel.

Emily apparently did not survive the marriage to have issue. Neither she nor her heirs were mentioned at the 1883 settlement of her father's estate.

JULIA ANN M. ODELL was born about 1843 in Calhoun County, Michigan, the daughter of Nathaniel A. Odell and Mahala Brace Odell. Julia Ann M. Odell married Martin L. Chapin on November 6, 1862 at Lodomville, Clayton County Iowa. The marriage license was issued from Delaware County. The bride's father Nathaniel Odell gave written consent to the marriage. They were married by Newell W. Bixby, Minister of the Gospel.

Julia apparently did not survive the marriage to have issue. Neither she nor her heirs were mentioned at the 1883 settlement of her father's estate.

AURILLA U. ODELL was born in Calhoun County, Michigan in 1847, the daughter of Nathaniel A. Odell and Mahala Brace Odell. Aurilla U. Odell married S. S. (Sam) Edwards on September 7, 1863, at Colony, Delaware County, Iowa. The couple was married by the Rev. N. Odell, the bride's father. They were the parent of one child, Effie M. Edwards, born about 1864.

At some unknown place and time Aurilla married Ruben Winston. The Winston family was found on the 1880 Iowa, Cerro Gordo County census, Mason Township. The 1885, Iowa, U.S. State census locates this family living in Niles, Floyd County. There are five children in the home at the time. Effie Edwards has also been included here but it must be noted she did not live in the home of her mother, but in the home of her grandparents Nathaniel and Mahala Odell.

1. Effie M. Edwards, born 1864
2. Eddie Winston, age 14 in 1885

3. Horace Winston, age 13, in 1885
4. Burt Winston, age 12, in 1885
5. Frankie Winston, age 5, in 1885
6. Minnie Winston, age 1, in 1885

MARY E. ODELL was born in Calhoun County, Michigan in 1849, the daughter of Nathaniel A. Odell and Mahala Brace Odell. Mary E. Odell married Edwin Gilmore on August 1,1867, near Colesburg, Iowa. They were married by a Geo. Larkin. The Rev. N. Odell did not perform this marriage. Silas Gilmore gave testimony to the groom's competent age and condition.

An Ed Gilmore sold Nathaniel A. Odell 160 acres in Montgomery in 1875. This man was probably Odell's son-in-law, but this is not known with certainty.

The Gilmore family was found on the 1880 Nebraska, Nuckolls County census, living in the Nelson Precinct. There were five children in the home, all listed as born in Iowa. The youngest child was 1 ½ years old. So, this means the family moved to Nebraska sometime after the youngest child was born. The children are listed below, and the ages are from the 1880 census.

1. Liddy Gilmore, age 11
2. Nettie Gilmore, age 8
3. Violet Gilmore, age 6
4. Lalice (sp) Gilmore, age 3, female
5. Adelbert Gilmore, age 1 1/2, male

AMELIA G. ODELL was born in Calhoun County, Michigan in September 1850, the daughter of Nathaniel A. Odell and Mahala Brace Odell. Amelia was found in her parent's home for the 1870 census. A boarder in the home at that time was John W. D. Foot.

Amelia G. Odell married John W. D. Foote on December 27, 1874, "at the Brides Residence." They were married by "N. Odell, Minister of the Gospel," the bride's father. The marriage license was issued from Delaware County. John was born in Darke County, Ohio in 1849 the son of William M. Foote and Rhoda Swisher Foote. John's younger sister Rhoda later married Amelia's brother Orville. More about the Foote family may be found in the biography of Orville B. Odell.

John W.D. Foote

The J.W.D. Foote family was found on the 1880 Iowa, Montgomery County census, Pilot Grove, living near Elliott, Iowa. John was recorded as a school teacher; there were no children in the home.

ELANORA ODELL was born in Calhoun County, Michigan in 1853, the daughter of Nathaniel A. Odell and Mahala Brace Odell. At some unknown place and time, she married William McGuire. The family was found on the 1880 Iowa, Montgomery County census living in Pilot Township. There were three children in the home at that time, names are listed below.

1. Clarence McGuire, age 4
2. Mary McGuire, age 3
3. Olrith McGuire, age 1; this child's name was drawn through, difficult to read

ORVILLE BIRT ODELL was born in Delaware County, Iowa on April 23 1858, the son of Nathaniel and Mahala Brace Odell. Orville grew up on the family farm near Colesburg. The family lived in Delaware County, Iowa for about 21 years before moving west all the way across the state of Iowa to Montgomery/Cass County. When Orville's father purchased 160 acres of land there in 1875, Orville moved with his family to the new area. However, his heart had already been lost to a young lady from Clayton County before he made the move.

Orville B. Odell married Catherine Rhoda Foote on June 24, 1877, in Milford, Montgomery County, Iowa. Catherine, who went by the name of Rhoda, was born October 28, 1859, in Greenville, Darke County, Ohio, the daughter of William M. Foote and Rhoda Swisher. The community of Milford, Iowa does not exist anymore and is now known by the name of Grant, Iowa. Orville was twenty years old while Rhoda was seventeen at the time of the wedding.

Rhonda's brother John W. D. Foote was found living in the Nathaniel A. Odell household for the 1870 Delaware, Iowa census. Rhoda and her parents, recent arrivals from Ohio, were then living in Elk Township, Clayton County, Iowa. Delaware County and Clayton County border one another, so they must have been living in communities close by one another. John W. D. Foote eventually marries Orville's sister Amelia and Orville later marries John's sister Rhoda.

The 1880 Iowa, Cass County census shows Orville and Rhoda were then living in Pleasant Township and they had one child, Scott S., who was then one year old. Orville's parents were also listed within this enumeration. Orville's parents sold him about 80 acres of land in Cass County on September 29, 1880. When Orville's father passed away on August 19, 1882, Orville was assigned the administrator of the estate by the Montgomery County Court.

Orville was given a Quit Claim by his mother Mahala Odell on June 12, 1883, for the property she and her husband had sold Orville on September 29, 1880. Orville, in turn, sold this land to Augusta Johnson on June 15, 1883. Orville and his family by then had already departed Cass County and were living in Superior, Nuckolls County, Nebraska. Orville's sister Mary E. Gilmore and her family were by this time also living in Nebraska. She and her family were living in Nelson, the county seat for Nuckolls County when the 1880 Nebraska census was taken.

Orville and Rhoda Odell purchased lots 13, 14, 15 and 16 in the village of Superior, Nuckolls County, Nebraska on March 13, 1883. Lot 13 was purchased from H. W. Young and wife. Lot 14 was purchased from James F. Young. Lots 15 and 16 were purchased from H. W. Young and wife and J. H. Todd.

On April 1, 1885, Orville and Rhoda sold lot number 16 to his brother-in-law Edwin Gilmore. On October 29, 1885, they sold lot number 15 to Milton A. Elliott and on February 5, 1886 sold lots number 13 and 14 to the same Milton A. Elliott. For some unknown reason about the year 1894 or 1895 the family moved to Amos, Missouri living there for about a year and a half. Their son Irvin M. Odell was born in Amos, MO on July 30, 1896. Shortly after this birth, the family returned to Superior, Nebraska.

Back row, Mahala May and Sylvester Scott Odell
Front row, Orville William and Ira Nathanial Odell

The family was found for the 1900 census living in Beaver Precinct of Nuckolls County. The date of the census was June 26, 1900. Orville's occupation was given as farmer. Orville's son Ira Odell was not found in the family enumeration for that year's census. Ira's name was last listed for the school census in 1897, suggesting Ira had by the time of the census left home either for work or school. Rhoda was noted on the census as being the parent of twelve children with ten still living. A 1900 plat of the Beaver Township shows Orville owned a section near the tracks of the Missouri-Pacific railroad line north of Superior, Nebraska. On that plat was a sorghum mill drawn on Orville's property. So, it appears Orville was a little more than a farmer; he may have been in the milling business as well.

Orville and Rhoda Odell sold "Lot one (1) in block number twenty (20) of North Superior, Nebraska" on November 5, 1900 for $150.00 to Emma K. Gittings. The record of when this property was purchased has not been found. The sale of this property at this late date suggests the family was leaving the area for good.

The family again moved to Amos, Missouri near Stotesbury in the fall of 1900. Rhoda Foote Odell died here on January 25, 1903, at the age of 42 years, two months and twenty-eight days. She was buried at the Underwood M.E.S. Church in Vernon County, Missouri. Rhoda's death left Orville with six young children, three of them quite young. Mahala May Odell, the oldest daughter in the home, married Roy Hicks at her home at Amos on November 9, 1904. This took her out of the home and away from any help she may have been able to give Orville with his underage children.

*Back Row, James Ross Odell, Orange Bert O'Dell, Orville William Odell, Irvin McClain
O'Dell, Victor Francis O'Dell and Sylvester Scott Odell
Front row, Ira Nathanial Odell, Mahala Odell Hicks, Orville Birt Odell, Ada Odell
Miller and Selden Jay Odell*

Why the Odell's were living in Amos, Vernon County, MO at this time is not known with certainty. However, research suggests it probably had to do with the railroad. The Kansas City Southern Railroad ran straight through Amos. A 1903 map of the area shows Amos had only about six or seven buildings in the whole town. Four of Orville's sons, Scott, Victor, James and Irvin eventually worked for the railroad. There may have been one final reason why the Odell's were in the area that was because there was other Odell's living in the area at the time. Vernon County marriage licenses for William Odell, O. M. Odell, Ira E. Odell and Flossie Odell have been located for this same time period. None of these people where Orville's children and it must be remembered that Orville had a son named Ira and there was an Ira in this crowd. The Odell family these Odell's belonged to is unknown.

There are no probate records for any Odell found in Vernon County. Nor are there any deeds for that name found in the records. Like the trains on the Kansas City Southern Line at Amos, Missouri, the Odell's were just passing through.

A family source states Orville married two more times after his wife's death and at about 1910 moved to California with his four youngest children where Orville and his son Selden Jay Odell had a store in Watts, California. There is no town named Watts in California unless it was Watts the infamous subdivision of Los Angles. The 1910 Los Angeles County, CA census fortunately does shed some light on the family at this time.

'Orvil' B. Odell and his wife of three years Arabella Odell were found living in the San Antonio Township. Enumerated within this family were Selden J., Ada K., Irvin Mc., and Orange B. Orvil (sic) and Selden were working as grocers. The family source further states that at about 1915, Orville moved to Montana where he was part owner of a farm or ranch with his son Victor Francis Odell located north of Great Falls, Montana. This assertion is backed up with the fact Orville's daughter Ada married at Great Falls, Montana on June 20, 1915. No information about where Orville married Arabella or if he was married a third time has been found.

Back row, James Ross Odell, Victor Francis, and Irvin McClain O'Dell
Front row, Ada Odell Miller, Orville Birt Odell, Mahala Odell Hicks and Orange Bert
O'Dell

It appears that it was sometime between 1903 and 1915, Orville's sons Victor, Orange and Irvin started spelling their name as O'Dell. One of the few tidbits of information about the Odell family passed down through the Ira N. Odell family states there was talk of a family rift over the written form of the Odell name. Orville B. Odell throughout his life consistently spelled his name as Odell.

There is a photograph circa 1920 in the possession of Priscilla Whitehead McCloud that shows the entire Odell family at that time. This photo was taken in Great Falls, Montana at a family reunion held in 1920 on a ranch twelve miles north of Great Falls. There were eight sons and two daughters along with the father in the photo. This appears to be the only family reunion that Ira N. Odell family was able to attend. There were other Odell reunions, one held in Yellowstone Park in Wyoming in 1929 and another held at May Odell Hicks place in Colorado in 1932.

During the later days of his life Orville Odell lived either at Victor's home in Lewistown, Montana or at Scott's home in Kansas City, MO. The 1930 Missouri, Jackson Country, census shows him living with Scott in Kansas City.

159

It was while he was at Scott's home at 3507 Windsor in Kansas City that Orville Birt Odell died at the age of 81 on February 8, 1939. A brief death announcement appeared in the *Kansas City Star* on February 10, 1939. It stated services were held at the C. H. Blackman & Sons funeral home at 9 a.m. and again at 2 p.m. at the Underwood Methodist Church near Hume, MO. His body was removed to Vernon County, MO where he was interred beside his wife Rhoda Foote Odell in the Underwood M.E.S. Cemetery.

The Underwood Methodist Church was established in 1870, on the east side of Amos. MO. Regular services were held at the church until the 1960's when it was closed and then only funerals were held there a couple of years after that. The church was destroyed by fire shortly after this time. The cemetery does have regular maintenance and is in good order. There is a stone for Rhoda that says, "Rhoda C., wife of O. B. O'Dell; October 28, 1859 – Jan. 25, 1903." Orville does not have a stone.

Orville Birt Odell and Rhoda Catherine Foote Odell were the parents of twelve children with ten living to adulthood.

1. Sylvester Scott Odell
2. Edward G. Odell, 1881, died Sept. 8, 1882, buried with Odell grandparents
3. Ira Nathaniel Odell
4. Orville William Odell
5. Mahala May Odell
6. Victor Francis Odell
7. James Ross Odell
8. Selden Jay Odell
9. Ada Catherine Odell
10. Irvin McClain Odell
11. Infant boy, born Jan. 19, 1899, died age 1 mo 7 days, buried Superior, Nebraska
12. Orange Bert Odell

SYLVESTER SCOTT ODELL was born in Cass County, Iowa on March 8, 1879, the son of Orville B. Odell and Rhoda Catherine Foote Odell. Sylvester, known to the family as Scott, married Alice Trowbridge in Nelson, Nebraska on November 26, 1899. Alice was born in Nebraska at about 1881.

Sylvester S. Odell was found on the 1900 Nebraska, Nuckolls County census records in Beaver District, District 190. Sylvester was a farmer, he and Mary had been married one year and there were no children listed in the home. The family was enumerated several listings from his parents listing. The same family, this time under the name of Scott Odell, was found on the 1910 Kansas, Crawford County census, 4Wd Pittsburg, District 102. Scott was working for the railroad as a water foreman. There were six children in the home. The family was found on the 1920 census living in Kansas, Crawford County, with six children in the home.

Sylvester S. Odell was recorded on the 1930 Missouri, Jackson County, Kansas City Township census. Alice E. Odell and Orville Odell were also listed in the home. Scott's occupation was given as "water service foreman" working for the railroad.

Sylvester Scott Odell

Scott Sylvester Odell of 3507 Windsor, Kansas City, MO, died at the home of his daughter Mrs. A. B. Hancock in Shreveport, LA on October 15, 1943. A death announcement appeared in the *Kansas City Star* dated October 16, 1943. Services were held at Blackman's Guardian Home; however, no cemetery was noted. The article further stated Scott was survived by his wife Alice, two sons, John H. Odell of Alliance, NE, and Bert B. Odell of Lake Lotawana and two other daughters, Mrs. C. M. Miller of Caliente, NV and Mrs. Fred Geier of Girard, KS.

Scott S. Odell and Alice Trowbridge were the parents of seven known children. The order of the children was taken from the 1910 and 1920 Kansas census.

1. John H. Odell, born 1900
2. Freda E. Odell, born 1902
3. Bert B. Odell, born 1904
4. Jessie J. Odell, born 1906
5. Frances E. Odell, born 1908
6. Paul L. Odell, born 1909
7. Bob, born 1919

IRA NATHANIEL ODELL was born on January 13, 1882, the son of Orville and Rhoda Foote Odell probably near Elliott, Montgomery County, Iowa, where the Odell family was then residing. The county seat of Montgomery County, Iowa is Red Oak which has been given as Ira's place of birth passing incorrectly down through his family for years. Ira moved with his family to Nuckolls County, Nebraska in 1883.

Ira was last listed in the Nuckolls County school census for the year 1897. He was not found with the family for the 1900 Nuckolls County, Nebraska census and he was not found on the 1900 Nebraska census soundex. It is known that Ira moved to Chicago sometime before 1906 and became a member of the Salvation Army. It was apparently while serving with the Salvation Army that he met his future wife.

Ira Nathaniel and Johanna Schultz Odell

Ira N. Odell of Glen Ellyn, Illinois married Johanna Wilhemina Schultz on February 6, 1906, in Chicago, IL. The marriage ceremony was performed by Colonel Charles Miles of the Salvation Army. Both Johanna and Ira were working for the Salvation Army at the time of their marriage. Johanna's sister Ida Schultz and Clarence A. Ryan were witnesses to the marriage. Johanna was born in Detroit, Michigan on August 13, 1879, the daughter of Johann and Albertine Schultz. A copy of the Salvation Army marriage certificate was mailed from the Salvation Army office at 120, 122, 124 W. 14th Street, New York. The small mailing tube used to ship the certificate was addressed to Lieut. Schultz at 4061 Dearborn Street, Chicago, Ill. This document was undoubtedly mailed to Johanna and she held the rank of Lieutenant. (Schultz family see page 180)

A family story states that following their marriage the young couple moved to San Francisco, California where they worked in an orphanage, probably for the Salvation Army. They were in San Francisco when the earthquake of April 18, 1906, devastated the city. They were tossed about in their beds while the earth trembled and shook. They remained in California for a while after the quake because their son Ira Stewart Odell was born in California on November 16, 1906. The family eventually moved back to Chicago date unknown.

Winona Ruth and Ira Stewart Odell

The Ira N. Odell family history states Ira was quite successful as an electrical contractor in Chicago. He came into the electrical business just as electricity was replacing gas as the medium for light and power in homes and businesses. The 1920 Illinois, Cook County census agrees with this assertion. The Odell's were found living at West 66th Place. There were two children in the home at that time, Stewart, age 13 and Winona, age 9. Ira's occupation was "electrician- own business."

Ira and family attended an Odell family reunion sometime in 1920 at a ranch located 12 miles north of Great Falls, Montana. The ranch was probably the home of Ira's sister Ada Miller. An excellent family photograph was taken at this time, see page 149. There were also several snapshots taken that included Ira's children, Stewart and Winona. This was the only reunion Ira and his family was able to attend.

Top left, Ira Nathanial and Johanna Schultz Odell   Top right, Ira Stewart and Winona Ruth Odell   Bottom photo, Odell home in Chicago, Illinois

By the time of the 1930 Illinois, Cook County census, Ira has become a "Realtor - Broker." Winona was the only child in the home; she was 19 years old and working as a stenographer- manufacturing. The family was then living on West 104th Street in District 759.

Ira N. Odell was only seventeen days from celebrating his 49th birthday when he died on January 30, 1931, at the conclusion of a basketball game at the YMCA located on 6545 S. Union Ave. During the first half of the game between the First Nazarene Church and the Englewood Methodist Church, Ira started feeling ill. During the half time break he went outside for some fresh air. As he left the building, he found two small children trying to siphon gas from his car. Ira gave chase and caught one of the youths who was then given a well-deserved spanking. Ira started feeling sick shortly after this but continued to watch the game which was very close. With only a few seconds left the Methodist team shot the winning basket. Ira jumped up to shout with the rest of the crowd and just as he did, he slumped to the floor. A physician attending the game was called to examine him and pronounced him dead.

Johanna Schultz, Ira Nathanial, Winona Ruth and Ira Stewart Odell

The newspaper article about the incident stated, "Mr. Odell, for many years a businessman in the 63rd and Halsted Sts. district, had suffered a nervous breakdown recently according to members of his family and his death is attributed to over excitement caused by a series of disturbing events on the evening of his death." The article concluded with the statement that the deceased had been "active in church and Y.M.C.A. boys work for many years and formerly affiliated with the Englewood Business Men's Association." Services for Ira N. Odell were held at the First Nazarene Church on 64th and Eggleston Ave. with interment in Mount Greenwood Cemetery.

Back row, Irvin McClain O'Dell, Orange Bert O'Dell, James Ross O'Dell and Selden Jay Odell
Middle row, Ada Odell Miller, Ira Nathanial, Orville Birt and Johanna Schultz Odell
Front row, Ira Stewart and Winona Ruth Odell

The death certificate for Ira N. Odell stated he was then employed as a salesman in the Real Estate business. His birthplace was given as "Don't know" and his mother's name was written the same way. Orville B. Odell was given as his father's name. Ira died of angina pectoris with a secondary condition of arteriosclerosis. The doctor's statement said Ira had been treated for his condition since September 22, 1930. The personal information for the death certificate was given by Johanna Odell.

Johanna W. Odell's daughter Winona Ruth Odell married Dr. William B. Whitehead on January 1, 1934, at the First Church of the Nazarene. Members of the Schultz family in attendance at the wedding were Louise Hudenburg, Roy and Catherine Hudenburg, Bertha Van Dyk, Mr. and Mrs. Stanley A. Van Dyk, Joyce Van Dyk, Jay Van Dyk and Albert H. Schultz. There were no members of the Odell family in attendance for the wedding.

Johanna Schultz Odell continued to live at her home on 1641 W. 104th St. Winona, several years after her 1934 marriage to Dr. William Bray Whitehead, moved her family in with her mother where they lived for about eight years. In 1943, shortly after Winona and her family moved to Fayetteville, North Carolina, Mrs. Odell became very sick with pneumonia. Winona returned to Chicago to nurse her mother back to health and it was then decided that Mrs. Odell would sell her apartment and move to North Carolina and live with her daughter's family.

Left photo, Ira Nathanial, Johanna Schultz, Winona Ruth and Ira Stewart Odell Right photo, Johanna Schultz Odell with Priscilla Ruth and William Odell Whitehead

Johanna Schultz Odell died on February 22, 1946, at the home of her daughter on 2610 Pecan Drive, Fayetteville, NC. Mrs. Odell's body was returned to Chicago where she was buried beside her husband at Mount Greenwood, block 22, lot # 68. A brief announcement appeared in the *Fayetteville Observer* and an obituary appeared on page 16, of the Monday, February 25, 1946, issue of the *Chicago Daily Tribune*. The article in the Chicago paper mentioned her son Ira Stewart Odell and her daughter Winona Whitehead. It also mentioned Johanna's sisters Mrs. Emma Klix, Mrs. Ida Hammond and their brother Albert Schultz.

The services in Chicago were performed by The House of Lanyon, Undertaker, located at 415 W. 63 Street, Chicago. A Memorial Record was kept by the funeral home for the family which is now in the procession of Johanna's granddaughter Priscilla W. McCloud. This book records the services were held at the First Church of the Nazarene at 2:00 PM on February 26, 1946. Bearers listed were Roy Hudenburg, Harvey Grund, Charles Hammond, Richard Needles, Walter Eichenberger and Paul Ashby. In the family record section Johanna's parents were listed as Albertina (d) and John (d). Siblings were Albert, Emma, Ida, Louise (d) and Bertha (d). The (d) indicated the individual listed were then deceased.

Ira N. and Johanna Schultz Odell were the parents of two children.

1. Ira Stewart Odell
2. Winona Ruth Odell

IRA STEWART ODELL was born in California, probably at San Francisco, on November 16, 1906, the son of Ira N. and Johanna Schultz Odell. Ira, better known by the family as Stewart, was found within his family on the 1920 Illinois, Cook County census. He was 13 years and no occupation was recorded by his name.

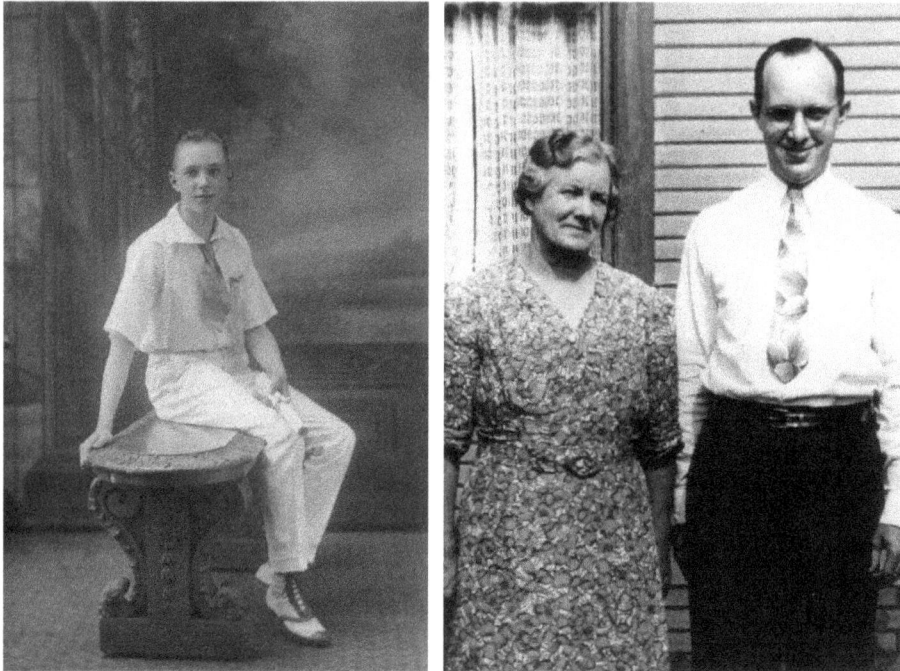

Left photo, Ira Stewart Odell Right photo, Johanna Schultz Odell and Ira Stewart Odell

Ira married Kathryn Jeanette Schiethe sometime around 1929. She was born in Chicago, Illinois on November 4, 1908, the daughter of Arthur E. and Jessie N. Schiethe. The Schultz family book gives her date of birth as November 4. This young couple was found on the 1930 Illinois, Cook County census living on Green Street in District 659. Census records show they had been married one year and he was working as a bookkeeper in an office and she was working as a clerk in a bank. Kathryn stated her father had been born in Illinois and her mother had been born in Scotland.

Ira worked many years for Montgomery Wards of Chicago and eventually retired from that company. Ira Stewart Odell died on February 8, 1994, at Winfield, Dupage County, Illinois. He was 87 years old. Visitation was held at Hultgren Funeral Home and services were held at College Church in Wheaton, IL. Ira was buried adjacent to his parents at Mount Greenwood Cemetery, Chicago, IL.

Kathryn J. Odell died Wednesday at home on April 13, 2005, at the Delnor Glen Assisted Living in St. Charles, IL. Services were held at College Church in Wheaton, IL where she had been a member for many years. She had a lovely voice singing in the choir for many years. She was a devoted wife and mother.

Kathryn was survived by the following grandchildren; Mark (Vivica), Eric (Mary), Adam (Kate), Todd, Dr. Sean Odell, Charles (Juli) Burroughs and one granddaughter Liz (Rick) Spaker.

Ira and Kathryn were the parents of two children.

1. Stewart Ira Odell
2. Jeanette Odell

STEWART IRA ODELL was born on December 14, 1938 or 1939, the son of Ira S. and Kathryn Schiethe Odell. Stewart graduated from University of Illinois College of Medicine in 1963. He completed residency at Rush Presbyterian St. Lukes Medical Center. Dr. Odell is board certified in Obstetrics and Gynecology. He is currently practicing at Dukane Obstetrics & Gynecology, St. Charles, IL. Has been in practice for 54 years. He married Vivian _____, at least five children, all sons.

JEANETTE ODELL was born on September 6, 1942, the daughter of Ira S. and Kathryn Schiethe Odell. Jeanette married Deane Perry Burroughs II, born September 2, 1964, believed to have had two or three sons, living in Kankakee, IL.

WINONA RUTH ODELL was born in Chicago, Illinois on May 8, 1910, the daughter of Ira N. and Johanna Schultz Odell. Winona graduated from Englewood High School, then attended business school. The 1930 Illinois, Cook County, census shows Winona working as a stenographer for a manufacturing company.

Winona Ruth Odell

Winona Ruth Odell

Winona Ruth Odell married Dr. William Bray Whitehead in Chicago, Illinois on January 1, 1934. They were the parents of three children. More information about Winona and her family may be found under her husband's name. See page 37.

1. William Odell Whitehead
2. Priscilla Ruth Whitehead
3. Lawrence Joseph Whitehead

ORVILLE WILLIAM ODELL was born in Superior, Nuckolls County, Nebraska on January 8, 1884, the son of Orville B. Odell and Rhoda Catherine Foote Odell. Orville W. Odell married Bretta Marshall on January 20, 1907 at Union Valley.

This family was found on the 1920 Kansas, Republic County census, Washington Township. Orville's name on the census was spelled Orval and he was listed as a farmer. There were three children recorded in the home at that time. They are listed below.

Orville W. Odell died of lung cancer on January 1, 1922. He was buried at Union Valley Cemetery in Belleville, Kansas. A copy of his death certificate states he had been under a doctor's care since June 1921. An obituary was found in the January 12, 1922 issue of the *Republic City News* of Belleville, Kansas that stated he was the parent of four children with one Benard Louis Odell passing away at the age of nine months.

1. Vera May Odell, born about 1909
2. Orville Glen Odell, born about 1910
3. Oscar Bert Odell, born about 1915

MAHALA MAY ODELL was born in Superior, Nuckolls County, Nebraska on February 27, 1886, the daughter of Orville B. and Rhoda Foote Odell. Mahala, also known as May, married Roy Hicks on November 9, 1904, at her home at Amos, Vernon County, Missouri. Roy Hicks was from Hume, Bates County, MO. The Hicks moved to Colorado from Missouri in the fall of 1909. The 1910 Colorado, Montrose County census shows this family. Roy was a farmer and there were two boys in the family, Basil R. Hicks, age 4 and Chester, age 1. Both boys had Missouri listed as their place of birth.

Mahala May Odell Hicks

Both the 1920 and 1930 census for Montrose County gave Roy's occupation as 'Ditch Rider' working for the U. S. Reclamation service. A ditch rider is someone who helps regulate and control the use of irrigated water to the ranchers and farmers. This was a very important job because of the drought conditions that existed at times in Colorado. The family lived on Kinikin Heights until the spring of 1937 when they moved to California Mesa, Montrose County. Mahala May Odell Hicks died on December 24, 1937, at her home on California mesa located three miles west of Olathe, Colorado. The *Montrose Daily Press* published an obituary on December 27, 1937 and a short article about the funeral on December 30, 1937. The obituary noted Mrs. Hicks had been "active in church and community work and one of the most widely known and best loved women of the community."

Services were held at Ormsbee Chapel in Montrose with the Rev. W. H. Muston of the Olathe Baptist Church in charge. "The entire front of the chapel was banked with flowers and the two rooms filled to capacity with friends of the kindly woman and her family." A quartet sang three songs; "Beautiful Isle of Somewhere", "Old Rugged Cross" and "What a Friend We have in Jesus." Interment was in Grand View cemetery.

The obituary mentioned one baby had preceded her in death; the baby's name and date of birth was not mentioned. Her surviving children were Basil of Montrose, Chester of Olathe, Mrs. Mildred Bond of Shavano Valley, Raymond and Russell, twin boys at home and Clara and Clarence, also twins at home. There were four grandchildren noted.

Mahala Odell and Roy Hicks were the parents of eight children with seven known children.

1. Basil Roy Hicks
2. Chester C. Hicks
3. Mildred M. Hicks
4. Raymond E. Hicks
5. Russell M. Hicks
6. Clara M. Hicks
7. Clarence R. Hicks

<u>VICTOR FRANCIS O'DELL</u> was born in Superior, Nuckolls County, Nebraska on October 23, 1887. Victor left home when he was about fifteen years old. He went to Sheridan, Wyoming and hired out as a brakeman on the Chicago, Burlington and Quincy Railroad. Victor came to Montana in August 1908 and was hired by the Jaw Bone Railroad as a trainman working between Lombard and Lewistown. He was promoted to work train conductor in 1909 participating in the construction of the Milwaukee Railroad to Roy, Winifred, Winnett and Great Falls.

Victor married Fannie Bob Cardwell on September 16, 1914, at Lewistown, Fergus County, Montana.

Left to right, Victor William, Victor Francis, Bobbie Glen, Woodrow Bert and Fannie Cardwell O'Dell

The 1930 Montana, Fergus County, Lewistown, District 4 shows this family that also included five children, all sons. Victor's occupation was listed as "Conductor-railroad." Victor was conductor on the Lewistown to Winnett train for many years until 1947 when he moved to Missoula, MT. He was conductor on the Olympian – Hiawatha line until his retirement in October 1952.

Victor F. O'Dell died suddenly at his home on 718 Russell Street, Whittier, CA on February 9, 1961. Local services were held at the chapel of White–Emerson Co. He was then removed for burial to Lewistown, Montana. Services were held on February 16 in Lewistown at the Creel Funeral Home. The songs "In the Sweet Bye and Bye" and "When They Ring Those Golden Bells" were featured in the service. Interment was in the Sunset Memorial Gardens.

Victor Francis O'Dell

Victor was survived by his wife Fannie of Whittier, CA and five sons; Victor William O'Dell of Centralia, Washington; Bobbie O'Dell of Lewistown, MT; Woodrow O'Dell of Oakhurst, CA; Leonard O'Dell of Lewistown, MT; and Doyal O'Dell of Urbana, IL and twelve grandchildren.

Victor F. O'Dell and Fannie Caldwell O'Dell were the parents of five children.

1. Victor William O'Dell
2. Bobbie Glenn O'Dell
3. Woodrow Bert O'Dell
4. Leonard Francis O'Dell
5. Doyal Dawson O'Dell

JAMES ROSS ODELL was born in Superior, Nuckolls County, Nebraska on December 9, 1889, the son of Orville B. and Rhoda Foote Odell. James, known to family members as Ross, married Florence Furman in Utah on July 8, 1915.

The family was located on the 1920 Montana, Gallatin County census, Three Forks precinct. James was the working as "Conductor-electric railroad." James was 30 year-old while Florence was 26 years old.

The family was found on the 1930 Washington, Cowlitz County census, Longview Township. James was working as "Conductor-Railroad." There were the two daughters recorded in the home.

James Ross Odell of 810 S. Nevada Drive, Longview, Washington died at a local hospital on July 27, 1953. An obituary found in the *Longview Daily News* dated 28 July 1953 stated he had worked for the Milwaukee Railroad on the Rocky Mountain division from 1910 until 1923. After that he came to Longview and joined the Longview, Portland and Northern Railroad. He was a yard master. He was a member of the Masonic Lodge at Three Forks, Montana and a member of the Brotherhood of Trainmen. He was survived by his wife Florence and two children Miss Phyllis R. L. Odell of Centralis and Mrs. Beverley R. Luhrs of Seattle and six grandchildren. He was interred in the Kelso IOOF Cemetery.

There were two known children of this family.

1. Phyllis L. Odell, born about 1917
2. Beverly Odell, born about 1920

SELDEN JAY ODELL was born in Superior, Nuckolls County, Nebraska on March 29, 1892, the son of Orville B. and Rhoda Foote Odell. The 1920 Montana, Lewis and Clark County, census shows Selden living with his younger brother Orange B. Odell. Both Selden and Orange were working as "laborers-general farm."

Selden never married and moved to Chicago where he became an electrician, date and time unknown. Selden was not found on the 1930 Illinois, Cook County census, but living the life of a single man he could have been easily missed. It is quite possible that Selden and his brother Ira were close and may have worked together as Ira was an electrical contractor in Chicago. On February 22, 1946, S. J. Odell, undoubtedly Selden, was recorded attending the Chicago funeral of his sister-in-law Johanna Schultz Odell.

During the time Selden lived in Chicago, he developed a close relationship with his nephew Stewart Odell, Ira Odell's son. In July 1953 when his brother James Odell died, Selden was noticed as living in Chicago. In June 1858 when his brother Irvin O'Dell died, he was living in Downers Grove, IL.

Eventually, because of failing health, Selden moved to Arizona where he lived with his sister Ada. When Uncle Selden passed away in Phoenix, Arizona on January 15, 1962, his nephew Stewart Odell flew from Chicago to attend the funeral. An obituary for Selden appeared in *The Arizona Republic* on January 18, 1962. It stated he had moved to Coolidge, AZ to live with his sister three years before his death. He was a retired electrician from Chicago. Services were held in the Church of Jesus Christ of Latter-Day Saints. He was buried in the Valley Memorial Park in Coolidge, AZ.

ADA CATHERINE ODELL was born in Superior, Nuckolls County, Nebraska on December 13, 1893, the daughter of Orville B. and Rhoda Foote Odell. Ada was reared in California and came to Lewistown, Montana in 1913. She eventually moved to Great Falls, MT.

Ada married Harry V. Miller on June 20, 1915, in Great Falls, Cascade County, Montana. This family was found on the 1920 Montana, Powell County census, Lincoln Township. Ada was 26 years old and Harry was 29. His occupation was listed as "General-Farm." There were three children in the home plus an adopted daughter named Josephine Miller.

Ada Catherine Odell Miller

The family moved into Great Falls from the wheat farm they had been operating located north of Great Falls in 1924. The 1930 Montana, Cascade County, Great Falls, census enumerates this family. Josephine Miller was no longer in the home, but the three other children from the 1920 census were. Harry Miller was then working as a mechanic, farm machinery.

The May 1954 obituary for Orange B. O'Dell states his sister Ada was then living in Great Falls, MT. The June 1958 obituary of her brother Irvin O'Dell states she was still living in Great Falls. When her brother Selden J. Odell died in Phoenix, AZ in January 1962, his obituary noted he had been living with Ada at nearby Coolidge, AZ. Ada died only four short months later in Fullerton, California, the last surviving child of Orville B. and Rhoda Odell ending nearly one hundred years of that family's history.

Ada Odell Miller died on Monday, April 29,1962, in Fullerton, CA. She had been hospitalized for three weeks after suffering a paralytic stroke. Funeral services were held in Great Falls with the Croxford Mortuary in charge. An article about Mrs. Miller appeared in the May 1, 1962 issue of the *Great Falls Tribune*. It noted she had worked for the paper in the composing room for fourteen years. She had retired in 1960 and was an active member of the Church of Jesus Christ of Latter-Day Saints.

Ada was survived by her husband and four children; Mrs. R. H. Ostergren of Fullerton, CA, Mrs. Harold Sewell of Helena, MT, Glenn P. Miller of Fullerton, CA and Harry V. Miller of Great Falls, MT.

Ada Odell and Harry V. Miller were the parents of four known children and one adopted child.

1. Sylvia M. Miller, born about 1910
2. Harry Miller, born about 1916
3. Evelyn M. Miller, born about 1917
4. Glenn P. Miller, not found on any census

IRVIN McCLAIN O'DELL was born in Amos, MO on July 30, 1896, the son of Orville B. and Rhoda Foote Odell. Irvin married Jessie Alice Graham on September 23, 1918, time and place yet unknown.

This family was found on the 1920 Montana, Powell County census, Deer Lodge City precinct. Irvin was working as a "car inspector-railroad. He was 23 and Jessie was 29. There was one child in the home, an eleven year-old step-daughter named Patricia O'Dell. The 1930 Montana, Powell County census, Deer Lodge, enumerates this family. Irvin was working as a "machinist-garage." There were two boys in the home, LeRoi, born about 1921 and Jackie, born about 1927.

Irvin "Pat" M. O'Dell of Silver Lake, WA died on June 27, 1958, in the Longview Hospital, Longview, Washington. An obituary dated Friday, June 27, 1958, found in the *Longview Daily News* states he had lived in the Silver Lake area for ten years coming there from Bremerton. He was a member of the Fraternal Order of Eagles and of Plumbers Union Local 695. He was survived by two sons, LeRoi of Woodruff, SC and Jack of Greenacres and four grandchildren. Services were held at Hubbard Funeral Home at Castle Rock. Internment was to be in Whittier cemetery (California or Washington-unkown).

As of the 1930 census there were two children in this family, their names are found listed below.

1. LeRoi O'Dell, (m) born about 1921
2. Jack (probably John) O'Dell, (m) born about 1927

ORANGE BERT O'DELL was born in Superior, Nuckolls County, Nebraska on December 28, 1899, the son of Orville B. and Rhoda Foote Odell. Orange married Marion A. Spratt on December 30, 1919. This family was found on the 1920 Montana, Lewis and Clark County census living in School District # 28, Lincoln. Orange's brother Selden was also living within this family enumeration. Both Orange and his brother Selden were working as "laborers-general farm."

The 1930 Montana, Sweet Grass County census, Big Timber-District 1, shows this family. They appear to be living in and working at a hotel in Big Timber managed by Orange's wife's former father-in-law G. R. Amsberry. Orange was working as a clerk for the hotel and his wife was working there as a chambermaid. There were two children in the enumeration at that time, their names are listed below.

Orange B. O'Dell died suddenly of a heart attack at his home in Big Timber on May 15, 1954. He was at the time having dinner with friends and family. He had complained of slight chest pains several days before the attack. The May 20, 1954, issue of *The Big Timber Pioneer* featured a front page article about O. B. O'Dell. It stated he had attended school in California and Lewistown. He moved to Lincoln, MT in 1920, and later to Sweet Grass County, ranching at Glasston. Later he was for a time part owner of the Cort Hotel in Big Timber.

In recent years Mr. O'Dell was a livestock buyer traveling throughout Montana, Idaho, Wyoming and Alberta, Canada. For the past four years he had been employed as a buyer by the Western Livestock Producers Assn. in Billings. He was survived by his wife Mrs. Marion O'Dell and four sons; Kenneth O'Dell of Helena, Harold O'Dell of Lewistown and Donald and Richard O'Dell of Big Timber.

Services were conducted from the Congregational Church followed with burial in Mountain View cemetery. Services included music with pallbearers and honorary pallbearers in attendance.

Orange Bert O'Dell and Marion Spratt O'Dell were the parents of four known children.

1. Kenneth N. O'Dell, age 7 in 1930
2. Harold P. O'Dell, age 5 in 1930
3. Donald O'Dell
4. Richard O'Dell

.

THE JOHANN SCHULTZ FAMILY

The only information about this family from a descendant comes from the great-granddaughter of Johann Schultz Odell, Priscilla W. McCloud. The Johann Schultz family, according to this source, was a member of an extended family from Germany who came to the United States in 1871. Following their arrival, the family settled in Detroit, Michigan. Part of this extended family after they had been living in this country for a while decided not to stay, so they returned to Germany. Johann Schultz and his wife Albertine Schultz are the only known members of this extended family.

The research effort on this family has been primarily the work of Cheryl A. Helm, the daughter of Priscilla W. McCloud. The public documents associated with this family have been found to offer different spellings for Johann's given name, Johann in German and John in English. The surname Schultz was also found written as Schulz. The name was, eventually, written as Schultz by all later family members.

One written source of family information has survived. A small devotional book entitled *Christian Forget Me Not* was given by Ida Schultz to her sister Johanna Schultz in 1904. Written on the second page of this book are the words "Merry Christmas, To Jo from Ida, New York, Dec. 25/04." This little book contains the handwriting of three generations, Johanna Schultz Odell, her daughter Winona Ruth Odell Whitehead and her granddaughter Priscilla Ruth Whitehead McCloud. It records the day of births for family members and close friends but, unfortunately, not always the year.

JOHANN SCHULTZ was born on January 11, 1843. He was christened on January 22, 1843, in Minkhaus, Pommern, Pruessen. Johann Schultz married Albertine Marie Kersten on March 18, 1870, in Mickrow, Pommern, Pruessen. Albertine Marie Kersten was born on January 21, 1847, and christened the same day at Of Wolfnogge, Pommern, Preussen. Albertine in German is pronounced "Albertina." The German letter 'e' has the sound of 'ah.' That is why her name is recorded on her children's documents as 'Albertina,' while on some public records it was written Albertine.

Pommern, Pruessen in English is Pomerania, Prussia. Pomerania was one of thirteen provinces of the Kingdom of Prussia whose capitol was Berlin. The province borders the Baltic Sea and at one time in its history was part of Sweden. The Germanic language spoken by these people was more like the Dutch language than the High German spoken by most other Prussians. Following the end of World War II, most of Pomerania was made part of Poland. The mostly Protestant inhabitants of the area were removed and those who could not flee to West Germany became part of the Communist East German society. The community of Mickrow became Mikorowo, Poland. The communities of Minkhaus and Of Wolffnogge have disappeared.

Research has found the record of Johann Schultz, Albertine Schultz and an infant Emma Schultz arriving at the Port of New York on April 18, 1872. They arrived on the ship, the *S. S. Hermann,* from the German port of Bremen. Johann's occupation was recorded as

"Joiner." A joiner is a wood worker usually associated with making furniture. Johann was 29 years old and Albertine's age was given as 25.

Left to right, Emma Marie Schultz, Albertine Kersten Schultz, Bertha Klara Schultz, Johann Schultz and Louise Schultz

The Johann Schultz family arrived in New York years before the Statue of Liberty was erected. The statue was dedicated on October 28, 1886, some fourteen years after they arrived in this country. The family did not arrive at the famous immigrant port of Ellis Island in New York harbor. The immigrant epoch of Ellis Island was from 1892 until 1924. The Schultz family went through what immigration procedures there were at the time at the New York Port Authority. It does appear that the only information recorded at the time of their arrival in this country for immigration was the ship's manifest or passenger list.

After arriving in the U. S., the family settled in Detroit, Michigan. There is every reason to believe the family lived in a largely German speaking community in Detroit. At that time Detroit had a large German speaking population sufficient enough to support a German language newspaper called the *Volksblatt*. The Schultz children were known to speak German until they started school where they began to learn English.

There were small scraps of the Schultz family history found in the public documents associated with the lives and deaths of their children. The names of John (sic) and Albertine Schultz were found on the 1942 Illinois death certificate of their daughter Louise Schultz Hudenburg. Their place of origin was noted on the 1930 Illinois, Cook County census of their daughter Ida Schultz Hammond, who gave both of her parent's country of origin as "Germany-Berlin." Another daughter Emma Schultz Klix's death certificate dated April 11, 1964, from Wayne County, MI recorded her parent's names as Johann Schultz and Marie Kersten.

The fact that Johann Schultz and Albertine Kersten were married in Germany came from the 1930 Michigan, Wayne County census information of their daughter, Emma Schultz Klix. Emma recorded her place of birth and that of her parents as Germany and that they had immigrated to the United States in 1871, which was also the year of her birth. This means she came to this country as an infant. She further stated she had been naturalized but did not record the date of that naturalization. It seems highly probable, since she was a minor, she and her parents may have been naturalized at the same time. Wayne County records have been searched for their naturalization without success. Existing Federal records, which may be incomplete, have also been searched, and nothing found. Immigration and naturalization procedures appear to have been loosely screened and records poorly kept at this time in U. S. history.

Priscilla W. McCloud has a photograph of the Schultz family that was taken when there were only three children in the family. This photograph shows the parents Johann and Albertine Schultz with their three children who had to be Emma, the oldest, Louise, the second oldest and Bertha, the baby. This photograph has to be dated sometime after June 30, 1877, because that was the date of Bertha's birth and since she is clearly shown easily setting up, therefore, it seems probable that it was taken either in late 1877 or early in 1878.

The 1880 Michigan, Wayne County census, Detroit City, District 315, page 614, list this family. The name was recorded under the spelling of Schulz. John (sic) Schulz was a 37 year old Carpenter from Germany. His wife was Albertine Schulz who was 32 and also from Germany. This fact is interesting because John (sic) and Albertine's son Albert gave this version of the name on the 1920 Illinois, Cook County census when he was living with his sister Louise Schultz Hudenburg.

There are, however, three glaring problems with this family listing on this census. The first problem is that the oldest daughter, Emma, was listed as being born in Michigan, not Germany. The second problem is that the second child's name looks almost like Elizabeth, but certainly not Louise. The third child listed was Bertha which is correct. The ages of the children were 8, 5 and 2, which are about right for the children's known ages. The third problem has to do with the fact that Johanna Schultz was not recorded on the census. Family records state she was born in 1879 and she should have been recorded on that census but was not.

There is an 1890 Detroit City Directory and the only Albertine Schultz recorded was the widow of Julius Schultz. There were many John Schultz and John Schulz listed, but there were no points of delineation, so the directory was of no help.

On May 14, 1893, Johann Schulz purchased six grave lots for $32.00 at The Trinity Lutheran Church Cemetery, 5210 Mt. Elliott, Detroit, MI. The deed for the six lots was issued on June 9, 1893. These lots may have been purchased in the name of Johann

Schultz because he may have been the first to need a grave site. Albertine Schultz died on February 2, 1897 and was buried in the family section there.

Albertine Kersten Schultz and Johann Schultz

William Klix, Albertine Schultz's son-in-law, was buried in the Schultz family section on about July 23, 1926. Emma Schultz Klix, William Klix's wife, was buried there on April 15, 1964. Two of Emma's children, Laura Klix and Stanley Klix, purchased two lots from the Johann Schultz estate, on May 21, 1964. This was about one month after the death of their mother Emma Schultz Klix in 1964. Stanley Klix was buried there about February 24, 1970 and Laura A. Klix was buried there about May 12, 1977. There is one remaining grave where no information was noted in the records. This is, most likely, the grave of Johann Schultz, who would have been buried there when the lots were first purchased on May 14, 1893.

It is not surprising to find the Schultz family buried in a Lutheran cemetery. Most Protestant Germans from the time frame of Johann and Albertine Schulz were Lutheran. The area where the Trinity Lutheran Cemetery is located is in what is now considered part of the urban blight of Detroit. The cemetery is situated about a mile or a mile and a half from the church. Surrounded by a heavy wrought iron fence, the cemetery has many lovely old stately hard wood trees that offer the grounds an impression of a tranquil setting. The stones of the cemetery have primarily German names carved on them, indicative of the community that formerly existed there over a hundred years ago. The Trinity Lutheran Church is still there but the church sold off the cemetery about twenty years ago and it is now under private management.

One final rhetorical question about this family needs to be asked. Why did all the children except Emma move to Chicago very soon after their mother's death in 1897?

Emma Schultz had married William Klix in Detroit on April 11, 1891 and made Detroit her home. Bertha Schultz married John W. Nelson in Detroit on April 14, 1898, and then, shortly thereafter, moved to Chicago. Her son Stanley A. Nelson was born in Chicago on September 19, 1899. Bertha and her son Stanley along with her brother Albert H. Schultz were found on the 1900 Chicago census. Louise Schultz married William Hudenburg in Chicago on July 3, 1900. Taking into consideration that it took time for a courtship to develop, then, Louise had to have been in Chicago a bit before she was married. Johanna Schultz was also found on the 1900 Chicago census, as was Ida Schultz, both living independent lives. If this was not a mass family migration it certainly has to be close to the definition of one.

Johann and Albertine Schultz were the parents of nine known children. Five of these nine children are buried in the Mount Greenwood Cemetery in Chicago, IL. The eldest child, Emma, is buried with her parents in Trinity Lutheran Cemetery in Detroit, MI.

1. Emma Marie Schultz
2. Louise Schultz
3. Emilia Augusta Schultz, born December 12, 1874, died December 19, 1875
4. Bertha Klara Schultz
5. Johanna Wilhemina Schultz
6. Klara A. W. Schultz, born January 13, 1882, died January 4, 1895
7. Ida E. Schultz
8. Albert Herman Schultz
9. Wilhelm Schultz, born July 14, 1890, died December 8, 1890

EMMA MARIE SCHULTZ was born in Of Minkhaus, Prussia on January 7, 1871, the daughter of Johann and Albertine Schultz. Emma was a baby when she and her parents immigrated to the United States in April 1872. She did become a naturalized citizen, date unknown.

Emma married William Charles Klix on April 11, 1891, in Detroit, Michigan, probably at the Trinity Lutheran Church. Their marriage license stated he was the son of August Klix and she was the daughter of John Schultz. He was 21 while she was 20. The bride and groom's mother's names on the marriage license were stated as "not given." Martha Klix was the witness for the groom and Johanna Schultz was the witness for her sister. They were married by the Minister J. A. Huegli of the Trinity Lutheran Church. Johannes Adam Huegli had been the minister at Trinity since 1860. He served the church for some 42 years, retiring in May 1902.

Emma Klix and William C. Klix were found on the 1890 Detroit City Directory boarding at the home of William's father, August A. Klix, on 464 Brewster. August A. Klix was a tailor; Emma Klix's occupation was a "tailoress," while William's occupation was that of a finisher.

The 1900 Wayne County, Michigan census, Detroit City shows this young family. The family was living on Scott Street and William, who was born about the year 1870, was working as a "wood finisher." They were both recorded as being born in Germany and had been married nine years with three of their four children still living.

The Klix family was found on the 1920 Michigan census, Wayne County, living in Ward 9, Detroit City on Dubois Street. William was working as a finisher in a factory. Emma did not work and was listed as a wife. There were six children in the home, all born in Michigan.

William C. Klix died on July 23, 1926. He was buried in the Schultz family section of Trinity Lutheran Church Cemetery. The church eventually sold the cemetery and it is now known as the Trinity Lutheran Cemetery.

The Klix family was found on the 1930 Michigan census, Wayne County, living in District 828. Emma Klix was listed as head of household. There were still four children in the home at this enumeration, Laura, age 38, who worked as a machine operator in an overall factory; Harry, age 24, a foreman in civil service; Stanley, age 24, a clerk in a jobbing shop and Russel, age 22, a mechanic in civil service. The census records noted Emma owned her home.

Emma Schultz Klix died at her home on 12122 Whithorn Ave., Detroit, MI of a coronary occlusion on April 11, 1964. She was 93 years old. The informant for her death certificate was her son Stanley Klix of the same address as his mother. Emma was buried on April 15 in the Schultz family section of Trinity Lutheran Cemetery, Detroit, MI between her mother and her husband. A death notice for her appeared in the *Detroit Free Press* on April 13, 1964. The notice stated, "Emma M. Wife of the late William C.; dear mother of Laura, Mrs. Elsie Fisher, Mrs. Esther Benignus, Harry, Mrs. Mable McKirdy and Stanley." Three grandchildren and 11 great-grandchildren were noted as was her sister Ida Hammond. The A. H. Peters Funeral Home, 12057 Gratiot Ave., officiated at the services.

Emma Schultz and William Klix were the parents of eight known children

1. Laura Alberta Klix
2. Elsie M. Klix
3. Lizzie Klix born April 18, 1896 and died April 18, 1896
4. Esther Helen Klix,
4. Harry William Klix
5. Mabel Ethel Klix
6. Stanley Herman Klix
7. Russel Charles Klix, born about 1908, last record 1930 census

LAURA ALBERTA KLIX was born at Detroit, MI on February 19, 1892, the daughter of William Charles Klix and Emma Schultz Klix. Laura never married. She was found with her parents on the 1920 Michigan, Wayne County, Detroit City census. She was working as a "sticher" in a factory. The 1930 Michigan, Wayne County, Detroit City census shows Laura still within her mother's home. She was working as a machine operator in an overall factory.

Laura enrolled for Social Security on December 1, 1936. Her address at that time was 12122 Whitmore, Detroit, MI. She was then working for W. M. Fink & Co.

On May 21, 1964, Laura and her brother Stanley Klix purchased two lots at Trinity Lutheran Cemetery from the Johann Schultz estate.

Laura A. Klix died May 12, 1977. A death notice for her was found in the *Detroit Free Press* dated May 13, 1977. The notice mentioned her sisters Esther H. Benignus and Mable McKirdy. Services were handled by the A. H. Peters Funeral Home. Laura A. Klix was buried in the Schultz family section of Trinity Lutheran Cemetery.

ELSIE M. KLIX was born at Detroit, MI on January 26, 1894, the daughter of William Klix and Emma Schulz. Elsie was living with her parents for the 1920 Michigan, Wayne County census. She was working at a factory as a box poster. It appears she married Norman Fischer about the year1923. This family was found enumerated next to her sisters Esther Benignus and Mabel McCurdy (sic) on the 1930 Michigan Wayne County, Detroit City census. There were no children listed and her husband Norman Fisher (sic) was listed as a part owner of a tool factory.

Elsie Fischer was noted in the death notice of her mother in April 1964. However, she was not mentioned in the 1977 death notice of her sister Laura A. Klix. It can be assumed that she was deceased by this time. In fact, if this is the right person, Elsie Fischer died in August 1972, from SS death records, Ancestry.com. She was last living at 49267 Ottawa Lake, Monroe, MI.

ESTHER HELEN KLIX was born in Detroit, MI on July 2, 1897, the daughter of William Klix and Emma Schulz Klix. Esther was married to Carl August Benignus about the year 1917.

The 1930 Michigan, Wayne County, Detroit City (Districts 751-879, actual District 824) census shows this family. There was one child, a daughter named Jean Benignus who was born on September 25, 1925, in the home who was 4 1/2 years old. Carl Benignus was a conductor for the city railroad. Esther was enumerated just above the listing of her sisters Elsie Fisher (sic) and Mabel McKirdy.

Esther Benignus was mentioned in the May 13, 1977, death notice for her sister Laura Klix. A SS death record found on Ancestry.com states Esther Benignus died in January 1985. Her address at the time of her death was 48225 Harper Woods.

Esther was the parent of one known child.

1. Jeanne Ruth Benignus, married Robert Brooks Taliaferro

HARRY WILLIAM KLIX was born in Detroit, MI on February 9, 1901, the son of William Klix and Emma Schultz Klix. Harry was found on the 1900 Michigan census living within his family. He was noted as a laborer working for the city.

The 1930 Michigan, Wayne County, Detroit City, census shows Harry still within his family home. He was a foreman in civil service.

On August 20, 1956, Harry filed for Social Security giving his address as 15400 Promenade, Detroit, Mich. He was working for the City of Detroit at that time.

Harry Klix died September 11, 1971. A brief death notice appeared in the *Detroit Free Press* on September 12, 1971. He was noted as the "beloved husband of Angeline." No children were mentioned. Services were handled by the A. H. Peters Funeral Home. Harry was buried at Forrest Lawn Cemetery, Detroit, MI.

MABEL ETHEL KLIX was born at Detroit, MI on January 8, 1904, the daughter of William Klix and Emma Schultz Klix. For the 1920 Michigan, Wayne County, Detroit City census, Mabel was living within her parent's family and working as a cashier in a department store.

Mabel married Stanley McKirdy about the year 1928. This couple was found for the 1930 Michigan, Wayne County, Detroit City census living in the home of her sister and her husband, Norman and Elsie Fisher. Stanley was then working as a wire maker in a wire cage factory. There were no children listed.

Mabel was mentioned in the May 13, 1977, death notice for her sister Laura Klix. A SS death notice from Ancestry.com states Mabel McKirdy died in April 1985. Her last benefit address was 48213 Detroit, Wayne MI.

STANLEY HERMAN KLIX was born in Detroit, MI, on February 16, 1906, the son of William Charles Klix and Emma Schultz Klix.

On December 3, 1936, Stanley enrolled for Social Security giving his address as 12122 Whithorn Ave. Detroit, Mich. At that time, he was working for Arrow Tool and Reamer Co. on 418 Livernois Avenue, Detroit.

Stanley H. Klix died on February 24, 1970. He was buried in the Schultz family section at the Trinity Lutheran Cemetery, Detroit, MI.

LOUISE SCHULTZ was born in Detroit, MI, on December 12, 1874, the daughter of Johann and Albertine Schultz. Louise had a twin sister named Emilia Augusta Schultz. Emilia died on December 19, 1875.

Louise married William Hudenburg in Chicago, IL on July 3, 1900. William was 48 years old while Louise was 30. William was born in Germany on February 2, 1852.

Information gained from census information stated he emigrated to the U. S. in 1855 and was naturalized in 1875.

The Hudenburg family was found on the 1920 Illinois, Cook County census in the 31st Ward. William was 67 years old and noted on the census as a Teamster. Louise was listed as a 45 year old wife. There was one child in the home named Roy who was 15 years old. There one additional person within the home and this was Albert Schulz (sic), who was Louise's brother. Albert was 33 years old and worked as an electrician in a store, probably the store of his brother-in-law, Ira N. Odell.

William Hudenburg died at what appears to be his residence on 6305 Racine Ave., in Chicago, IL, on June 6, 1923. He was buried in Mount Greenwood Cemetery, Chicago, IL. There was no death notice found for William in the Chicago newspapers. It appears that at the time the cemetery lot was purchased for William, a whole section containing eight graves lots were purchased which also included a lot for Louise's brother Albert H. Schultz.

The 1930 Illinois, Cook County, census list this family in District 205 and living on East 92 Street Avenue. Louise was head of household. Roy Hudenburg, age 25, was still in the home and his occupation was given as "Editor - Paper." Louise's brother Albert Schultz was also in the home and his occupation was given as "Electrician - Building."

Louise Hudenburg along with Roy Hudenburg and Catherine Hudenburg attended the wedding of her niece Winona Ruth Odell at Chicago, IL on January 1, 1934, to Dr. William B. Whitehead. Albert H. Schultz was also in attendance as was Bertha Van Dyk, Mr. and Mrs. Stanley A. Van Dyk, Joyce Van Dyk and Jay Van Dyk, all members of the Schultz family.

Louise Schultz Hudenburg died January 15, 1942, of what was termed "Bronchitis" and "Complete Dilation of heart." There was a death notice for her in the Chicago Tribune dated January 17, 1942. It mentioned that she was the loving mother of Roy and the fond grandmother of Don and Margaret. Services were held at the First Church of the Nazarene on 64th and Eggleston, Chicago. She was buried at Mount Greenwood Cemetery, Chicago, IL. A death certificate for Louise shows she was living at 727 East 92 Street at the time of her death and that she owned her own home. There are still, at this date, four grave plots open at Mount Greenwood Cemetery that the descendants of the Hudenburg family still own.

Louise and William Hudenburg were the parents of one known child.

1. Roy Paul Hudenburg

ROY PAUL HUDENBURG was born in Illinois on June 4, 1904, the son and the only known child of Louise Schultz and William Hudenburg. He was given the name of Percival Roy Hudenburg but was always known as Roy. Roy was still residing in the home of his mother for the 1930 Illinois, Cook County census. He was 25 years old and his occupation was "Editor - Paper."

Roy married Catherine McHugh on May 4, 1933. Catherine McHugh is the daughter of Mr. and Mrs. Edward McHugh formerly of Sioux Falls, Iowa. At the time of the marriage Catherine worked for THE TRIBUNE in the promotion department as editor of The Trib, a magazine of THE TRIBUNE.

Roy Hudenburg and Catherine Hudenburg along with his mother Louise and other Schultz family members attended the January 1, 1934, Chicago wedding of his cousin Winona Ruth Odell to Dr. William B. Whitehead.

Roy Hudenburg along with Harvey Grund, Charles Hammond, Richard Needles, Walter Eichenberger and Paul Ashby were bearers at the Chicago funeral of his aunt Johanna Schultz Odell on February 22, 1946. Mrs. Roy Hudenburg along with Albert H. Schultz, Mrs. Stanley Van Dyk and Eleanor Grund were also in attendance at the funeral.

Catherine McHugh Hudenburg died on June 26, 1973 in Scarsdale, New York and is buried in Mount Pleasant, New York.

Roy signed over a lot in Mount Greenwood Cemetery to Harvey Grund, the husband of his cousin Eleanor Hammond Grund for her burial, on August 18, 1984. Roy was at that time, according to information on the cemetery records, living in Richmond, VA.

Information found in the Social Security death records state Roy Hudenburg died in Richmond, VA on October 6, 1989. Information noted on his death certificate gives his wife's name as Mrs. Suzie McHugh Hudenburg. His occupation was noted as "retired consultant for York and Sawyer in New York." He was interred at the Mount Calvary Cemetery.

Roy and Catherine were the parents of two children.

1. Donald P. Hudenburg
2. Margaret Hudenburg

BERTHA KLARA SCHULTZ was born in Detroit, MI on June 30, 1877, the daughter of Johann and Albertine Schultz. Bertha married John Warwick Nelson in Detroit, MI on April 14, 1898. John was born in England about 1863, the son of John Nelson and Sarah Worswick. Bertha K. Schultz's parents were given on the marriage license as John Schultz and Christina Kerstaen. They were married by the Pastor Charles Haass. The witness for John was William Klix and the witness for Bertha was Emma Haass.

Bertha was found on the 1900 Illinois, Cook County census living in Chicago. She was listed as Bertha Nilson (sic) and there was one child recorded, a son named Stanley A. Nilson (sic). Also listed in this home was her 12-year-old brother Albert Schultz. A Delayed Certificate of Birth dated August 26, 1946, for Cook County, IL has been found.

It states that Stanley Albert Nelson was born in Cook County on September 19, 1899. His parents were John Warwick Nelson and Bertha Clara Schultz. The document was signed by Stanley's uncle Albert Herman Schultz.

Bertha Nelson married Sebo Van Dyk on May 16, 1902 in Chicago, IL. Sebo Van Dyk was born in Holland about the year 1851. He immigrated to this country in 1882 and was nationalized in 1885, time and place unknown.

This family was found on the 1920 Cook County, IL census living on West 69th Street. Sebo was a 69-year-old repairman who worked for the city railroad. Bertha was 42 and a housewife. The only child recorded on this enumeration was Stanley Van Dyk, who was twenty years old and was working as a salesman in a department store.

Sebo Van Dyk died at his home in Chicago, IL on November 1, 1922. He was buried on November 4, at the Forest Home cemetery. He was buried in the Biel Family section of the cemetery next to someone named Jeanette Biel Van Dyk, 1890 – 1914. Sebo's occupation on his death certificate was given as 'Mechanic' and he was working at the Chicago Surface Lines. The family's address at the time of his death was 1140, W 68th Street. Stanley A. Van Dyk, who was the informant for the death certificate, gave that same address as his own.

Bertha Van Dyk, Mr. and Mrs. Stanley A. Van Dyk, Joyce Van Dyk and Jay Van Dyk attended the January 1, 1934, Chicago, IL wedding of Bertha's niece Winona Ruth Odell to Dr. William B. Whitehead. Albert H. Schultz, Louise Hudenburg, Roy Hudenburg and Catherine Hudenburg were other members of the Schultz family in attendance at the wedding.

Bertha Schultz Van Dyk died of "Carcinoma of Breast" and "Chronic Myocarditis" on April 19, 1944. Her death certificate states she was living at 1140 W. 68th Street, Chicago, IL at the time of her death. She was buried in the Mount Greenwood Cemetery, Chicago, IL, in one of the Hudenburg's grave sites. At the time of Bertha's death, her son Stanley was living in Chicago on 6945 Oglesby Ave., and there was no mention of any grandchildren.

1. Stanley Albert Van Dyk

STANLEY ALBERT VAN DYK was born Stanley Albert Nelson in Chicago, Cook County, IL on September 19, 1899, the son of John Warwick Nelson and Bertha Klara Schultz. No additional information about Stanley's father has been found.

Following his mother's marriage to Sebo Van Dyk on May 15, 1902; Stanley assumed his stepfather's surname. A Delayed Certificate of Birth for Stanley dated August 26, 1946, has been found that gives his name as Stanley Albert Nelson. The document was signed by Stanley's uncle Albert Herman Schultz. Information on this document states that at the time of Stanley's birth his father was working as a Real Estate Salesman.

Stanley was found with his parents on the 1920 Cook County census. He was working as a salesman in a department store at the time.

Stanley A. Van Dyk married Minnie Isabelle Evemeyer on October 19, 1920 in Chicago, Illinois. Minnie was born on August 3, 1900 in Beardstown, Illinois, the daughter of Henry Fred Evemeyer and Ella Louise Koch Evemeyer.

Stanley Albert Van Dyk and Minnie Isabelle Evemeyer Van Dyk

The family was found on the 1930 Cook County, IL census living on South Sangamon Street. Stanley was 30 years old working as a cashier in a bank. Minnie was 29 years old and a housewife with one child in the home Joyce M. Van Dyk aged 3. Also, in the home was his sister-in-law Frances Herbert aged 22 years old.

Mr. and Mrs. Stanley Van Dyk attended the January 1, 1934, Chicago wedding of his cousin Winona Ruth Odell to Dr. William B. Whitehead along with his mother and other Schultz family members. The names of Joyce Van Dyk and Jay Van Dyk, the children of Stanley, were also recorded in the bride's 'Wedding Memories' book.

Mrs. Stanley Van Dyk attended the February 22, 1946, Chicago funeral of Johanna Schultz Odell. Stanley's name was not recorded in the Memorial Record of the funeral.

An obituary article found in the Tuesday, September 14, 1976 issue of *The Miami Herald* giving notice of the death of Stanley A. Van Dyk. Stanley died at his home on 4410 San Amaro Drive, Coral Gables, FL on September 13, 1976. The article stated he was chairman of the board of S. A. Van Dyk Inc., an insurance firm in Chicago. He had stepped down as president of the firm when he moved permanently to Florida in 1968. He was survived by his wife Minna Evemeyer Van Dyk and two children and five grandchildren. Stanley was cremated at the Van Orsdel Crematory in Miami, FL.

Stanley's daughter Joyce Dieffenderfer was noted in the article about her father's death as the Dade County Election Supervisor and residence of Coral Gables, FL. His son Jay was noted as a residence of Chicago, IL.

Minnie Van Dyk died on March 15, 1990 in Dade, Florida.

Stanley A. and Minnie Van Dyk were the parents of two known children.

1. Joyce Van Dyk died December 29, 1980, Dade, FL
2. Jay Stanley Van Dyk died January 20, 1985, Chicago, IL

JOHANNA WILHEMINA SCHULTZ was born on August 13, 1879, in Detroit, Michigan, the daughter of Johann and Albertine Schultz. A wonderful story passed on by Johanna's daughter Winona Odell Whitehead relates that during the festive evening when Johanna was christened, conviviality was so great she was given the name of Johanna Wilhemina Henrietta Augusta Louisa Schultz. Some validity is given to this story because the christening name for Johanna was found recorded as "Johanna A. H. L. Schultz." She was christened on August 30, 1879. Thankfully, however, she signed her name simply as Johanna W. Schultz.

Johanna Wilhemina Schultz

Johanna was witness to the marriage of her sister Emma Schultz to William Klix in Detroit on April 11, 1891. She was probably living at home with her mother Albertine Schultz until she passed away on February 2, 1897.

There is information that suggests Johanna Schultz was living in Chicago by the time of the 1900 Illinois, Cook County census. The census records relate that this Johanna

Schultz was 22 years old and had been born in Michigan in July 1879, which fits our Johanna perfectly. She was a boarder living in the home of Samuel and Harriet Beery in Hyde Park. Her occupation was "Clerk-Bakery."

Johanna W. Schultz eventually went to work for the Salvation Army, and it was during this time she met her future husband. Johanna W. Schultz married Ira N. Odell in a Salvation Army ceremony on February 6, 1906, in Chicago, IL.

Johanna Schultz Odell died at the home of her daughter Winona Odell Whitehead in Fayetteville, NC on February 22, 1946. She was buried beside her husband Ira N. Odell in Mount Greenwood Cemetery, Chicago, IL. Four of Johanna's siblings are also buried nearby in the Greenwood Cemetery. See Ira N. Odell, page 164, for more information about this family.

IDA E. SCHULTZ was born in Detroit, MI on June 11, 1884, the daughter of Johann and Albertine Schultz. Ida married Charles C. Hammond on January 14, 1914, in Chicago, IL. Charles was born on October 24, 1894, at Rouses Point, Clinton, NY, the son of Charlotte and Frederick J. Hammond.

This family was found on the 1920 Cook County, IL, census living in Hyde Park, Kenwood Ave. Charles was 28 years old and worked as chief engineer at a hotel. This undoubtedly had to do with the boiler system and furnace at the hotel. Ida was a 30 year old housewife. There were two children in the home at that time, Eleanor, age 4 7/12 and Charlotte, age 8/12. The family rented their home.

The 1930 Illinois, Cook County, census shows this family still living on Kenwood Avenue, property which they rented. Charles was then working as a "Stationary Engineer" at a grain elevator. There were two children in the home, Eleanor, age 14 and Chas. C., age 5. It appears that Charlotte had passed away sometime between 1920 and 1930. On this census, Ida stated both her father and mother were from "Germany-Berlin."

On both the 1920 and the 1930 census Charles and Ida were enumerated next to his parents Frederick J. Hammond and Charlotte R. Hammond. Frederick J. Hammond did the same kind of work as his son.

Charles C. Hammond, who was a little over 50 years of age, died on December 7, 1945. He was buried in Mount Greenwood Cemetery in Chicago, IL. A death notice for Charles appeared in the Chicago Tribune on December 9, 1945. The notice stated he lived on 8407 S. 79th Avenue. Three children were mentioned, Mrs. Eleanor Grund, Charles F. Hammond and the late Charlotte Hammond. A brother George W. Hammond was also mentioned. Charles was buried in Mount Greenwood Cemetery in a lot purchased by Ida Hammond very near the lots belonging to the Hudenburgs'.

Ida died of acute myocardial infarction on January 15, 1971. She was buried in the Mount Greenwood Cemetery, Chicago, IL. No notice of death for Ida was found in the Chicago newspapers. Ida and Charles were the parents of three known children.

1. Eleanor Ida Hammond
2. Charlotte Hammond, was born on December 13, 1919, died February 25, 1923
3. Charles Frederick Hammond, born July 8, 1924, died July 5, 2005, married to Lucille Galbert.

ELEANOR IDA HAMMOND was born in Chicago, IL, on May 11,1915. She was christened on August 22, 1915. She married Harvey Earnest Grund on September 18, 1938. Harvey was born on June 23, 1911, the son of Charles Grund and Mary Belle Hart.

Eleanor Hammond Grund died on July 24, 1984. She was buried in Mount Greenwood Cemetery. The lot in which she was buried in Mount Greenwood was either sold or given to her for burial by her cousin Roy Hudenburg as it was located in the Hudenburg section. Her husband Harvey Grund was also given or sold a lot in the same section however, he never used the grave site because he is not buried in Mount Greenwood Cemetery. Harvey died June 10, 1985 and is buried in Las Vegas, Nevada.

Eleanor Hammond Grund was the mother of two known children. In her death notice, there were two grandchildren mentioned, Carl and the late Paul.

1. Stephen D. Grund, wife Carol
2. Harvey D. Grund, wife Beatriz

ALBERT HERMAN SCHULTZ was born in Detroit, Michigan on June 14, 1887, the son of Johann and Albertine Schultz. Albert was christened on July 12, 1887. Albert was found living with his sister Bertha Schultz Nilson (sic) in Chicago for the 1900 Illinois, Cook County census. He was then 12 years old and noted as being in school and had been born in Michigan. Bertha later became Bertha Van Dyk.

Albert was physically a small man and never married. The 1920 Illinois, Cook County, census shows Albert living within the home of his sister Louise Hudenburg. He was 33 years old at that time and worked as an electrician in a store. The 1930 Illinois, Cook County, census shows Albert still living with his sister Louise Hudenburg and he was still recorded as an electrician. What Albert's circumstances were following the death of his sister Louise Hudenburg are unknown.

Albert H. Schultz died at Jackson Park Hospital in Chicago, IL, of a coronary occlusion on May 31, 1954. The arrangements for his funeral were taken care of by John A. and Marie R. Zimmerman. He was buried in Mount Greenwood Cemetery next to his sister Louise Schultz Hudenburg. Albert's sisters Bertha Schultz Van Dyk and Ida Schultz Hammond are both buried in the same section of the cemetery. There was no notice of death found in the Chicago papers for Albert.

Index

Index

Index

Index

Index

Margaret, 133
Margaret Marie, vii, 29, 77, 123, 124, 126, 127, 133, 134, 135, 136
Mary, 133
Mary Leonard, vii, 124, 125, 126, 127
Phillip, 130
Richard A., vii, 37, 129, 130, 167, 187
Rueben, 122
Sadie M., 127
Sally, 133
Sarah, 122
Simgessmer G. vi, 28, 122, 123, 124, 125, 126, 127, 128, 131, 133, 141
Thomas E., 133
William, 122
William, 130
William Bray, vii, 34, 35, 36, 124, 125, 126, 127, 128, 129, 130, 131
William J., vi, 122, 124
Nelson
John, 187
John Warwick, 182, 187, 188
Stella 94
Newman
Lydia, 145, 149
Nathan J. 90

-O-

Occhiene
Ernest, 129
Odel
Augustin, 144
O'Dell
William F., 143, 144
Odell
Ada Catherine, viii, 158, 159, 160, 163, 164, 175, 176
Adam, 169
Aeha., 146
Allen, 145
Amelia G., viii, 151, 152, 154, 156
Angeline, 148
Arabella, 159
Augustin, vii, 146, 147
Augustin, 145, 146
Augustin, 147
Augustine, vii, 145, 146, 147, 148, 149
Aurilla U., viii, 151, 152, 153
Austin, 145
Austin, 145
Austin Henry, 148
Austin M., vii, 146, 148, 149, 151
Astor May, 153
Azor, 148
Benajah, 144

Benajah, 145, 146
Benard Louis, 170
Bert B., 161
Beverly, 174
Bob, 161
Captain Augustine, vii, 144
Charles A., 147
Charles E., 153
David, 145, 146
Edward G., 152, 160
Elanora, vii, 151, 152, 155
Elisha Brace, viii, 149, 152
Ellen, 148
Emily E., viii, 152, 153
Eric, 169
Flossie, 158
Frances E., 161
Freda E., 161
George, 147
Ira E., 158
Ira Nathaniel, viii, 36, 39, 157, 158, 159, 160, 161, 163, 164, 165, 166, 167, 168, 169, 174, 191
Ira Stewart, viii, 162, 163, 164, 165, 166, 167, 168, 169, 174, 175
Isaac Henry, viii, 146, 147, 148, 149
Isaac Henry, Jr., 147, 148
Jacob, 144
Jacob, 144
Jacob, 147
James, 145
James, 147
James Ross, viii, 158, 159, 160, 164, 174
Jane A., 148
Jane A., 149
Jeanette, viii, 169
Jeremiah N., 151, 152
Jessie J., 161
John C., 153
John H., 161
John L., 149
Julia Ann M., viii, 152, 153
Kate, 169
Lucy, 145
Lydia, 146, 147
Lydia A., 149
Lydia O., 152
Mahala May, viii, 157, 158, 159, 160, 171, 172
Mark, 169
Mary, 147
Mary, 148, 149, 151
Mary, 169
Mary E., viii, 151, 152, 154, 156
Minne L., 153
Nathaniel, 144
Nathaniel, 145
Nathaniel A., 153
Nathaniel Alvin, viii, 146, 147, 148, 149, 150, 151, 152, 153, 154, 155, 156

O.M., 158
Orville Birt, viii, 150, 151, 152, 154, 155, 156, 157, 158, 159, 160, 161, 166, 170, 171, 172, 174, 175, 176, 177
Orville Glen, 170
Orville William, viii, 157, 158, 160, 170
Oscar Bert, 170
Paul, 161
Phyllis L., 174
Reuben, 147
Robert L., 153
Rosada, 147
Samuel, 145
Samuel, 147
Sarah, 147
Sarah, 148
Sean, 169
Selden Jay, viii, 158, 159, 160, 166, 174, 175, 176, 177
Stephen, 149
Stewart Ira, viii, 169
Susan A., 148
Sylvester Scott, viii, 151, 156, 157, 158, 159, 160
Tilinghast S., 151, 152
Vera May, 170
Vivian, 169
Vivica, 169
Wallace S., 153
William, 149
William, 158
Winona Ruth, viii, xi, 36, 37, 38, 39, 40, 41, 42, 48, 50, 60, 92, 163, 164, 165, 166, 167, 169, 170, 178, 186, 187, 188, 189, 190, 191
Odell/O'Dell
Bobbie Glen, 172, 173
Donald, 177
Doyal Dawson, 173
Harold P., 177
Irvin McClain, viii, 156, 158, 159, 160, 166, 174, 175, 176
Jack, 176, 177
Kenneth N., 177
Leonard Francis, 173
LeRoi, 176, 177
Orange Bert, viii, 158, 159, 160, 166, 175, 177
Patricia, 176
Richard, 177
Victor Francis, viii, 158, 159, 160, 172, 173
Victor William, 172, 173
Woodrow Bert, 172, 173
Odle
Augustin, 144, 145
Augustin, 145
Augustus, 144
Augustin, Jr., 145
Jacob, 145
Nathaniel, 145
Zakia, 146

197

Index

Index

Index

Index

www.ingramcontent.com/pod-product-compliance
Lightning Source LLC
Chambersburg PA
CBHW041612260326

41914CB00012B/1471